P9-DNM-141

Islam in America

The Columbia Contemporary American Religion Series

Columbia Contemporary American Religion Series

The United States is the birthplace of religious pluralism, and the spiritual landscape of contemporary America is as varied and complex as that of any country in the world. The books in this new series, written by leading scholars for students and general readers alike, fall into two categories: Some titles are portraits of the country's major religious groups. They describe and explain particular religious practices and rituals, beliefs, and major challenges facing a given community today. Others explore current themes and topics in American religion that cut across denominational lines. The texts are supplemented with carefully selected photographs and artwork, annotated bibliographies, concise profiles of important individuals, and chronologies of major events.

—

Roman Catholicism in America
CHESTER GILLIS

Islam in America
JANE I. SMITH

Buddhism in America
RICHARD HUGHES SEAGER

ISLAM

in America

Jane I. Smith

COLUMBIA UNIVERSITY PRESS

NEW YORK

COLUMBIA UNIVERSITY PRESS
Publishers Since 1893
New York, Chichester, West Sussex

Copyright © 1999 Columbia University Press
All rights reserved
Library of Congress Cataloging-in-Publication Data
Library of Congress Cataloging-in-Publication Data
Smith, Jane I.
Islam in America / Jane I. Smith.
p. cm. — (Columbia contemporary American religion series)
Includes bibliographical references (p. 219) and index.
ISBN 0–231–10966–0 (cloth) — ISBN 0–231–10967–9 (pbk.)
1. Islam—United States. I. Title. II. Series.
BP67.U6S6 1999
297.'0973—dc21   98–31943

Casebound editions of Columbia University Press books are printed on
permanent and durable acid-free paper.
Printed in the United States of America
c 10 9 8 7 6 5 4 3
p 10 9 8 7 6 5 4 3 2 1

To Peg and Bruce

CONTENTS

INTRODUCTION

"I hadn't gone shopping for a new religion. After twenty-five years as a writer in America, I wanted something to soften my cynicism. I was searching for new terms by which to see. . . . I could not have drawn up a list of demands, but I had a fair idea of what I was after. . . . There would be no priests, no separation between nature and things sacred. There would be no war with the flesh, if I could help it. Sex would be natural, not the seat of a curse upon the species. Finally, I'd want a ritual component, a daily routine to sharpen the senses and discipline my mind. Above all, I wanted clarity and freedom. I did not want to trade away reason simply to be saddled with a dogma. The more I learned about Islam, the more it appeared to conform to what I was after."[1]

These words, written by a convert to Islam whose father is Jewish and whose mother is Christian, suggest some of the ways in which Islam has appealed to many Americans. It is perceived as a religion that is direct, natural, straightforward, and disciplined. Malcolm X and others who came to the faith initially through movements like the Nation of Islam felt that appeal, and it is the substance of the call to Islam made by those immigrant Muslims who believe their duty is to bring others into the Islamic fold. Through that call, and by the arrival of Muslims from virtually everywhere in the world to the shores of the United States, Islam has come to constitute one of the three major religions in America.

It has become commonplace to note that in the West in general, and the United States in particular, Muslims no longer can be thought of as "over there." Increasingly, they are a visible and vocal part of the fabric of Western society. Still, only recently have many Americans begun to grasp that Islam, along with Christianity and Judaism, is itself a "Western" religion. Most scholarly as well as popular writing continues to slip easily into the dichotomy of "Islam *and* (or, over against) the West." But information about Islam and Muslims is increasingly available through the media, and it is difficult not to notice the presence of Muslims in American cities and towns. Most Americans, however, remain only vaguely aware of the size and significance of the Muslim community in America and know little if anything about the religion itself. Before an introductory talk I gave on Muslim faith and practice recently a woman asked me, "Where is Islam?" supposing it to be a country. For the most part, Americans have little concept that approximately as many Muslims as Jews live in America and outnumber many of the mainline Protestant denominations.

Harvard historian of religion Diana Eck's Pluralism Project, available on CD-ROM,[2] provides a fascinating look at what she calls comparative religion in the making. Eck's students have documented and photographed evidence of the recent and not-so-recent arrival of Muslims, Hindus, Buddhists, Jains, Zoroastrians, and many others to the urban and rural areas of America. A major segment of her project deals with Muslim communities across the continent, and the viewer is treated to the contrast of Muslim farm workers and day laborers with physicians and other highly successful professionals, and to images of storefront mosques alongside some of the striking new Islamic centers constructed in the last several decades. Such resources as this, along with the sharp rise in scholarly studies in the field of American Islam, the addition of materials on U.S. Muslims in a number of university courses, the increased attention to Islamic religion and culture in high school curricula, and opportunities for Muslim children to talk about their holidays to their classmates at the grade-school level, will make it difficult for those coming through the American educational system to need to ask, "Where is Islam?"

"Today, the American Muslim community is comprised of people drawn from a wide-ranging ethnic and professional mix. Whether they are immigrants, indigenous Americans, or converts, all are united in the unique theistic experience that is Islam. Whether they are physicians, lawyers, entrepreneurs, professors, cooks or factory workers, all of them are making a contribution to America's future."[3] These observations, from an address given at the Thirty-Fourth Annual Convention of the Islamic Society of North America (ISNA) in 1997, suggest both the heterogeneity of the American Muslim community and the concern of many of its members and leaders that Islam be recognized as a legitimate, and contributing, sector of American society. What is this religion whose presence in the United States is so visible, and so permanent, that many Muslims are asking for America to be called a Judeo-Christian *and* Muslim country? Is it simply a foreign religion somehow transplanted into Western soil, or is it emerging as a genuinely American phenomenon?

The faith of Islam arose in seventh-century Arabia when, as Muslims believe, God chose a religious visionary named Muhammad to be the last prophet of the monotheistic religions. It spread rapidly throughout the greater Middle East, North Africa, and Southern Europe and within a century was a vital force in much of the known world. For most of their history, Muslims have been creative contributors to the development of science and art, literature and philosophy, technology and culture. Major Muslim empires ruled over vast areas of the world until the beginning of the twentieth century. Today there are more than a billion Muslims across the globe, found in virtually every country, and Islam is considered one of the five or six "great world religions." Muslims understand the Qur'an, the holy book of Islam, to be the verbatim revelation of God to Muhammad, and it is now available in translation (Muslims would say "interpretation") in most of the world's languages.

The growth of Islam during the early centuries of its existence was a difficult phenomenon for Western Christianity to comprehend, and misunderstanding, prejudice, fear, and, in some cases, hatred have characterized much of the history of encounter between the two faiths. This legacy, along with current fears and concerns about supposed "Islamic extremism," forms part of the context in which to understand the experience of Muslims in what has been a mainly Christian America. "Though Islam is an Abrahamic faith alongside Judaism and Christianity," argues a Muslim historian from the University of Chicago, "it is usually seen as threatening both 'mom and apple pie' as well as basic 'Judeo-Christian values.' "[4] This sentiment is increasingly balanced in the United States, however, by efforts on the part of non-Muslim Americans, working with Muslims, to achieve a fairer presentation of Islam in the media, the classroom, and the common imagination.

Much of the development of Islam in the twentieth century, detailed in the last part of chapter 2, has been in reaction to what is perceived by Muslims as Western imperialism—in its political, economic, and even religious aspects. In recent decades a number of movements have arisen in different parts of the Muslim world calling for a renewed intentionality about the role of Islam in the running of the state and in the public as well as private lives of Muslims. The Western press has persisted in labeling these movements "fundamentalist," seeing in them common characteristics of extremism, hostility to the West, and sometimes even violence. In truth, neither the word *fundamentalist* nor the assumption of commonality are accurate. A better umbrella term for such movements may be *revivalist*, and sometimes they are known simply as *Islamist*, a term covering a great range of interpretations and actions, which only rarely manifest themselves in the kind of violence that is so frightening to the average American. The challenge for the American Muslim is to try to live and practice an Islam in which the values of justice, morality, and peaceful coexistence with people of other faiths and persuasions are seen to overshadow the image of the militant Islam that is so often publicized in the U.S. media.

It has been part of my professional responsibility as a teacher of Islamic studies as well as my personal pleasure over the past several decades to share with American audiences what I understand about the historical, ethical, and spiritual dimensions of Islam. In this many Muslim friends and associates have patiently helped me see what it means to be Muslim individually and congregationally. I have spent a great deal of time in conversation with Muslims, in both academic and interfaith settings, and have shared many meals in which Muslim hospitality and generosity have been much in evidence. Some of my most meaningful experiences have occurred when I have been invited to share in the ritual of prayer, in both private homes and the more public space of the mosque or Islamic center. Not all American Muslims find themselves in a position to be open to interaction with those who are not Muslim and, at least for the time being, feel that they need separation so as to devote their attention to determining how to preserve their Muslim identity in a Western culture. Many others, however, are eager to share their beliefs and practices with friends who genuinely want to learn and understand. In this volume I present the perspectives of as many American Muslims as possible and allow their voices to determine the important issues and illuminate the presentation of material.

Three decades ago there were fewer than half a million Muslims in America, including immigrants and African Americans. While the projections range widely in terms of the current population, and there is sometimes disagreement as to who should properly be identified as Muslim, the consensus is that somewhere around six million Muslims live permanently in America and that the community is growing steadily. For the most part, Muslims themselves estimate the number to be somewhat higher. Many factors account for the significant increase over the years, as the succeeding chapters will illustrate. The largest group of Muslims in America is comprised of first-, second-, and third-generation immigrants, as well as some numbers of Muslim students who stay for a while and return, often to positions of leadership, to their home countries.

While it is difficult to determine exact proportions, many scholars of American Islam project that perhaps 40 percent of the Muslim community is African American. That number includes followers of Imam W. D. Mohammed, members of other Sunni organizations, and those who belong to heterodox groups that adhere to some interpretation of Islam, such as Louis Farrakhan's Nation of Islam or the Ansar Allah. The picture of American Islam is greatly complicated by the many sectarian movements that want to identify themselves as "Muslim," an identification often seriously challenged by other Muslims. American Muslims are deeply involved in formulating what it means to be part of the "*umma* (community) in the West," and through the development of Islamic organizations, increasing numbers of local and national meetings and conferences, and rapidly proliferating communications, they are in the process of determining the nature and authenticity of an indigenous American Islam.

This volume provides a general introduction to the religion of Islam as American Muslims experience and practice it and to the range of communities and groups that are part of the faith. The opening chapters help the reader locate the experiences of American Muslims within the history of Muslim beliefs, institutions, and developments. Chapter 1 introduces the beliefs and rituals that have characterized the Islamic community from the time of the Prophet and frame the religious life of American Muslims. It sets the five articles of Muslim faith and the five elements of formal religious practice within the context of community life and suggests some of the reasons why Muhammad continues to be a model for the faithful. "Following the Sunnah [way of the Prophet] does not mean just imitating the outward appearance of the Prophet, but it means creative learning from his character and example," says the president of the Islamic Society of North America. "He is our paradigm because he was closest to Allah in his relationship and lived his life fully and totally for the sake of Allah. That was the secret of his moral excellence and his life became a paradigm for this reason."[5]

Chapter 2 looks at the lives and personal experiences of people who have played significant roles in the past and recent history of Islam. It describes the swift and broad spread of the religion during the early years of its existence and the development of the main Islamic disciplines, including law, theology, philosophy, and mysticism. This section illustrates some of the ways in which the lives of individual Muslims, their influence, and their decisions about what Islam means and how to live ethically and religiously have shaped the faith and practice of those trying to determine what it means to be Muslim in today's Western society.

Chapters 3 and 4 consider some of the many ways in which Islam has come to be a significant and highly visible part of American history and culture. Chapter 3 sketches the complex history of immigrant Islam in America, describing the ways in which Muslims have arrived in America or have chosen to adopt Islam as their religion. It traces the immigrant movements from the middle of the last century, primarily from the Middle East, through the several waves of immigration, to the present time in which Muslims come from virtually everywhere in the world. It illustrates the broad range of cultural contexts represented by Muslim immigrants, their great variety of educational and professional levels, and the different ways in which they believe Islam should be practiced in America. Adding to this already complex scene is the phenomenon of growing numbers of converts to Islam from among the white, Hispanic, and Native American population, sometimes coming to the faith through affiliation with one of the many Sufi movements in the United States and Canada. Chapter 4 begins with the introduction of Muslim slaves to America and their (in most cases) forced conversion to Christianity. Their story includes a detailed discussion of the rise of African American Islam, from the early expressions of black nationalism through the appearance and development of the Nation of Islam to contemporary manifestations of both orthodox and heterodox Muslim movements.

The next three chapters look at the range of issues that confront Muslims who want to live faithfully in the context of America. Many Muslims in the West do not attend a mosque or participate in religious observances, considering themselves Muslim primarily by heritage or cultural affiliation. Others are observant, practicing, and mosque-attending. These chapters describe the concerns these Muslims face in relation to worship and religious life, family and personal matters, the role of women in American Islam, the raising and educating of children, care for the elderly and for those in the military and in prison, the use of Islamically acceptable products, appropriate dress and behavior, and many other issues related to life in a country in which Islam is often misunderstood and unappreciated. Particular attention is given to the development of mosques and American Islamic organizations, the propagation of the faith, Muslim participation in the political process, and the ways in which both Muslims and non-Muslims are identifying and addressing instances of prejudice and unfair treatment. The phenomenon of Islamic outreach activity is discussed in some detail, reflecting the intent of some Muslims to make America their mission field. "The Islamic vision endows North America with a new destiny worthy of it," said Ismaʻil al Faruqi, irrepressible Palestinian professor from Temple University. "For this renovation of itself, of its spirit, for its rediscovery of a God-given mission and self-dedication to its pursuit, the continent cannot but be grateful to the immigrant with Islamic vision. It cannot but interpret his advent on the shores except as a God-given gift, a timely divine favor and mercy."[6]

The final chapter suggests some of the concerns facing Muslims in America—immigrant, African American, and convert—as they look to the next decades. The issues are those that Muslims themselves are raising in their literature, conversations, and local and national meetings. These concerns reflect the complexity of the American Muslim scene as reflected in its racial-ethnic and cultural mix, in the changes from early immigrants to those who are second- and now third-generation Americans, in the ways in which Muslims are and are not allowing themselves to be influenced by trends and movements overseas, and in the many different understandings of what it means to affirm and maintain an Islamic identity in a context in which one represents a still small minority faith.

"Profiles" offers biographical sketches of some Muslims who have contributed to the definition and formulation of American Islam from a variety of historical and cultural contexts. It suggests the range of people and experiences that constitute the rich and variegated picture of Islam in the United States, describing Muslims who are prominent in the academy and the organizational side of the community as well as sports personalities and those who figure in other aspects of American public life. Following is a chronology of events in the history of American Islam, a glossary of relevant terms, and a listing of resources that may be helpful to readers wishing to know more about Islam in the United States and Canada, including a briefly annotated bibliography of books, as well as a listing of Muslim journals and periodicals, Islamic educational organizations, videotapes about American Islam, radio and television broadcasts, and Internet resources.

The picture of American Islam changes each day as new people join the community, new information becomes available from a range of resources, and new interpretations are developed to help Muslims know more about their faith and how it can be practiced in a pluralist society. "The time has come for the American Muslim community to take full responsibility for their affairs," insists one Muslim commentator. "We must lay the foundation for our younger generation to live and prosper in this country as political and economic equals."[7] That task will be easier to the degree that Americans know more about, and can come to better appreciate, the religion of Islam as a vital contributor to its religious landscape. This book is intended as one way to facilitate that task.

Islam in America

CHAPTER ONE

Muslim Faith and Practice

On Friday shortly after noon in the small inner-city mosque, primarily African American, the worshipers slowly gather. A man who has volunteered to vacuum before each prayer service makes certain that the carpets are clean to receive the foreheads of those who will soon bow in prostration to God. Each person removes his or her shoes before entering the worship hall, placing them in a wooden rack near the front door. The carpets, which are really thin runners, are arranged so that those gathered for prayer will be facing in the direction of Mecca, indicated by a plaque in the front of the hall. The room is bare of furniture except for a lectern in the front and a few folding chairs in the back for those who are unable to sit on the floor. Arabic calligraphy on the wall proclaims the Basmalla, or invocation— "In the name of God, the Merciful, the Compassionate"—with which all chapters of the Qur'an save one begin. The vacuum stops. Worshipers, who have performed their ablutions in the basement before entering the prayer hall, individually prepare themselves for participation in the communal worship. A man rises, faces front, puts his hands behind his ears, and sings out the call that will begin the service: "Come to the prayer, come to the time of felicity. . . ." The imam steps forward, and the ritual begins.

For the Muslim, prayer is not simply a mental or spiritual attitude or even just a matter of thanksgiving of the mind and heart. It involves a total bodily response, not simply sitting but putting oneself through a series of complete prostrations. For that reason, mosques do not have chairs or pews. Each of the five daily prayers consists of a series of ritual bowings and bendings (each called a *raka'*) accompanied by the appropriate prayers and invocations. Standing shoulder to shoulder, feet to feet, the worshipers are lined in rows facing the imam, or leader, of the prayer, men in the front and women in the back. Children, who are almost always present, remain more or less quietly with the women, the older ones learning the steps of the prayer ritual. Boys who are past early childhood sit with their fathers. Most of the men are wearing small woven or embroidered caps, and the women have long sleeves and skirts or pants, with their hair fully covered. Together they perform the several sets of prayer prostrations, which include standing, bowing at the waist with hands placed near the knees, and kneeling and placing one's forehead on the carpet in full supplication. "When you are in that position of complete vulnerability," explains the imam, "you really get a feel for what it means to submit yourself fully to God."

The ritual includes the common recitation of the Fatiha, the brief opening chapter of the Qur'an, that functions for the Muslim much as the Lord's Prayer does for the Christian when it is said in unison. The imam renders the phrases of the ritual as much in Arabic as possible so that his congregants can become more familiar with the language. Because it is Friday, the service includes a sermon given by the imam, in English, generally on a topic related to living as faithful Muslims in America or learning to relate to people of other faiths. Listeners remain seated on the carpets during this homily. At the end of the prayer the worshipers say the *taslim*, or salutation, invoking peace, by which one both greets those who are worshiping around him or her and again signals one's absolute submission to God. When the service is over, worshipers stand, greet one another, and file out to return to their daily activities.

Meanwhile, across the city, an identical ritual is being carried out, but under quite different circumstances. This mosque, whose congregation is made up mainly of professional immigrant Muslims, has been built on a classical Islamic model. A dome on top, mounted with a visible crescent, leaves no doubt that this is a Muslim house of worship. The prayer hall is large, and thick carpets cover its floor. Women come into the mosque through a separate entrance and worship on the second level in a kind of balcony, from which they can watch the imam and the men through a latticework railing. Children roam freely and feel less constraint to be quiet than when they are in the same room with the men and the imam. Most of the women participate in the prayer ritual, although some prefer to sit and talk quietly with one another in the corner. They too are dressed conservatively, generally in the traditional clothing of their country of origin.

But while the surroundings are different, the ritual is the same—washing, standing, sitting, prostrating, reciting. Muslims take great pride in the fact that despite architectural and other kinds of variations, no matter where in the world one goes to worship, the essentials of the ritual will be the same. In both the African American and immigrant mosques, those who are not Muslim are welcome to attend the service and even to participate if they so wish, although this is not true of all mosque communities, either in the United States or elsewhere. When the service in the immigrant mosque is over, the men stay and talk with the imam and one another for a while, sometimes about the sermon but more often about community affairs. The women gather the children, greet and hug their neighbors, retrieve their shoes, and leave, they too ready to get on with the business of the day.

How have rituals such as this become part of the fabric of Islam? What binds Muslims around the world in recognition of the importance of the ritual prayer, whether or not they actually participate in it regularly, and of the other elements of Islamic faith and practice? The answer that American Muslims will give to such questions is clear and direct. Muslims believe what they do, and practice as they do, because of the example of Prophet Muhammad, who established his community in Mecca and Medina according to the directives he received from God. Before looking more specifically at those elements that make up Muslim faith and practice, it is important to get an

Muslims praying on Madison Avenue in New York City prior to Muslim Day parade.
© JOLIE STAHL

idea of how important the figure of the Prophet is to Muslims, and why many American Muslims pattern their own lives as closely as possible after the model he set for all succeeding generations.

> By the star when it sets, your companion is not in error, nor is he deceived, nor does he speak out of his own desire. Truly this is a revelation revealed, taught to him by one who is strong and mighty in power. He was on the cusp of the uttermost horizon, then he drew near and approached until he was the distance of two bows' lengths or even closer. Thus did [God] reveal to His servant that which He revealed.
>
> *(Sura 53:1–10)*

With this stirring description of the appearance of the angel Gabriel to a man named Muhammad ibn (son of) Abdullah in the Arabian desert more than fourteen centuries ago, the Qur'an, the Holy Book of Islam, confirms that God himself chose to send his revelations to this the last of his messengers and prophets. Nothing is more sure for a people who are accustomed to the regularity of nature than the setting of the morning star, and the chapter of the Qur'an in which this early meeting between Muhammad and Gabriel takes place bears the title "The Star." Muslims believe that as this daily event is utterly reliable, so is the affirmation made here that Muhammad himself, identified in the verse as the "companion," is truly the recipient of divine revelation.

Muslims accord the highest respect to Muhammad, seeing in him the prototype of spiritual guidance, wise leadership, and moral example for the best of human living, both communally and in relation to God. American Muslims are often particularly conscientious about adding the phrase "may the blessing and peace of God be upon him" whenever mentioning the name of the Prophet. "The tense and delicate balance between the glory of Muhammad's prophethood, his closeness to God and his visionary gifts, the Herculean tasks he undertook and accomplished in the world, and the warmth and liveliness of his household is at the heart of the Muslim view of life; if this is understood, Islam is understood," writes an American convert attempting to convey to those who know little of Islam how important Prophet Muhammad is to Muslims.[1]

And yet subsequent history was to bear out the implicit concern expressed in these verses of the Qur'an that Muhammad indeed would be charged with the three things specifically denied here. Over the centuries he has been accused, especially by Christians, of being in gross error, of being led astray (deceived) by the powers of Satan, and of being so overcome with his own desires for power that he invented a false and diabolic religion with which to dupe his people. Some have even suggested that he must have suffered from epilepsy, citing the testimony that he was quite overcome with the early revelations he received from God through the angel. Muslims in America today still find that these three accusations characterize the opinions most non-Muslims have about the Prophet. Was he well meaning but simply wrong? Somewhat less charitably, was he somehow in the grip of a kind of malignant power that led him to such erroneous claims? Or worst of all, was he a self-aggrandizing seeker of personal glory who fabricated divine revelations to secure a position of political leadership?

While most Americans decry the negative assessments of Muhammad that have characterized most Western judgments over the centuries, blatant examples of them still appear. AT&T WorldNet Service, the largest direct Internet service provider in the United States, in June 1998 removed a website that referred to Muhammad as a lecherous hypocrite who clearly was no man of God.[2] Non-Muslims who are uncomfortable with viewing Muhammad as misguided, opportunistic, or simply wrong may with some hesitation allow Muhammad's status as a prophet of God, although generally without the essential Islamic understanding that his was the last and final divine revelation, or without conceding that the message to Muhammad could in any way contravene the truth of the Bible. Muslims are saddened and puzzled that non-Muslim Americans still seem to have little understanding or appreciation of the finest human qualities exemplified in the founder of Islam. It is to him, however, that American Muslims continue to look as the recipient of the final and lasting word of God, and the exemplar for their own modes of public and private behavior. And it is to him that are credited the bases of Muslim belief and practice as they have come to structure the life of the faithful Muslim.

The Elements of Islamic Faith and Practice

The articles of belief and practice that structure the life of the faithful American Muslim today have been developed out of the experiences of Prophet Muhammad (detailed in chapter 2) and drawn from the basic teachings of the Qur'an. Muslims understand that as there are five responsibilities that all the faithful are expected to perform, often referred to as the five "pillars" (*arkan*) of Islam, so there are five articles of faith that together constitute the

Muslim affirmation of divine being and human responsibility. Many struggle to practice all of these as faithfully as possible and to make them evident in their daily life. Others exercise the freedom to pick and choose, and to modify them when they feel it is appropriate to life in America.

The Five Elements of Faith

From an early age Muslim children learn from their parents and mosque schools that Islam is based on five specific beliefs:

1. *Faith in God*. Implicit in the Islamic understanding of God is the notion of an unqualified difference between divine and human. The very recognition of God is often expressed by the term *tawhid*, meaning both God's oneness and the human acknowledgment of it. It presupposes that no other being is like God and that humans must not only testify to God's uniqueness but also must reflect their belief in it through their own lives and actions. As God alone is Lord and Creator of the universe, so the Muslim acknowledges God's oneness by living a life of integratedness, integrity, and ethical and moral responsibility. In the Islamic understanding, the greatest sin a human being can commit is to impugn the oneness of God, to suggest by word or deed that anything else can in any way share in that divine unity. This sin is called *shirk*, association or participation. Over history, some Islamic mystics have, in the eyes of the orthodox, come dangerously close to heresy in their affirmation of experiences of oneness with God.

Islam is the only major religion whose very name suggests a bidimensional focus of faith. On one axis it refers to the individual human response to God's oneness, and on the other it means the collectivity of all of those people who form a community of religious faith to acknowledge and respond to God. The religious response of all those people who have affirmed the oneness of God can fairly be understood as personal *islam*. It was only with the official beginning of the community at the time of the *hijra* to Medina, however, that there arose a specific recognition that Muslims together form a group, a unity, an *umma*, although the term *Islam* itself was not much used in that sense until considerably later. The struggle to identify what *umma* means in the Western milieu and to determine if there can be a distinctively American Muslim community is one in which American Muslims are deeply immersed, as succeeding chapters will illustrate.

2. *Faith in the reality of angels*. In the West, at the end of the twentieth century, angels have been the subject of much speculation. Their popularity

seems to have experienced a considerable revival, as depictions of angels even embellish the covers of popular magazines. Muslims might find this somewhat amusing, since the conviction that angels exist and play an active role in human life has been part of their religious awareness from the earliest days of Muhammad's encounter with God through the angel Gabriel. He is only one of a number of angels, one of the most dramatic being Israfil, whose blowing of the mighty trumpet at the end of time will signal the coming of the Day of Resurrection and Judgment.

3. *Faith in God's messengers.* Muslims understand that God has sent his revelation (*wahy*) through a series of communications to humanity in a variety of ways, through a variety of people. The recipients of these communications are referred to as both prophets and messengers. The distinction between prophet (*nabi*) and messenger (*rasul*) is that the words of the former are intended for specific communities of people, while those of the latter have universal significance. Thus all messengers are also prophets, though the reverse is not true. The Qur'an is full of references to those who are acknowledged to be prophets, many of whom Jews and Christians recognize for their role in Old Testament history. Only a limited number of prophets are also messengers, including Abraham, Moses, and Jesus, before the coming of the final prophet and messenger, Muhammad. In recent times, relations among Muslims, Christians, and Jews in America are often cultivated under the rubric "Abrahamic religions," suggesting that the common ancestry of the three faiths may be a more productive basis for interfaith conversation than the rehearsing of theological differences. Jesus is considered to be the greatest of the prophets and messengers of Islam before Muhammad, although not a son of God or in any way divine. With the revelation to Muhammad, God is said to have concluded the process of revelation. Muhammad is thus referred to as the seal of prophecy. This doctrine is of such great importance in Islam that for anyone to claim for himself or for another the designation of prophet is considered heresy.

4. *Faith in the Holy Books.* As the Qur'an makes quite explicit, God sent books, or complete revelations, to both the Jews and Christians before the coming of Muhammad. The message contained in those books is essentially that contained in the Qur'an. Unfortunately, Jewish and Christian communities either purposely or inadvertently changed or distorted God's messages, with the result that the revelation needed to be sent one last, and final, time. The Qur'an is that final revelation. However, Christians and Jews have a special status in the Muslim community because they were chosen by

God to be the recipients of his books. The Qur'an consistently refers to Jews and Christians as *ahl al-kitab*, the People of the Book. American Muslims sometimes suggest this commonality as a basis for affirming the United States as a Christian, Jewish, *and* Muslim country. The Qur'an itself is often referred to simply as The Book, a term relating it to the previous divine revelations and suggesting its own position as the final word of God to humanity.

5. *Faith in the Day of Resurrection and Judgment.* The basic revelation given to Prophet Muhammad was the double message of God's oneness and of a day of final assessment of human actions. In Islam, as the concept of *tawhid* ties together God's oneness and human responsibility, so God will gather together all people at the end of time for an accounting of how they have lived their lives. As the Qur'an makes abundantly clear, this will be a momentous occasion, signaled by the trumpet of the angel Israfil, the most amazing cataclysmic events, and the resurrection of all bodies, which will be joined with their souls for the judgment. Each person will be given his or her "book of deeds." If the book is put into one's right hand, then the

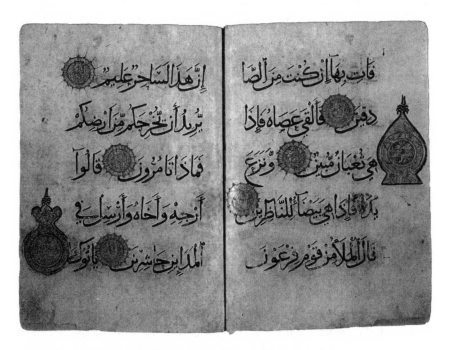

Pages from a manuscript of the Holy Qur'an dating from the twelfth century.
New York Public Library Picture Collection

reward will be the gardens of paradise near to God himself. If, however, the book is received in the left hand, the unhappy sinner will face the eternal fires of punishment. The coming Day of Judgment emphasizes the importance of living Islamically. American Muslims often discuss conduct, dress, and other issues in the context of God's final assessment of human actions.

These five articles of faith are all grounded in the message of the Qur'an and are non-negotiable for Muslims. They are elaborated upon in the literature available to the Muslim community in America and, according to the ability of the child to absorb them, are part of the religious education that is increasingly taking place in mosques and Islamic centers across the country.

The Five Pillars

Even before learning about these articles of faith, however, young Muslims are taught the essentials of living a good and responsible life according to the Islamic understanding. These essentials are expressed in the five pillars, which form the essence of the individual Muslim's personal piety (*taqwa*). Muslims actively working for the propagation of Islam in America understand that one of its most appealing aspects is the simplicity and clarity of the responsibilities that frame the Muslim life.

1. *Testimony concerning the oneness of God and the prophethood of Muhammad.* This twin affirmation is called the *shahada*—literally, "witness"—and comes directly from the articles of faith. While all of the five pillars, or responsibilities, are incumbent on every Muslim, the *shahada* is basic. One can lapse from any of the others and still be a Muslim, although, of course, one is strongly encouraged to be faithful to them all. But failure to believe in and articulate the oneness of God and the prophethood of Muhammad means that one is outside the community of Islam. Those who wish to affiliate themselves with Islam in America—or anywhere else—need only pronounce the *shahada* three times in a formal setting to be henceforth effectively and legally Muslims. Many buildings in the United States and Canada have been converted to function as mosques, and one indication of their new status is a calligraphic rendering of the two affirmations of the *shahada* painted on the walls or hung as a sign or banner in the front.

2. *Performance of the ritual prayer.* Formal prayer was part of the expectation of the Prophet for the members of his community from the beginning. "Worship at fixed hours has been enjoined on the believers. . ." (Sura 90:103); "Establish worship at the two ends of the day and in some watches

Calligraphic rendering of a Qur'an verse that reads: "Over every knowledgeable being is One more knowing." COURTESY MOHAMED ZAKARIYA

of the night. . ." (Sura 11:114). At first, Muhammad ordered believers to face Jerusalem in their prayer orientation, but sometime after the *hijra* he directed that orientation to Mecca. All mosques contain what is called a *qibla*, or indicator of the exact direction for the worshiper to face when performing the prayer. In America as in other non-Muslim countries, if a building has not been built specifically to serve as a mosque, the direction of prayer will most likely not coincide with the "front" of that building. Travelers can make use of small mechanical devices to help orient them toward Mecca. Many hotels in Islamic cities provide indicators of the prayer direction in the rooms.

Ritual prayer, *salat*, is not a casual thing for the Muslim but assumes a regularity and discipline. God is said to have prescribed to Muhammad the daily ritual of five formal prayers for every believer, although the Qur'an itself does not specify that demand. The exact times of day for performing the *salat* are clearly established in the *hadith*, or traditions, and have been codified in the law. Specifically, they are the *salat al-fajr* at dawn before the rise of the sun, the *salat al-ẓuhr* after the sun passes its highest point, the *salat al-ʿasr* in the late part of the afternoon, the *salat al-maghrib* just after the setting of the sun, and the *salat al-ʿisha* sometime between sunset and midnight. If one is ill or on a journey, combining the noon and afternoon prayers, or the sunset and evening prayers, is acceptable. As we shall see in chapter 6, Muslims have some difference in opinion as to what to do if one's workplace does not permit prayer at the appropriate time. Some Muslims who find the prayers difficult to perform in the workplace may combine the noon and afternoon prayers. Occasionally, and now more frequently, students in public schools will ask for the right to pray. "My cousin and I were the only two Muslims in the school, and the school did not want to give us permission to leave the room to pray," recalls a Palestinian woman. "I told my teacher that if he wouldn't let me pray, I was going to walk out of class and do so anyway. Finally, they backed down and let us go."[3] Some Muslim students are finding common cause with Christian students who want prayer in the public schools, working around the law by organizing prayer clubs after classroom hours.

Visitors to the Muslim world over the centuries have seldom failed to be struck, sometimes enchanted, by the call to prayer (*adhan*: literally, "proclamation" or "announcement") through which the faithful are reminded to interrupt their daily routines to remember God. So important is the ritual prayer in Islam that the one to give that call to prayer, called the *mu'adhdhin*, has been said to be worthy of special merit in many of the traditions of the Prophet. Throughout the centuries, the call to prayer has been sung from atop a minaret, or tower, of the mosque. While the *adhan* in some senses parallels such reminders in other traditions, as, for example, the *shofar* (ram's horn) in Judaism or the tolling of bells in Christianity, it is unique in its reliance on the human voice. The *mu'adhdhin* receives careful training as to proper intonation and vocalization, and his craft has been seen as one of the great arts of Islam. At the specified time he (and it is always a man who performs this function) ascends to his place on the minaret, or to some other appropriate spot, turns toward Mecca, and begins his recitation. In recent times, particularly in the major Islamic cities, the noises of traffic and industry have necessitated replacing the live human voice with a recording played over a loudspeaker. Some American cities have seen great controversy about whether the call to prayer should be allowed to "disturb" the other residents of the neighborhood in which a mosque is located. Different communities have come to terms with this problem in different ways. Most often in American mosques the call is given inside the prayer hall rather than outside, serving not so much as a reminder to the faithful to pray as a kind of beginning to the prayer ritual. The *adhan* itself sometimes functions as a kind of prayer, and as such is whispered into the ear of a newborn baby, first in the right and then in the left. Shi'ites sometimes add to the prayer a phrase of special respect for 'Ali.

The *salat* cannot be carried out without careful preparation on the part of the worshiper, including entering into a state of ritual purity, which involves both the cleansing of the body and the purification and readying of the mind and heart. Ritual washing (*wudu'*) is performed outside or inside the mosque and includes wiping water over the head, ears, neck, and feet. American buildings that have been adapted as mosques have had to designate certain facilities specifically to this purpose, normally with separate washing places for men and women. During prayer a man's body should be covered at least from his waist to his knees, and by most interpretations a woman should have only her face and hands uncovered. After washing, one performs the *niyya*, or intention, which serves as the transition from ordinary daily activity to the special state of prayerful attention.

Ritualized prayer can take place in the mosque, at home, or in any other place that is clean and appropriate. The congregational prayer is traditionally held on Friday, attended by men and sometimes by women (chapter 5 will deal with the topic of women's participation in the prayer). In America this communal ritual is often (also) observed on Sunday because of the difficulty some worshipers have in getting away from their work on Fridays. Muslims also practice a private, personal, and nonritualized form of prayer called *du'a*, in which the worshiper addresses God in praise and supplication.

Place for performing *wudu'* or ritualized washing before the prayer in the Islamic Center of Cleveland, Ohio. COURTESY ISLAMIC CENTER OF CLEVELAND, OHIO

3. *Almsgiving.* In a number of places the Qur'an specifically enjoins the believer to pay the alms tax (*zakat*, sometimes rendered *zakah*). "Truly those who recite God's book, perform the salat, and spend privately and publicly from what We have provided to them, are engaged in an enterprise that never fails" (Sura 35:29). From the earliest days the Prophet preached that those who call themselves Muslims have a responsibility to care for the less fortunate among them. The Qur'an particularly identifies the poor, widows, and orphans as needing attention. The responsibility of giving away a portion of one's personal property on a regular basis has served a number of purposes in the structure of the Islamic *umma*, not all of them, of course, functioning perfectly in all instances. In theory, however, it does indeed give support for the needy and assures a more equitable distribution of wealth. *Zakat* provides support for the maintenance of the Islamic state as a whole (a function especially important in the early days of Muhammad's community), and it is a means of thanking God for the blessings he has bestowed. The word *zakat* itself suggests both piety and purity, underscoring the relationship of financial responsibility to righteous living. Like all Islamic requirements, its observance helps assure the giver of a better chance for a felicitous reward in the hereafter.

Technically, *zakat* is a tax of 2.5 percent of what is estimated to be the sum value of all of one's possessions. It is not, therefore, an income tax as such but takes into consideration the totality of a person's holdings. In the early centuries the central authorities kept the monies collected through *zakat* and distributed them to run the state. *Zakat* earnings were used not only for charitable purposes but for education, the ransom of captives, and other purposes deemed important for the welfare of the community. Non-Muslims, specifically Jews and Christians who had "protected" status as People of the Book, had to pay a poll tax instead. The administration of *zakat* is considerably more difficult now than in earlier days, particularly since so many countries in which Muslims reside have a mandatory income tax. For the most part, giving to charity is considered voluntary today, although Muslims are strongly encouraged to understand regularized giving to worthy causes to be part of their religious responsibilities and an expression of their piety and righteousness. A few Muslim countries insist on the right of the government to levy a *zakat* tax on its citizens. In most of the Islamic world, the government runs and financially subsidizes the mosques. In America, of course, this is not the case, and the American Muslim community has had much discussion about how to understand and employ *zakat* to build and maintain mosques.

Increasingly, *zakat* is also being understood as a means of providing some kind of service to members of the community. Such service can be handled either by organizations and Islamic centers, small private groups, or even individuals. A Kansas high school senior talks about the work she and her friends do in hospitals, soup kitchens, and retirement homes: "Our youth group . . . visits these places and helps people. Many of them are very lonely, and they enjoy and appreciate having someone to talk to. Since many of them have never met Muslims before, we talk to them about our religion and tell them what we believe and why we dress the way we do. . . . It makes us feel good to do something."[4]

4. *Fasting during the month of Ramadan.* While the Qur'an contains a number of references, some direct and some oblique, to the other four pillars, in only one place does it specifically enjoin fasting during the month of Ramadan: "O you faithful, fasting is ordained for you in the same way that it was ordained for those who came before you, so that you may fear God. . . . It was during the month of Ramadan that the Qur'an was sent down as a guidance for humanity. . . . Whoever among you sees the moon, then he should fast, but the one who is sick or on a journey, [can fast] an equal number of other days" (Sura 2:183–85). Specifically, this passage means that everyone of an appropriate age (generally recognized to be past puberty) and not too elderly or infirm is expected to refrain from food, drink, tobacco, and sexual relations during the daylight hours of this month. In a kind of subsidiary fashion, Muslims are also expected to follow the strictest ethical codes during this time, being especially careful to be honest, thoughtful, and sensitive to the needs of others and to refrain not only from eating and drinking but also from using foul language and untruthful words. A frequently cited saying of the Prophet Muhammad is "God does not need the fast of a person who does not abandon false speech or acting according to his false speech."

Like many of the duties required of Muslims, fasting has both physical and spiritual dimensions. As prayer and pilgrimage involve the body as well as the mind and heart, fasting and the breaking of the fast engage the totality of one's faculties. To fast each day from the first morning light to the setting of the sun requires intense mental, emotional, and bodily discipline. The act of eating at the end of the day, when one smells and tastes the first fruits and sweets, involves the heart in thanksgiving and the senses in the enjoyment of food. In Islamic understanding, God has constructed the universe according to a balance (*mizan*, the same word used for the balance that will weigh one's deeds on the Day of Judgment). Thus each of the five

Advertisement from the Islamic Circle of North America suggesting how Muslims might spend their *zakat* or alms tax. COURTESY ICNA RELIEF

responsibilities balances and supports the others, and all of the constituent elements that go to make up the human person work together in balance and harmony.

"When I was growing up in Pakistan, we never thought of Ramadan as a month of spiritual reawakening. It was more a kind of cultural festival. It is good that our youth here are challenging the old customs and thinking about Ramadan from a fresh perspective," says a Muslim mother who lives in Chicago, when asked about the time of fasting. "Ramadan should be a time not only for focusing on our own obligations or even our own spiritual needs. We should use it as the occasion to introduce Islam to others, and even to organize special food drives for the homeless and poor," remarks a youth from Washington, D.C. "I eagerly wait for this month. I love being in the mosque every day listening to the divine message. I rediscover myself in this month. I think I grow in every aspect of my personality each year," says a young Muslima in southern California.[5] These comments suggest some of the ways in which Muslims experience the month of Ramadan in the American context.

Only recently have the American media realized that many Muslims in this country do something noteworthy during one month of the year. It comes as a refreshing change from the concentration of the press on so-called "Islamic extremism" to find some thoughtful and even appreciative coverage of this important time in the life of the Muslim community. Muslims themselves are devoting increasing attention in their journals, periodicals, and websites to sharing with one another the importance of this month-long event, and in particular to hearing the responses of the youth of the community to the experience of participating in it.

The rigorous and demanding discipline of the fast is exacerbated when it must be carried out in an area of the world lacking ready facilities for its support or understanding on the part of most non-Muslims about its purpose. Not all Muslims in the United States participate fully, or even at all, in this stringent exercise, although many of those who choose not to fast express the wish that they had either the discipline or the support to be able to do so. Those who do fast clearly believe that the rewards fully justify the rigors. "All of a sudden my sleeping and work habits change," insists a teenaged Muslim boy who has only recently practiced the full fast. "I sleep early and wake up early. I feel an urge to read the Qur'an and think about what it means. I really look forward to the breaking of the fast every day not so much because I am hungry, although of course I am, but because it is really the only time of the year when we are sure that the whole family will sit around one table sharing food." "I do fast," says a young woman. "It used to be that I would stop eating some meals, and in between I would smoke or drink a Coke or something. But since then I have begun coming to the mosque, and I realize that fasting really means a commitment to God. Now Ramadan is not just another month for me but a special time for developing self-control."[6]

Traditionally, the day is said to begin when one can distinguish a white thread from a black one by the early light of the morning, and to end when that distinction can no longer be made at the end of the day. The months of the lunar calendar, which are slightly shorter than solar months, in effect rotate around the Western calendar. Thus Ramadan may fall at any time of the year and "moves forward" a few days each year. Fasting in the winter is generally less arduous because the days are shorter and there is less heat, while strict observance during the summer can be particularly difficult. "I used to work in the lumber yards all day," comments an Arab student who used to live in the Pacific Northwest. "It takes a lot of energy, and particularly in the summer when the days are long and hot it is really hard not to even have any water. My boss sort of understood what I was doing, but not enough to let me take any time to rest like I would have been able to do back home."[7]

The many Muslim theologians and commentators who have thought, spoken, and written about the fast of Ramadan over the centuries have suggested that it leads to a number of beneficial ends. Considered both a physical and a spiritual regimen, fasting brings a greater appreciation for the blessings of God, which are so easily taken for granted; it ensures that one reflects on what it means to live in obedience to the commands of God; it reminds one that one's life is truly in God's hands; and it serves to unite in fellowship all of those who are participating in this observance. The month of the fast is also traditionally the time in which the faithful extend special forgiveness to anyone who might have offended them. That it may also be a time of reaching out to people outside the Islamic community, while not unknown to Muslims in other times and places, is a particular contribution of those who are living in America. Recognizing that fasting is a part of Jewish and Christian practice, some commentators have suggested that this month is a special time for the promotion of better interfaith understanding. The Washington, D.C.-based Council on American-Islamic Relations (CAIR) posts on the Internet detailed suggestions for publicizing the meaning of and the events related to Ramadan. Its "Ramadan Publicity Campaign Summary and Tips" includes proposals for contacting newspapers, television and radio stations, schools, libraries, and hospitals, as well as ideas for organizing daily *iftar* (breaking the fast) meals for the homeless and food drives for the needy.

Leaders of the various American Muslim communities currently are giving a good deal of attention to the importance of Ramadan as a time of charitable outreach. Noting that some Muslims, out of concern for their bodies during the fast, tend to go into a kind of hibernation, sleeping excessively and saving energy, they insist that the physical regimen of not eating combined with the proper mental and spiritual attitude should actually serve to give one new energy, which is then to be directed outward. Urging that Ramadan should be a month of increased physical activity, some turn to the example of the Prophet, who, during the nine Ramadans he experienced between the establishment of his community in Medina and his death in 632 C.E., engaged in a series of activities designed to illustrate the power of Islam and the example of sacrifice and submission to God. Particular efforts at outreach during Ramadan might include having young people from one Islamic center go to an orphanage to give out clothes and toys and talk with the children about Islam and the meaning of a month's fasting. With the growing numbers of Muslims in prison, the observance of Ramadan for the incarcerated is drawing increasing attention. Muslims are taking this special time to visit prisons to speak to Muslim inmates about the faith and about the significance of fasting. Some even stay to participate in the special prayers and Qur'an recitation of the Night of Power, which in some prisons may last all night.

The literature of Islam pays increasing attention to ways of sharing this important time with non-Muslims. Physician and Islamic scholar Dr. Hassan Hathout of the Islamic Center of Southern California, for example, wonders whether it might be possible to let non-Muslims actually experience the benefits of Ramadan, even if just for one day. In an article titled "Visions of a Fasting Muslim" in the Muslim journal *Islamic Horizons*, he notes that along with Mother's and Father's Days, Valentine's Day, and President's Day, we now have days for secretaries, bosses, and whomever else. "The wild dream that engages one's imagination is this: would it at all be possible for America at large to observe a similar day?" His suggestion is for a "Self-Control Day" with the slogan "Just Say No" prominently displayed to encourage various forms of abstinence. This day might significantly lower the incidence of violence, drunk driving, drug consumption, and crime in general. The purpose, of course, would be to instill in Americans the desire to extend such forms of self-control beyond a single day. "Can the Muslim then invite America to a national day of fasting?" he asks. While such possibilities are more rhetorical than concrete, they do suggest a growing feeling among American Muslims that others have something to learn from their observances.

5. *Performing the pilgrimage to the holy city of Mecca once during one's lifetime*. The Qur'an contains several references to the necessity of visiting Mecca on pilgrimage, as in the following: "Fulfill the pilgrimage and the visitation unto God" (Sura 2:196–97). Although the Prophet moved his community to Medina at the time of the *hijra*, it has always remained second in the worship life of Muslims to the place of his birth and the home of the Ka'ba, the most sacred shrine of Islam with its venerated Black Stone reportedly given by the angel Gabriel to Abraham. When Muhammad returned to Mecca, he cleansed it of all impurity from having housed idols. The Ka'ba

became the symbol of the victory of the Islamic community and regained its status as the central sanctuary for those who worship the one true God. It is the responsibility of each Muslim to make at least one ritual visit (*hajj*) to Mecca, and many choose to return more than once to experience the thrill of joining with literally millions of fellow worshipers in the adoration of the one God. The official time for the pilgrimage is during the month named Dhu al-Hijja, the last month in the lunar calendar. One may also choose to make an individual pilgrimage at any other time of the year, which is called not *hajj* but *'umra* and is known as the "lesser pilgrimage."

Those who have reported their experiences on the *hajj* generally attest to its enormous significance in their personal religious lives. "How was I to know this would be the journey of a lifetime," muses a Muslima from Philadelphia. "Tears poured down my face like a fresh spring shower. The air left a sweet taste in my mouth, as if I had eaten the most succulent piece of fruit. I am here, really here. My eyes scanned this canvas of buoyant faces, effervescent smiles and nodding heads affirming the peace felt in their hearts. The serenade of voices from many tongues, this a cornucopia of Allah's servants, made a soothing welcome. . . . My Hajj experience served as my vehicle for the placating of my soul. This excursion took me up the paths and down the trails of the human spirit. The internal strength I gained induced a genuine love of Allah."[8] The gathering of so many people in what is considered to be the most holy spot on earth—up to two million may be there at one time—is literally quite overwhelming. Some have expressed their awe as akin to a combination of intense reverence mingled with fear of both the power of the occasion and the practical reality of moving within such giant circles of humanity.

Because of the sheer numbers, the experience that is supposed to engender such great joy, however, can also be rather intimidating for some. A Pakistani Muslim who teaches high school in Denver, Colorado, relates that she made her first pilgrimage when she was only sixteen. "Even though I clung tightly to the hands of my parents," she said, "I was terrified that I might get swept away from them just because there were such great throngs of people. When I went again in my twenties I was better able to cope and appreciate the experience for its enormous awe and beauty."[9]

It is often said that during the pilgrimage the true idea of an egalitarian Islam is realized. All male worshipers, whatever their status or position in everyday life, don the same simple white cloth to symbolize a state of ritual purity and participate in the same set of ceremonial rituals. Women are allowed more flexibility in their dress.

The process of the pilgrimage begins when the pilgrim states his or her intention, *niyya*, and greets the city of Mecca with the cry "Here I am, Lord, here I am!" During the days of the *hajj* pilgrims circumambulate the Ka'ba, kiss the black stone, and reenact Hagar's legendary search for water to give her infant son, Ishmael. Toward the end of the pilgrimage, which lasts some ten days, pilgrims journey through Mina to the plain of 'Arafat, where the worshiper recalls the struggle of the patriarch Abraham against idolatry. Back in Mina, pilgrims throw seven stones at a small pillar in the main square said to symbolize the recalcitrant Satan. The last act of the pilgrimage is the sacrificing of an animal with its head facing Mecca. Some of the meat is eaten and the rest distributed to the needy. At this point the (male) pilgrim's head is shaved, and he begins the process of desacralization. Throughout the *hajj* ritual the worshiper says many prayers and listens to many sermons to help orient himself or herself to the proper attitude and response. Some pilgrims choose to visit the tomb of the Prophet in Medina, although that is not a formal part of the pilgrimage. Passengers on international airlines at the conclusion of the pilgrimage often see returning pilgrims carrying large plastic bottles of water from the well of Zamzam, a life-giving source said to have been provided by God for Hagar and Ishmael. These waters are believed to retain their restorative powers.

The Saudi state goes to enormous lengths to provide for the safety and welfare of pilgrims. Huge tent cities are erected to house them, many meals are prepared, and transportation to the outlying areas is provided for those who cannot walk. While occasionally accidents happen, there is generally remarkably little illness or other problems, given the massive numbers of people who must be accommodated. The "miracle" of the undertaking, however, is said to pale in significance compared with the personal "miracle" experienced by the individual worshipers during this ritual that is truly the event of a lifetime. Because non-Muslims are not allowed in Mecca, careful procedures are maintained to assure that those who participate are genuine Muslims, sincere in their *shahada*. The man or woman who has completed the pilgrimage is known, respectively, as a *hajji* or *hajja* and is accorded special respect by the members of his or her family and community.

In recent years, a number of books and films have chronicled the events of the *hajj*, providing access both for Muslims and non-Muslims to the events and emotions of the experience. Michael Wolfe, for example, in his book *The Hadj: An American's Pilgrimage to Mecca*, takes the reader through each stage and experience of the pilgrimage. It is recommended for those planning on making the pilgrimage themselves, as well as those who as outsiders can never have the experience but can benefit from the candid perspectives of this American Muslim.[10] As more educational material about the beliefs and practices of Islam becomes available to the American public, and as the media provide more coverage of the ritual observances of Islam, Muslims hope that other Americans can see Islam as a faith of beauty, rigor, and ethical responsibility rather than as the vehicle of terror and the inspiration of "Islamic bombs."

Some American Muslims are particularly critical of their fellows who do not observe the five ritual practices as diligently as they might. A practicing physician who writes about his understanding of the right way to practice Islam, for example, calls those whom he sees as too casual about their faith "Supermarket Muslims." Accusing such persons of being interested mainly in aspiring to the Western upper class, he says, "They don't pray on a daily basis, but usually on Fridays and always on the Festival days to the pre-scribed prayer. They do not fast for the fear of becoming weak (or have another excuse). They usually do not calculate the poor-due, but do give charity to ward off evil. They sometimes go for *umrah* but hardly go for the *hajj*. . . ."[11] Many Muslims are less than appreciative of having their reli-gious observances under such critique, and some are writing publicly about their right as individuals to respond to the demands of their religion in ways that reflect their own faith and understanding. Who has the authority to determine what constitutes the genuine practice of Islam in the American context is one of the many matters to which the community must turn its attention in the coming decades.

CHAPTER TWO

Contributors to the Development of Islam

What is Islam? For American Muslims, it means many different things, although the most immediate answer is that it consists of the revelation of the Qur'an, the experiences of its Prophet, and its requirements of faith and practice. This is Islam in its essential meaning. However, the many individuals who over the centuries have called themselves Muslim have shaped and developed Islam as a living faith. In the same way, the decisions American Muslims make about how to understand and practice the faith in a Western context will significantly define Islam in the next century. In this chapter we will learn about the development of the religion over the fourteen centuries of its existence as illustrated in the lives of people recognized to have helped mold Islam into its present reality. Included here are many of the men and women whose particular contributions to faithful living, understanding, and interpretation have shaped and determined the kinds of Islam to which American Muslims today adhere.

The Prophet Muhammad and the Revelation of the Qur'an

For the Muslim today, as has been true over the centuries, Muhammad is understood to have been fully human, in no way sharing in the divinity that is God's alone. Indeed, he had humble origins and was raised as an orphan by his uncle Abu Talib. While Muhammad was still in his early teens, it is said that a Christian monk recognized in him signs of prophecy. Another story relates that when a stone fell from the Ka'ba, the tribes of Mecca quarreled as to which one should have the honor of replacing it. The young Muhammad is said to have solved the problem by placing the stone on a cloth that representatives of all the tribes could lift up together. By the age of twenty-five he was employed in the lucrative camel trade of a well-to-do merchant woman named Khadija, whom he ultimately married. Muhammad and Khadija's marriage was apparently a warm and close one, and until her death his wife was his strongest supporter. She is considered the first to accept the call to Islam. They had four daughters, of whom the best known is Fatima. All of their three sons died as infants, complicating the matter of community leadership when the Prophet himself died in 632.

Mecca, where Muhammad lived and first preached, was a well-developed commercial town at the crossroads of major trade routes connecting Africa to the Far East. It was also the center of a pilgrimage route, providing a lucrative business for many of its inhabitants, which they did not wish to see disrupted by any new preaching. The century or so before the time of the Prophet, who received his first revelations circa 610 C.E., is generally known as the *jahiliyya*, or time of ignorance, a term highlighting the fact that worship of idols in and around the local shrine was the religious practice of the day. The shrine itself, the Ka'ba still visited by Muslims on pilgrimage and considered the holiest of shrines, is believed by Muslims to have been built by the Prophet Abraham with the assistance of his son Ishmael. The Prophet transformed the ancient practice of pilgrimage from a time of idolatrous adoration to the *hajj* described in chapter 1.

Arabia at the time of Muhammad's youth had a vague concept of a kind of supreme creator God called Allah (literally, Al-Lah, "The God"), but three goddesses, or "daughters" of Allah, named Al-Lat, Manat, and Al-'Uzza, along with a male god called Hubal, held sway. Among the many reasons why Muslims all over the world several years ago accused the notorious Salman Rushdie of blasphemy in his novel *The Satanic Verses* was his portrayal of the Prophet Muhammad as having acknowledged the existence of one of those goddesses on his deathbed.

> "Who's there?" [Muhammad] called out. "Is it Thou, Azraeel [the angel of death]?" But Ayesha ['A'isha] heard a terrible, sweet voice, that was a woman's, make reply: "No, Messenger of Al-Lah, it is not Azraeel." And the lamp blew out; and in the darkness [Muhammad] asked: "Is this sickness then thy doing, O Al-Lat?" And she said, "It is my revenge upon you, and I am satisfied. . . ."[1]

Tradition affirms that while Muhammad was on a retreat in a cave near Mecca, he was stunned to hear a voice commanding him to recite in the name of the Lord. The year was 610, and Muhammad was forty years old. The words of God to the trembling Muhammad, mediated through the angel Gabriel, are recorded in chapter 96 of the Qur'an, generally conceded to be the first of the divine revelations: "Recite in the name of your Lord who created man from a clot of blood. Recite, for truly your Lord is the most generous. He taught by the pen, taught man that which he did not know." A man with no pretensions to having achieved such a high state of contemplation as to have induced this experience, Muhammad was understandably terrified. It was on his descent from the mountain that he saw the figure of the angel Gabriel filling all the horizon and heard the voice declaring that he, Muhammad, was the Messenger of God. Covering himself with his cloak in fear, he ran home as fast as he could, begging his wife to protect him. Again according to tradition, she wisely encouraged him to heed the voice of God.

The Arabic word for "recite" is the same as the word for "read," and the response given by Muhammad in Arabic to God's first command, recorded not in the Qur'an but in the traditions, at once serves to express the question "What shall I recite?" and the statement "I cannot read." The dogma that he was unlettered is not developed in the Qur'an but is detailed in later commentaries. While it may seem difficult to support in light of his association with the caravan trade, it is important in portraying him as a pure recipient of divine revelation. Because he was illiterate, goes the argument, he could not have read and copied anything from other sacred writings circulating around Arabia at the time. He received the first revelation from God through the angel Gabriel during the month of Ramadan, on what is referred to as the "Night of Power." Coming near the end of the month, it is generally marked by special observances in the mosques of America.

With Khadija's support, and with the arrival of subsequent messages that he recognized as coming from God, Muhammad began to fulfill the vocation to which the angel charged him. He was to receive many more direct communications from God over the next twenty-two years. In the earlier days these were generally mediated through Gabriel, on the understanding that direct communication between human and divine is too overwhelming to be borne without training and experience. Later, as the Prophet grew in spiritual strength and wisdom, such mediation was no longer necessary.

The earliest revelations to the Prophet contained two messages that were foreign to the citizens of Arabia at that time. First, Muhammad preached that there is only one God, that the many deities and especially the daughters of God are a fiction, and that human beings have the responsibility to acknowledge God's oneness by their own submission. Second, he tried to convince his listeners that, contrary to their current beliefs, life does not end with death, that immortality is not only through progeny but that all will be resurrected and judged at the end of time. From the earliest days of his receiving these messages from God, he understood that one of his most important roles was to warn the heedless that they would ultimately be called to accountability for their actions.

Muhammad found few who were ready to appreciate his preaching. His own tribe, called the Quraish, opposed him at every turn, ridiculing his claim to prophecy. The death of his beloved wife, Khadija, and the loss of his uncle and protector, Abu Talib, made the Prophet's task even more difficult. Muslims today accord special honor to Muhammad for his faith and singleness of purpose in preaching the message of God during these dark and seemingly hopeless days. For years he was unable to persuade more than a small handful of believers of the essential truth of his teachings. In addition, the stringent moral content of the divine revelation required believers to help the needy, to care for the hungry and the orphans, and to offer hospitality to all. While these values were not unknown in *jahiliyya* society, they represented a new kind of social order, which constituted one more threat to an established and comfortable way of life in the community of Mecca.

Despite the extreme difficulties that attended the first decade of Muhammad's Meccan preaching, a small band of followers gradually formed. Others after Khadija came to acknowledge the truth of his teachings, including his cousin 'Ali and Abu Bakr, who was to be the first caliph, or leader, of the community after Muhammad's death.

Then came an event that was to change his fortunes dramatically. A delegation from a city several hundred miles north of Mecca invited him to arbitrate a matter deeply contested among its tribes. It is clear that the Prophet's reputation as a wise statesman was beginning to spread. Determining that the antagonism toward him personally as well as the opposition to his message was so great in Mecca as to make the revelations' propagation virtually impossible, Muhammad took the opportunity to migrate with his small band of followers to the new location. The city was Yathrib, later to be known as Madinat al-Rasul (the city of the Messenger) or Medina, and to become the second holiest city in Islam and Muhammad's final resting place. The year of this *hijra*, or migration, was 622, and it signals the formal beginning of the community (*umma*) of Islam as such. The Islamic calendar, which is based on lunar rather than solar cycles and consists of 354 days, starts at the moment of the *hijra*.

Those attempting to provide an appropriate historical antecedent for the Muslim community as a minority in America frequently invoke the example of the *hijra*. As the Prophet and his small band of followers were able to find a home in Medina and to establish a vibrant Islamic community, so Muslims today emigrating from their homelands see the *hijra* as a model for living together responsibly as Muslims in the new and often alien context of America.

The story of the growth and spread of Islam from this base in Medina is well known. Muhammad established himself as the true prophet-statesman, the religious leader who continued to share with his community the revelations that came regularly from God, and the political leader who gradually consolidated power over the whole of Arabia. Most of the tribes of Arabia came either to acknowledge the truth of his message, converting to Islam in faith, or to recognize his rising political power, converting out of expediency and a desire to throw in their lot with the victor.

Meanwhile, the revelations from God continued to arrive. Although those he received while struggling in Mecca were generally short and focused, Medinan revelations were longer and more concerned with the particular issues that the Prophet was facing as he moved to consolidate his community. During this time much of the legislation that was to become the basis for the establishment of the Islamic law, or *shari'a*, was set down. At the same time that the Prophet was advancing the political fortunes of Islam, he was also developing a structure for the religious and social life of his followers. He himself exhibited the virtues, many of which were extensions of the values of pre-Islamic Arabia, that have come to characterize the righteous Muslim. Among these are honesty, generosity, hospitality, charity, fairness, and modesty. It is on these qualities that many American Muslims seek to pattern their lives.

During the consolidation of the community at Medina the basic relationship between male and female followers of Muhammad was established. There is little doubt that women were considered full members of the *umma*, that they participated in its public as well as private life, and that they shared in both the developing set of religious obligations and worship activities. Many Muslim women in America today look to the time of the Prophet as one in which women's rights were fully acknowledged and implemented and in which women were encouraged to assume positions of leadership in the community. They challenge any of their coreligionists who want to continue excluding women from public spheres, pointing to the egalitarian practices of the Prophet and the example of many of his wives, who held positions of economic, political, and even religious leadership. The traditions of Islam insist that Muhammad extended every possible effort to treat his wives fairly and equally, although it seems clear that he most deeply loved his first spouse, Khadija, and his youngest wife, 'A'isha. It was in Medina that the regulations for marriage and divorce were established. It was also there that he received the revelation advising that, to protect their privacy, his wives stay hidden by a partition when he was visited by delegations of men. Some have argued that it was this verse, mistakenly extrapolated to apply to all other women, that served as the impetus for the seclusion and exclusion of women from public life that was to characterize many succeeding centuries of Islam.

Two years before he died, Muhammad succeeded in subduing Mecca, the city of his ancestry. Following his policy of charity whenever possible, the Prophet granted amnesty to all its inhabitants, despite their years of opposition to him and his message.

Before he died, he took his followers on a final pilgrimage to the Holy City of Mecca. On the way, God revealed to him the following message, which is now found in chapter 5, verse 3 of the Qur'an: "Today I have completed for you your religion and have fulfilled My favor to you, and have chosen for you al-islam as your religion." The Arabic word for "I have completed" (akmaltu) is also the word for "I have perfected," and Muslims see in these definitions the affirmation that Islam is both complete and perfect, the best and most appropriate way in which to acknowledge and worship the one God and to live in right relationship with one's fellows. Much contemporary Islamic apologetic turns to this verse as the final proof that Islam is indeed the right and true religion for all humankind.

In 632, after a brief illness, the Prophet of God succumbed. By then he had managed to consolidate virtually all of the Arabian peninsula under Islam and set the stage for what was to be the quick and remarkable spread of the faith across much of the known world.

Pioneers of Early Islam

Muslims in America today look not only to the Prophet as the exemplar of right and faithful living but also to many of Muhammad's family members, companions, and associates for inspiration. Though these people lived at the beginning of the history of Islam, they are held up as models by those in positions of authority today. Both men and women who are adopting the faith of Islam look to these early pioneers as they select Muslim names, and Muslims continue to refer to the early days of the community for guidance in their relationships with one another as well as with God.

When his beloved wife Khadija died, the Prophet suffered an enormous personal loss. Although for political reasons he later married a number of wives, he was never to find another who played quite the same role for him as had Khadija. It is said, however, that it was the daughter of Abu Bakr, 'A'isha, who captured his heart and held it to the end of his life. 'A'isha's most important religious role was as collector and recorder of traditions from and about Muhammad. By virtue of her position as the wife closest to Muhammad, her memories were particularly important. It is said that more than twelve hundred traditions are credited directly to her. Among record-ed instances of women leading prayers for other women in the early com-munity, 'A'isha is the most often mentioned. She was at the Prophet's side when he died, and she herself was buried a quarter of a century later in Medina. Of all the names taken by American women who convert to Islam, 'A'isha is one of the most popular.

Among the very earliest of the supporters of the Prophet, in the days in which support was very difficult to come by, was 'A'isha's father, Abu Bakr. Although Muhammad was three years his senior, Abu Bakr was to become his father-in-law when he married the young 'A'isha. Abu Bakr was one of the small group to accompany the Prophet in the *hijra* to Medina. Known for his wisdom and piety, he had been selected by Muhammad to perform the important function of leading the prayer when he himself was unable.

As the Prophet recited each revelation he received from God, one of the companions recorded it on whatever material was available. When Muham-mad died, those fragments were gathered into various collections. A few minor variations in these collections appeared, and soon it became clear that some kind of official version was necessary. Abu Bakr is said to have initiat-ed the production of a standard version, although it was officially complet-ed under the rule of the third caliph, 'Uthman b. 'Affan, some twenty years after the Prophet's death.

When Muhammad died, there was consternation in the young commu-nity not only at the loss of its beloved leader but also at the lack of a clearly established policy for determining future leadership. Blood succession through a son was not a possibility, as all of Muhammad's own sons died in infancy. The Prophet's companions gathered to make a decision, reassuring the followers that there would indeed be an orderly and wise transfer of authority. Because of his reputation for faith and piety, the companions chose Abu Bakr to assume official leadership as the *khalifa*, or caliph. Abu Bakr was followed by 'Umar (for ten years) and then 'Uthman (for twelve years) as caliphs of the young Muslim community.

Despite successes in the growth and spread of Islam externally, there were serious internal tensions. Both 'Umar and 'Uthman died by the knife. The community chose 'Ali to be the fourth caliph, but he faced serious challenge, from both 'A'isha and the forces of a Damascene governor named Mu'awiya. In what has been called the "Battle of the Camel," 'A'isha rode out with a small army to oppose 'Ali. It must have been a somewhat bizarre scene as the beloved wife of the Prophet engaged in battle against his also beloved cousin and son-in-law. Many men died defending 'A'isha, but in the end 'Ali was the victor. This incident, marking the first time that Muslim forces fought against one another, has served the designs of commentators who argue that a woman's place is not on the battlefield, in the political arena, or anywhere else outside the home.

All during the early days of Islam a number of Muslims felt that succession through the natural bloodline of the Prophet, not popular acclaim or election, should determine the leadership of the community. Thus they felt that the legitimate first leader should have been 'Ali rather than Abu Bakr, by virtue of his blood relationship as cousin to Muhammad. Muslims became irreconcilably split as supporters of 'Ali broke away to form what has become known as the party of 'Ali, or Shi'ites. Thus came into being the two major divisions of Islam, Sunnis (those who followed the Sunna of the Prophet and accepted the authority of the line of caliphs) and Shi'ites, or Shi'a. Unlike the Sunnis, Shi'ites have always believed that Prophet Muhammad designated 'Ali to be the leader of the *umma* after his death and that the first three caliphs were able leaders but not true spiritual guides.

Despite these internal divisions, all Muslims acknowledge the significance of 'Ali in the life of the early Islamic community. It is said that, after Khadija, either he or Abu Bakr was the first to recognize the prophethood of Muhammad. 'Ali was instrumental in facilitating Muhammad's flight to Medina, providing a ruse to cover his departure. In fact, it was 'Ali who later suggested that the *hijra* mark the beginning of the Muslim calendar. The Sunnis say that 'Ali was the transmitter of many traditions of the Prophet and a significant religious authority. The Shi'ites consider him the preeminent holy person of Islam after the Prophet, the first Imam, and the most saintly servant of God.

In the year 661 'Ali was to meet his end with the same violence that had done in his two predecessors. Entering a mosque for prayer, he was struck by a poisoned sword. The violence that claimed the lives of three of the four "rightly-guided caliphs" has been manifested all too often throughout the history of Islam and has stood in stark and unhappy contrast to the ideals of peace and communal support that are at the heart of the Islamic message. Despite the political turmoil and bloodshed that characterized their rule, Sunnis refer to the first four rulers as the "rightly guided caliphs," and their period in Sunni Islam (632–661) is often idealized as a time of near-perfection.

While the Shi'a have experienced various splits and divisions over their long history, they are united in their conviction that the greatest of injustices was done in the early days of Islam when Husayn, 'Ali and Fatima's son and the grandson of the Prophet, was gruesomely massacred in the fields of Karbala in Iraq. Sunni Muslims as well as Shi'ites have lamented the Karbala event, but it is among the Shi'a that the most regularized practices of remembrance and participation in the suffering of Husayn have become established. This event is memorialized in the observance of Muharram, one of the most important of holy days for American Shi'ites.

The largest number of Shi'ites believe that twelve Imams succeeded Muhammad, the last of whom disappeared in 873 at the age of four for reasons of political persecution. He remains alive but hidden, guiding the affairs of his community through his designated leaders. This branch of Shi'ites is known as the Ithna 'Ashariyya Shi'ites—in English, Twelver Shi'ites. They live in hope of the return of the hidden Imam to serve as the deliverer, under whom there will be a final rule of justice and peace.

Another group of Shi'ites split from the main body in 765 over the issue of which son of the sixth Imam, Ja'far al-Sadiq, should be considered the legitimate successor. The Twelvers believe that the one designated was the second son, Musa al-Kazim, while others are convinced that the legitimate leader should have been the first son, Isma'il. The latter are thereby known as the Isma'ilis, or more colloquially and in contrast to the Ithna 'Ashariyya, the Seveners. Twelver and Sevener Shi'ites together form about one fifth of the American Muslim community.

The Early Development of the Islamic Community

The community of Muslims in Medina established its presence and extended its domain first through a series of marauding expeditions, then through more serious and carefully planned encounters. Although Abu Bakr's rule as caliph lasted only two years, under the leadership of a talented commander of the armed forces he was able to see the lands of Islam begin their expansion. First, rebellions in Arabia were quelled, and Islam began to move into Palestine, Persia, and Byzantium. The final advance of the Muslim East into the Christian West came when Muslim armies crossed the Pyrenees from Spain into France. The northward spread of Islam was stopped at last in 632 when the legendary Charles Martel repelled Muslim forces outside Poitiers. By the beginning of the ninth century, however, the West had virtually lost control of the Mediterranean as a result of the expansion of Islam.

A little more than a century after the death of the Prophet, dramatic changes also came to the heartland of Islam. The 'Umayyad Caliphate, which had ruled since the death of 'Ali, gave way to the beginning of 'Abbasid rule in 750. This political change prompted a young 'Umayyad prince to flee westward and establish a separate caliphate in Spain, which was to rule the Iberian peninsula for the next two centuries. The 'Abbasids moved the capital from 'Umayyad Damascus to the newly created Baghdad, in Arabic called "the City of Peace." With this, the *umma* of Islam was to turn into an empire of enormous political power, great opulence, economic prosperity, and cultural achievement such as has scarcely been rivaled. Muslims in the West today take pride in recalling the glory of the 'Abbasid days, especially its accomplishments in the arts, sciences, philosophy, mathematics, and medicine, seeing such achievements as integral to the meaning and structure of Islam. The 'Abbasids called great attention to their support of religion and were active in the construction of new mosques and religious schools. The state supported the religious scholars, *'ulama'* (literally, "the learned ones"), as a professional elite with great prestige and power. Those trained in the Qur'an, the law, and other religious disciplines controlled many aspects of life in 'Abbasid society. Arabic was becoming a truly international language, and massive projects of translation were undertaken, especially by Christians employed at the caliphal court.

Soon after the death of the Prophet, the community began assembling narratives of what the Prophet had said and done during his lifetime, as collected by his close companions and confidants. This task involved determining the authenticity of each individual narrative (*hadith*) and arranging an enormous number of reports into categories of clearly authentic, probably reliable, and unsubstantiated. They were then gathered into six main collections of traditions, which are still of great importance to Muslims. These traditions constitute the Sunna, or way, of the Prophet, which many American Muslims continue to cite as their most important guide for conduct.

The term *hadith* can refer to both a single narrative and the whole body of accounts. Along with the verses of the Qur'an that describe proper modes of action and social intercourse, these narratives were to become the basis for the development of Islamic law, or *shari'a*. In the early days, the law differed considerably from place to place as the Islamic empire expanded into different geographic and cultural areas. By the eighth century, dissatisfaction with these legal variations led to the attempt to standardize the law. Four legal scholars who lived and worked in the eighth and ninth centuries have come to be known as the founders of the major Sunni schools of law. Abu Hanifa (d. 767) is the author of the Hanafite school, Malik ibn Anas (d. 796) of the Maliki tradition, and Ahmad ibn Hanbal (d. 855) of the Hanbali interpretation. Muhammad al-Shafi'i was the fourth of these legal giants whose influence continues so strongly today, and he is often referred to as the systematizer or architect of Islamic law. A fifth school is the Ja'fari school of Shi'ite law. Generally speaking, the Muslim world is divided into adherents of these schools of law, which now do not differ greatly in detail but suggest some regional variations. America, of course, with immigrants from around the world, represents a mix of them all.

Perhaps because he had traveled and been exposed to many different areas of the Islamic world, al-Shafi'i has been known as somewhat of an eclectic. While he emphasized strict adherence to the Qur'an and Sunna, which he saw as the foremost legitimate bases of the *shari'a*, he is nonetheless considered an advocate of an intermediate position between rigid traditionalism and too free rational interpretation of the law. To the Qur'an and Sunna (the one divinely revealed and the other, according to him, divinely inspired) he added, when necessary, two subsidiary sources of legal opinion. These are the consensus (*ijma'*) of those who are qualified to render judgment, and the use of analogical reasoning (*qiyas*) in very specific circumstances. In his emphasis on consensus he moved the focus away from individual interpretation to the importance of the community as a whole, asserting that God will not allow his community to agree on anything erroneous. His famous work, titled the *Risala*, stands as a monument to legal construction and has earned him the title of founder of *usul al-fiqh*, the foundations of the law. Today the Shafi'i school of law predominates in Southeast Asia, East Africa, and the southern part of Arabia. Muslims in America, like those in many other parts of the world, understand the importance of the Qur'an and Sunna as articulated by al-Shafi'i, and many attempt to live in as close accord as possible with the way of the Prophet. Some others, although still minority voices, hold that the traditions of the Prophet, while normative for behavior, need not necessarily be considered binding.

Meanwhile, as the forces of Islam were marching and gathering more lands and more wealth for the caliphal coffers, and the scholars and legists were struggling to find ways in which to adjudicate the lives of Muslims, some people found themselves restless with the directions in which the *umma* of Islam seemed to be moving. These pious men and women of the early community were becoming concerned that the acquisition of territories and wealth was leading Muslims far from the simple ideals propounded by Prophet Muhammad and practiced in the first days of Islam. They heeded the Qur'anic warning about the fires of eternal damnation for those who do not lead responsible lives and became increasingly concerned that such a fate awaited them, as well as those in leadership positions.

With this heightened awareness of the Day of Judgment, some of these pious souls began to express a repugnance even for the good things of the earth itself, a rejection that does not reflect the world-affirming nature of the Qur'an. This rejection manifested itself in intense self-denial and asceticism. Some chose to wear scratchy wool clothing, reminiscent of Christian hair shirts, to enhance their own discomfort. After the Arabic word for wool, *suf*, these folks came to be known as Sufis, a term that stuck. Sufism is the generic name for the ascetic/mystical movement that has played such a significant role in the history of Islam. Sufism has also served as the vehicle through which many Americans have come to Islam, and a number of different Sufi orders are now growing in popularity in the United States.

One of those greatly revered for her piety and her extreme God-consciousness, and who adopted quite severe ascetic practices, was Rabi'a al-Adawiyya, famed female mystic and lover of the divine. While she is one of the few women ascetics whose name has been recorded in history, a number of women found the pietistic-mystical path to God more congenial than strict adherence to the dictates of the emerging law. Many American women are attracted to the spiritual and communal dimensions of Sufism. Rabi'a, born around 717, is said to have lived alone in the most humble of circumstances, for a while remaining a recluse in a small cell. Many stories circulate about her spending days with no more than a morsel of bread and a few sips of water, so dedicated was she to the contemplation and adoration of God and so persuaded that he would provide for her basic needs. While some of the other early ascetics lived in fear of the fires of punishment, Rabi'a professed to be so overcome with God-consciousness that she had no time to consider either this world or the next. Asked once if she loved the Prophet, she replied that yes, of course, she did, but in fact her whole consciousness was so devoted to the reality of God that she really did not have time to think about the Prophet.

One of the issues illustrated by Rabi'a, as well as by others who believed that they had a kind of direct access to God, was that of possible antinomianism, or the tendency to circumvent the legal prescriptions. As we have seen, Rabi'a lived at a time when great attention was being paid to the importance of law in binding the community. While there is little evidence that she necessarily ignored the formal responsibilities of Islam, clearly they were of less importance to her than the direct love of God. Rabi'a was one of the first to espouse the kind of love-mysticism that often leads to a coming together of lover and beloved, human and divine, in ways that threaten the sanctity of *tawhid*, or the affirmation of God's unicity (uniqueness). Later Sufism developed two schools of approach to God, sometimes called the "sober Sufis" and the "intoxicated Sufis," the latter in their extreme proclamations of intimate association with the divine often earning the severe disapprobation of the orthodox.

In the centuries after Rabi'a lived, despite the misgivings of orthodoxy, Sufism developed as a highly significant movement within the faith of Islam. It came to represent a kind of parallel to the *shari'a*, or law—which is often known as the external path to God—in its emphasis on the internal path, called the *tariqa*. This term applied to both the journey of the individual mystic in his or her quest to draw near to God and the different orders that ultimately developed as distinguished Sufis gathered disciples and formalized their teachings. These movements grew up in all the Islamic lands and found adherents among every social and economic class. After some four centuries a number of Sufi orders were permanently established, their followers still maintaining affiliation with them today.

The *tariqa* is understood to provide a practical way in which an individual aspirant learns how to gain heightened God-consciousness. A spiritual master, a *pir* or *murshid* claiming lineage from the Prophet Muhammad, heads each order, and each has its own set of particular teachings, involving a series of states and stages in the spiritual quest along which the master guides the disciple. In later centuries Sufism came to be an important vehicle for the teaching of Islam, and the orders included not only those dedicated to pursuing the mystical path but also followers who wanted Islamic training and the collegiality of the congregation.

The Development of Philosophy, Theology, and Mysticism

As the first several centuries of Islam passed, the community moved into a new phase of its existence. The immediate expansion was completed, the Qur'an was gathered and authorized, the *hadith* collections were determined, and the law was becoming formulated. Islamic civilization was moving toward the height of its glory, with new developments in the arts and sciences illustrating a wide range of intellectual and artistic creativity. The third and fourth centuries of Islam saw amazing developments not only in the specifically religious sciences but in mathematics, art and architecture, medicine, literature, and philosophy as Islam absorbed, assimilated, and developed the many concepts it encountered through its rapid geographical spread.

One of the signal achievements of this period was the flourishing of Islamic philosophical sciences. Most of the works of Plato and Aristotle were known to Arab Muslims, and it has long been recognized that the medieval Muslim world made a lasting contribution to Christendom by providing Western scholars with access to the great classics of Greece and Rome through Arabic translations, from which they were rendered into European languages. In addition, Muslim philosophers used the tools of Greek philosophical thought to develop their own reflections, sometimes supporting the dogmas of orthodoxy and at other times providing serious challenge and engaging in significant debate and even controversy. Into this scene came Ibn Sina, known to the West as Avicenna, one of the great intellectual giants of Islamic philosophy and science.

Ibn Sina is said to have early exhibited those qualities of intellectual curiosity and achievement that were to serve him so well through his distinguished career. By the time he was ten years old he had memorized the entire Qur'an and was well on his way with the study of grammar, logic, and mathematics. By sixteen he had taught himself physics, metaphysics, and medicine and was already well known as a philosopher, astronomer, and physician, as well as one well versed in the law. For a number of years he wandered through Persia, meeting and engaging with mystics, philosophers, and men of letters. He finally settled in the magnificent city of Isphahan, where during a long period of relative peace he wrote some of his most important works. He died in 1037 in Hamadan, and there modern travelers may visit his tomb.

Ibn Sina's writings cover a great range of subjects. A devout Muslim, he understood his own philosophy as supporting rather than contradicting the central doctrines of Islam. One important exception was his denial of the notion that physical bodies will be resurrected at the end of time and be subject to a final judgment. He argued instead for the immortality of the soul, one of the primary areas of disagreement between Islamic philosophers and theologians. Later scholars have noted the relationship of his philosophy-theology to his own mystical leanings, and his writings always insist that the first reality is God and it is on him that the existence of all other creatures and things depends. If the genius of Islamic civilization at its height was indeed the flowering of arts and sciences and their integration into a common body of knowledge, surely Ibn Sina was the quintessential representative of both that range and that integration. Still acknowledged as an intellectual and philosophical giant in the development of Islam, he occupies as great a place of respect and veneration in the West as any figure in the history of the Muslim community. As Muslims in America continue to move increasingly into positions of professional leadership, they may well look to Avicenna as a model of scientific as well as artistic creativity and range.

Some half-century after Ibn Sina appeared another extremely influential figure who was to serve as the great "integrator"—or perhaps more appropriately, "reconciler"—in the history of Islamic thought. That person is the renowned theologian, philosopher, and mystic Abu Hamid al-Ghazali. As al-Shafi'i had provided a kind of middle way between the legal extremes in his day, and Ibn Sina in his very person brought together a range of disciplines, so al-Ghazali served as a reminder to the sometimes fractured Islamic *umma* that true Islam both integrates and reconciles and that the umbrella of the faith has room for a range of interpretations. Like many others in the history of Islam, including the current African American Muslim leader Warith Deen Mohammed, al-Ghazali was considered a *mujaddid*, or renewer of the faith, who, according to tradition, appears once in every century to restore the faith of the community.

Al-Ghazali was born in the Iranian city of Tus in the year 1058, three years after the Turkish Seljuks had taken over as rulers of Baghdad. By this time the rapid growth of the faith and the incorporation of such a range of peoples and cultures into the *umma* had made the ideal of unity difficult to achieve. The caliphate had fallen on difficult days, and the 'Abbasid ruler in Baghdad was virtually powerless. Isma'ili Shi'ites were seriously challenging Sunni leadership of the Islamic community. Differences between philosophers and theologians were driving a notable wedge between the religious and intellectual leaders of the community. Those who followed an esoteric Sufi path were, by the time of al-Ghazali, finding themselves often at dangerous odds with those who espoused a more "orthodox" interpretation of the faith. Into this complex set of communal tensions came this young scholar and theologian, who took it upon himself to bring as much harmony as possible through example and intellectual endeavor.

By al-Ghazali's time, Islamic theologians had resolved some of the more sticky issues, though not without some attending violence. Several centuries earlier a philosophical-theological school called the Mu'tazila had tried unsuccessfully to defend the notion of human free will, on the grounds that divine justice must necessitate human choice and agency. The orthodox "conclusion" was that while humans have responsibility, only God creates; thus, God is the author of human actions. Al-Ghazali himself was part of what was known as the Ash'arite school of theology, after the name of one who tried to reconcile human responsibility with divine authority and knowledge. Interestingly, much twentieth-century Islamic theological reflection finds itself in sympathy with Mu'tazili presuppositions.

If he was a theologian, al-Ghazali was also a philosopher, and it was his particular genius to incorporate the philosophical sciences into the study of theology in a way that really had not previously been done. Then in 1095 al-Ghazali went through a spiritual crisis that changed his life. Through his teaching and writing he had achieved great fame as one of the outstanding theologians of the time. But his dissatisfactions ran deep, and as he relates in a later autobiography, God ultimately forced him to take stock of his life in a completely new way. In a final moment of crisis, God actually froze his tongue so that he was unable to do what he did best, lecture in a public forum in his classroom. Suddenly, he saw his teaching as insignificant, his motives insincere, and his whole life apparently leading to disaster. "I saw for certain that I was on the brink of a crumbling bank of sand and in imminent danger of hell-fire unless I set about to mend my ways," he wrote in his autobiography. "Worldly desires were striving to keep me by their chains just where I was, while the voice of faith was calling, 'To the road! to the road! What is left of life is but little. . . . If you do not prepare *now* for eternal life, when will you prepare? If you do not now sever these attachments, when will you sever them?' "[2]

With this unavoidable challenge, Abu Hamid al-Ghazali began serious engagement in the practices of Sufism. Gradually, he became persuaded that it is neither through the mind nor the senses that truth is to be obtained, but in the realization of God's presence in one's life and heart achieved through careful training and disciplined spiritual activity. During this period of his life al-Ghazali wrote what was to be his most enduring and significant work, titled *The Revivification of the Religious Sciences*. He brought law and theology together with philosophy so as to give each a place in the fabric of Islam, all through the lens of a deeply mystical faith. Perhaps most important, he demonstrated how Sufi practices responsibly observed were not dangerous or antithetical to orthodoxy but provided a base of religious experience through which the living breath of God could truly enliven the heart of the believer. Conflicts between "intoxicated" Sufis and sober theologians never fully abated, but al-Ghazali had given assurance of a way in which to understand all these strands of religion as integrated into the full fabric of Islamic faith. Significant as al-Ghazali's mystical reflections are, his greatest gift was in fact the coordination of the intellect with the heart and the presentation of this integration in a rigorous and persuasive set of treatises.

Other mystics, however, gave themselves completely to highly poetic utterances that told of their intimate experiences with the divine Lord. The literature of Islamic mysticism is replete with Sufi love poetry, from Egypt to Persia to India and beyond. Many of these poets have captured the imagination of readers and pious aspirants to the Sufi path, and they continue to be read today in many versions and translations. Probably none has fired the hearts of those with religious sensibility and a longing for communication with the divine in quite the same way as the famous mystic of Anatolia, Jalal al-Din Rumi.

Rumi, who lived about a century after al-Ghazali, came originally from the area of Balkh in Khorasan, a melting pot of many cultures and forms of religious expression. Probably because of the threat of Mongol invasions from the East, his father fled with his family through such famed Islamic cities as Baghdad and Mecca, and finally into Asia Minor. They settled in the ancient city of Konya, which today lies in the central part of the modern state of Turkey. Like al-Ghazali, Rumi became extremely popular as a teacher, gathering large numbers of disciples and followers. The most stunning event of Rumi's life was his encounter with the enigmatic and charismatic Shams al-Din of Tabriz. A Sufi of great spiritual discipline who normally shunned social contact, Shams, it is said, swept into Konya seemingly from nowhere and quite overwhelmed Rumi with the power of his presence. In later years Rumi was to write of Shams as both his beloved teacher and spiritual confidant. His relationship with Shams symbolized that between lover and beloved, the divine aspirant and the Lord who is the object of adoration, and engendered some of the most beautiful mystical love poetry ever written. Though their relationship lasted only a few short years, its impact on Rumi was so intense that he was able to draw on it for inspiration and spiritual power throughout his life. It is said that he received death with the joy of knowing that he would at last be in the presence of his beloved Lord. His tomb in Konya is a place of great importance as a pilgrimage site and is revered as the spiritual center of Turkey.

Rumi's poetry has a rhythmic character that easily allows it to be put to music, as when the haunting melody of the flute portrays the reed-soul. Although the use of music and dance have raised the hackles of the orthodox over the centuries as a too-easy method of God-intoxication, it has continued as an important mode of mystical expression in many orders. None, perhaps, is more famous than that adopted by the order of Mehlevis founded by Jalal al-Din Rumi, often referred to as the Whirling Dervishes. While "whirling" would seem to connote a kind of frantic spinning, in fact the participants, who are dressed in long skirts and conical hats, turn slowly and gracefully, their motion intended to reflect the movement of the planets around the axis of the universe. This spiritual dance has continued to attract devotees and is gradually being attempted by groups of Sufis in America, although in many cases its resemblance to the Mehlevi dance might well be questioned. Rumi himself remains one of the most beloved figures of Islamic mystical piety, with his poetry and teaching reflecting the most profound aspects of the divine-human relationship.

"Whirling Dervishes" of the Sufi order of Jalal al-Din Rumi at Konya, Turkey.
Courtesy Turkish Tourist Office

The Intervening Years

Over the ensuing centuries, many developments too complex to detail here took place in the vast lands of Islam. The Mongols did, in fact, arrive, and in 1258 Baghdad was destroyed and the 'Abbasid caliphate with it. The year 1492 saw not only the venture of Christopher Columbus to America but also the beginning of the Christian Inquisition in Spain and the death or expulsion of its Muslim citizens. The Crusades, ill-fated adventure of the West to reconquer Jerusalem—which resulted in so much slaughter and car-nage—staggered to an end by the middle of the second millennium. Chris-tians gained little but the legacy of some illegitimate progeny, while suc-ceeding centuries of Muslims would long remember what they now label as the first of a long series of Western imperialist ventures into Muslim lands.

After occupying Baghdad, the Seljuk Turks, who had adopted Islam as their religion, moved gradually to establish control over all of Anatolia. In 1453 Western Europe saw one of its worst fears realized when Turkish Mus-lim forces seized and occupied the ancient city of Constantinople, establish-ing the Ottoman Empire, which was to continue until the end of World War I. Under Sulayman the Magnificent, Constantinople, then called Istanbul, became one of the glorious cities of the world with its Blue Mosque and other monuments to Islam, a place of fascination for Westerners who were becoming increasingly intrigued by Muslim culture. In the early 1500s, with the ascension of Babur as the first Moghul emperor of India, Islam became

Richard the Lion-Hearted and his Christian troops watch as Muslims are massacred at Acre during the Fourth Crusade. BIBLIOTHEQUE NATIONALE

a permanent feature of the Indian subcontinent. His successors continued the construction of Islamic edifices, the most notable being that great masterpiece of Islamic architecture the Taj Mahal.

As early as the thirteenth century, merchants from the southeastern coast of Arabia established trade routes across the Indian Ocean into the lands of Indonesia, where they brought the word of Islam and intermarried with the women of that country. The spread of Sufism also played a major role in the introduction of Islam to the area, and Indonesia was to become what is today the largest Islamic country in the world. Malaysia and other parts of Southeast Asia also became major centers of Islamic life, with the first Southeast Asian Islamic state established in the early 1600s. Under the Safavid Kingdom in Persia in the sixteenth and seventeenth centuries, the great Islamic sciences, still strikingly evident today in the glorious art and architecture of the city of Isphahan, flourished.

Islam, of course, had established itself across North Africa soon after the death of the Prophet. Many centuries of exploration, trade, and wandering Sufi teachers and preachers to the lands of Africa also brought Islam to a number of areas of the sub-Saharan continent, most notably in the west. All of these areas into which Muslim faith and culture spread are represented today in the many faces of American Islam.

At the beginning of the Western colonialist venture, three huge Muslim empires controlled a significant portion of the world: the Turkish in much of the Middle East, the Safavid in Persia, and the Moghul in India. Starting perhaps with Napoleon's invasion of Egypt in 1798, the West entered into an unfortunate phase of its collective history in which economics and the desire for expansion of territorial control combined with a strikingly parochial sense of manifest destiny. The West convinced itself of its mission to civilize and educate much of the rest of the world, particularly those areas under Muslim control, a venture that took the form of military, political, and Christian missionary interventions. Over the course of the nineteenth century the British took India and Malaysia, the Dutch occupied Indonesia, and the Russians moved into Turkestan. In 1830 France seized Algeria and from there extended control over the central Sahara and much of the Islamic West and equatorial Africa, and in 1881 took Tunisia. Egypt fell to Britain in 1882, and by the end of the century British control extended up the Nile into the Sudan. Spain, Germany, and Belgium also participated in the feast, although with fewer obvious results. Italy's largest conquest was that of Libya in 1911. At the same time the Ottoman Empire was being dismantled, with Eastern European lands one by one taken away by the West. Even the Middle East came heavily under Western influence.

By the end of World War I the Ottoman Empire was history. Arabs who had thrown their support to the West against their Turkish coreligionists, believing promises of an independent Arab state, found to their horror that Britain and France had no intention of keeping such a promise and, in fact, had agreed in secret to divide the Middle East into their own separate spheres of influence. Britain, which was still in control of Egypt and India, took Iraq, Palestine, and Transjordan. France, in addition to its North African territories, moved into Lebanon and Syria. These arrangements were called "mandates," sanctioned by the newly created League of Nations. Turkey itself was divided into a number of areas under different forms of Western control, with only a fraction of its former empire still in Muslim hands. Iran, which had tried to be neutral in the war, only to find itself violated by a number of Western forces, was unstable, with Britain the most significant presence there, as in much of the rest of the Middle East. To add to the humiliation and disillusionment of Muslims came another blow to the Islamic world, the Balfour Declaration, which provided for the establishment of a homeland for Jews in the heart of primarily Muslim Palestine.

It would be difficult to overestimate the devastating effects these Western incursions into the lands of Islam had on the deep sense of pride Muslims held in their faith and culture. While during the nineteenth century the responsibility for what is seen as unqualified Western imperialism lay mainly with Europe, primarily Britain and France, in the twentieth century the burden in the eyes of Islam has shifted to the United States. Throughout the century European powers have relinquished their political control of Muslim countries one by one, although the boundaries drawn around many of them remain those arbitrarily set at the end of World War I. The United States, however, through its support of the state of Israel, its collaboration with Muslim rulers considered to be working against the interests of true Islam, its economic exploitation, and its Christian missionary endeavors that seem to be aimed at the extermination of Islam, has become the target of great criticism on the part of many Muslim leaders, especially in the last half of this century. Muslims emigrating to America find themselves caught between the political or economic need to make a new home here and the psychological burden of coming to a place they have perceived as the cause of much exploitation and pain.

Framers of Twentieth-Century Islam

Muslim leaders throughout the century have struggled to recover pride in their religion as a faith and a cultural foundation. The many movements they have initiated, influential among both American Muslims and Muslims who have trained in America and then returned home, are too numerous and complex to detail here. They can be extrapolated, however, from the lives of a few of the people who have significantly contributed to the formation of an Islam designed both to recover lost glories and to provide an effective counter to what Muslims generally perceive as continuing, if less overt, forms of Western (American) imperialism.

At the end of World War I the Muslims of Turkey were forced to abandon all thoughts of an empire and concentrate on rebuilding their state. They did this under the exceptional leadership of Mustafa Kemal, later called Ataturk, who has been considered the founder of the modern state of Turkey. Many Muslims, and many Turks, felt strongly that the appropriate leadership of the Islamic community was still the caliphate. Mustafa Kemal came quickly to realize that the future of Turkey lay not in an antiquated institution but in the swift identification of itself as a national entity with power and influence. When the Turkish Republic was officially formed in 1923, Mustafa Kemal proclaimed that it was to be governed by a president elected by the National Assembly. Not surprisingly, Ataturk himself was the first to hold the office. In 1924, despite strong urgings to the contrary by other world Muslim leaders, the Assembly ratified Ataturk's proposals for a completely secular state and officially abolished the caliphate. While the office of caliph had long since lost the authority originally invested in it after the death of the Prophet, it had remained as a symbol of pan-Islamic governance and authority. That it came to such an end deeply shocked much of the Islamic world and has had a lasting effect on Muslim political thought.

Ataturk did not believe that he was abandoning Islam. His goal was to further the state as such, and religion was seen as one highly significant force in that process. But it was to be a moral rather than a political force. Kemal is notable not only for his success in establishing Turkey as a major player in the twentieth century but also for being a major proponent of restricting religion to private life. His actions have been much debated and criticized, and in general, secularism has not emerged as a popular choice for most Muslims engaged in rethinking the role of Islam in the modern world. Muslims in America watch with great interest as Turkey struggles to legitimate itself as a member of the European assembly of powers at the same time that some of its leadership and much of its population refuse to relinquish what identifies it as a state in which Islam continues to play a role of great significance.

Among those who expressed concern over Ataturk's secularism and the abolition of the caliphate were several prominent Muslim leaders in India. From the late nineteenth century through all of the twentieth, Indian (and later Pakistani) Muslims have been among the most articulate of those attempting to design a proper course for a modern Islam. Some were strongly influenced by the West and European rationalism, while more traditional religious leaders objected strongly to such Western leanings. By the middle of the twentieth century a number of strong currents in Islamic thought were to contribute to the creation of the state of Pakistan in 1947.

Muhammad Iqbal is the name most commonly associated with the idea of forming a separate state in which Islam would be the official religion. That he died nearly a decade before the realization of that vision in 1947 does not detract from his influence. It was Muhammad 'Ali Jinnah who, in fact, was the architect of the new state, though he lived only long enough to see its creation. Jinnah became so convinced by Iqbal's arguments that as leader of the Muslim League Party, he led the way to the founding of a new nation, despite the desperate pleas from many of his countrymen, including Mahatma Gandhi, that India not be divided.

While events of extreme significance for the future of Islam were occurring in Turkey and the Indian subcontinent over the first half of the century, other areas were experiencing the tension as well as the excitement of new and creative thinking. One of the most fertile grounds for this kind of regenerative theological adventure was Egypt. The most prominent pioneer of reform in the early 1900s was Muhammad 'Abduh. 'Abduh was a practical reformer who chose to work through the evolutionary process that he hoped would bring about steady change. He fostered a series of reforms in religious education at the traditional al-Azhar University, worked as the *mufti*, or chief legal official, of Egypt to bring about the new developments he advocated, and with Rashid Rida authored a commentary on the Qur'an that is still foundational for understanding Islam in the twentieth century.

As the early decades of the century unfolded in Egypt, however, 'Abduh's legacy (he died in 1905) came to be challenged by some who saw him either as too progressive, too accommodating to Western ideas, or too unwilling to advocate a more radical solution to the problems of a somewhat dormant Islam. One of those who proposed a quite different approach was Hasan al-

Mustafa Kemal Ataturk, founder of the modern state of Turkey. ARCHIVE PHOTOS

Banna, whose insistence on dramatic change led to the formation of the still very powerful Muslim Brotherhood, an organization that is influential in many segments of American Islam today. He saw in Egyptian society not the steady change that 'Abduh had hoped for but increasing secularism, a disregard for the heritage of Islamic law and tradition, and the development of an upper middle class thoroughly enchanted with Western culture. In the late 1920s al-Banna and several associates began the Muslim Brotherhood as a call to return to a God-centered political and social life. Largely an urban movement, it appealed to both the masses and a large segment of educated professionals. While not a political party, at least in the early days, it quickly earned the disfavor of the ruling parties. In 1949 the Egyptian government had Hasan al-Banna assassinated after the Brotherhood mounted a public challenge for the establishment of an Islamic state. In 1954, after an attempt on President Nassar's life, the Brotherhood was outlawed, although it continued to be active. Its fortunes have risen and fallen over the decades, while its political philosophy remains attractive to many contemporary Muslims.

Developing as a kind of parallel to the Muslim Brotherhood in Egypt is a movement called the Jama'at-i-Islami (literally, "the Islamic Society") in Pakistan. Like the Brotherhood, it has looked to a conservative interpretation of Islam for a social framework in which religion and the state are unified under the *shari'a*. Also like the Brotherhood, it has considerable influence on American Islam, and the writings and ideas of its founder, Abu'l-A'la al-Mawdudi, are more easily accessible to Western audiences because they are available in English.

Al-Mawdudi was born in 1903 in India into the Sufi order of the Chistiyya, which claims a lineage of descent through the Prophet's daughter Fatima. Known as a strong Indian nationalist, Mawdudi began to speculate on the nature of a true Islamic state, which, as in Brotherhood ideology, would look to the community of the Prophet as a model. Invited by Iqbal to move to Lahore, he there founded the Jama'at-i-Islami organization in 1941. Also like the Brotherhood, the Jama'at saw itself not as a political party but as an ideological fraternity with a growing network of branches and cells. Its members were committed to religious training and to the development of a range of social projects designed for a new generation of young people dedicated to Islamic morality.

Mawdudi became increasingly convinced that Western influences endangered Islam and that the best hope for Pakistan was a sound religious basis. He criticized both modernists and conservative traditionalists who paid more attention to their own legal deductions than to the true sources of Islam, the Qur'an and Sunna of the Prophet. His ideas became extremely popular, and the Jama'at spread rapidly across Pakistan. Unlike the more populist Brotherhood, it was basically an elitist movement designed to train new leadership for an Islamic state and society: ". . . the objective of Islamic Jihad is to put an end to the dominance of the un-Islamic systems of governments and replace them with Islamic rule," he wrote in an article on the meaning of *jihad* (holy war).[3] In many ways Mawdudi is the father of Islamic revivalism, the set of movements that have become so influential in the Islamic world in the last part of the twentieth century and that the Western media erroneously label "Islamic fundamentalism." He envisioned Islam as invigorated, pure, and unwilling to compromise with the forces of Westernization or secularization or with those who stressed Indian nationalism over Islamic identity. Politically, the Jama'at often opposed official government policies and, again like the Brotherhood, was suppressed and finally officially banned, its activists sometimes imprisoned.

Although al-Mawdudi died in 1979, his international influence and the popularity of his ideas have not flagged. His many writings are internationally consumed and in the American context provide a significant model for Islamic living in the contemporary world. Many find him too conservative, while others perceive his urgings to return to the Qur'an and Sunna to be extremely persuasive. Mosques and Islamic centers in the United States regularly feature his books and pamphlets, as do Islamic bookstores, grocery and convenience stores, and other establishments selling and distributing Islamic materials. Al-Mawdudi's call for what many interpret as the virtual seclusion of women has appealed to some and outraged others. For conservative Muslim communities in America, both immigrant and African American, it is clear that the prescriptions of Abu'l-A'la al-Mawdudi will be influential for some time to come.

Among the most significant events in the Islamic world in the latter part of the twentieth century, and one that resulted in the migration of many Muslims to the United States, was the Iranian revolution of 1979, effected by the hand of the Ayatollah Ruhollah al-Musavi Khomeini. In many ways it has come to symbolize the Islamic revivalism that has manifested itself in Egypt, Pakistan, and many other places in the modern world. While the original hope of some of Khomeini's supporters that he might be the returned Imam so long expected by Twelver Shi'ites was not fulfilled, he became a symbol of great pride to Shi'i and Sunni Muslims everywhere for having established an Islamic state and, perhaps especially, for having done so in the face of strong American opposition.

Khomeini was born in central Iran two years after the turn of the century. After studying in several centers of Islamic learning, he was accepted as a *mujtahid*, one credited with determining a methodology for legal interpretation. Later, he was to achieve the status of *ayatollah* (literally, *ayat Allah*, "sign of God"), the highest and most learned authority over the religious, social, and political life of Shi'ite Islam. By the 1960s Khomeini had emerged as one of the most articulate spokesmen in opposition to the policies of Mohammed Reza Pahlavi Shah. During Muharram in 1963 Khomeini went so far as to compare the shah with the murderer of 'Ali's son Husayn at Karbala, triggering massive demonstrations against the shah in Tehran. Such activities led to Khomeini's arrest and exile to Turkey, then to Iraq and Paris. He became a hero to leftist youth movements opposed to the shah as he advocated the authority of the jurist as the appropriate rule for the state.

From exile, his messages continued to be transmitted to his public in Iran through illegal pamphlets and cassettes. His image as the personification of opposition to the shah grew, as did his popularity. In 1979 he returned

Ayatollah Ruhollah al-Musavi Khomeini, supreme leader
of Iran, 1979–1989. ARCHIVE PHOTOS

triumphant to Iran, sent the shah into exile, and founded the conservative
Islamic Republic, whose clerical rule continues today. America had never
imagined that its "island of security in the Middle East" could fall. The
holding of American hostages for 444 days by the revolutionary "students"
added to American revulsion, reinforced by Ayatollah Khomeini's claims,
still repeated today if more rhetorically, that America is the land of Satan.

Iranian Americans evidence extremely mixed feelings about their home
country. Some, uprooted from a land they loved, rue the day that Khomeini
came to power and believe sincerely that his austere rule, mitigated only
somewhat by his successors, does justice neither to Islam nor to the heritage
of Iranian leadership in all of the great sciences and arts of Islam. Others
applaud the ability of a committed Muslim leader to challenge the power of
what they perceived as an American-supported dictatorship, though regret-

ting the repression that still makes the lives of many Iranians difficult. Still others look with increasing pride at the new thinking and interpretation that they see evidenced in the works of Iranian intellectuals, both men and women, as they struggle to balance support for an Islamic state with the need to survive both ideologically and economically in the contemporary world.

These, then, are some of the people and movements that have influenced the shaping of twentieth-century Islam and whose heritage continues to influence the lives of Muslims in America. As we shall see later, the influence is often two-way, as Muslim students, diplomats, and businesspeople bring American Islamic influences back to their home countries. Those who then return to the West, often in positions of national leadership, add through their international connections yet another dimension to the formation of American Islam.

What is that Islam—or, perhaps more accurately, what are the many forms of Islam—that have come to characterize the American scene? To that diversity and complexity we now turn.

CHAPTER THREE

Islam Comes to America

The First Muslims

Commentators on the emergence of Islam in the North American scene have looked for the most part to the middle and latter part of the nineteenth century as signaling the first real arrival of Muslims in the United States. Indeed, at this time the first Muslim immigrants, primarily from the Middle East, began to come to North America in hopes of earning some kind of fortune, large or small, and then returning to their homelands. We will return to their story shortly. Going back considerably further, some scholars currently argue that for nearly two centuries before the time of Christopher Columbus's venture in 1492, Muslims sailed from Spain and parts of the northwestern coast of Africa to both South and North America and were among the members of Columbus's own crew. African Muslim explorers are said to have penetrated much of the Americas, relating to and sometimes intermarrying with Native Americans. Some hypothesize that Muslims set up trading posts and even introduced some arts and crafts in the Americas. Evidence to support such claims, cited from artifacts, inscriptions, and reports of eyewitness accounts, is still sufficiently vague that the thesis remains somewhat hypothetical.[1]

The date of 1492 is of historical significance not only because of the Columbian exploits. It also signals the official end of the presence of Islam in the Iberian Peninsula, now known as Spain and Portugal. After having enjoyed a glorious rule in the ninth and tenth centuries in Cordoba, and a more checkered overlordship under North African rule in the succeeding centuries, Muslims saw their fortunes decline rapidly. In 1474 the husband-and-wife team of Fernando of Aragon and Isabella of Seville succeeded to conjoint but separate thrones. Known as the "Catholic monarchs" for their dedication to reuniting all of Spain under Christendom, they captured the last stronghold of Muslim occupation in Granada in 1492. By the turn of the fifteenth century, Muslims (generally referred to as Moors) throughout the peninsula were forced to choose among the unfortunate alternatives of conversion to Christianity, emigration, or death. Many who chose the first continued to practice their faith in secret, maintaining a hidden conclave of Islam for centuries. Others tried openly to rebel and were subsequently expelled from the land that some centuries earlier had been one of the few historical examples of Christian and Muslim (and Jewish) cultural harmony.

Evidence is coming to light indicating that some of those Moors forced to leave managed to make their way to the Caribbean islands, with a few even getting as far as the southern part of the present United States. As scholars representing a variety of disciplines continue to explore these theories, some American Muslims see in them proof that Islam played a role in the early history of this country. The possibility of such connections with Spanish cultures is particularly appealing to those U.S. Hispanics who are attracted by Islamic teachings.

Early Muslim Immigrants in the American Context

With this combination of evidence and conjecture in mind, let us turn to the well-documented history of immigrant Muslims. Migrations occurred in a series of distinguishable periods. The first was between 1875 and 1912 from rural areas of what was then called Greater Syria under the rule of the Ottoman Empire, currently Syria, Jordan, Palestine, and Lebanon. The vast majority of immigrants from the Middle East at that time were Christian, often somewhat knowledgeable about America because of training in missionary schools. A small percentage was comprised of Sunni, Shi'i, 'Alawi, and Druze Muslims. By the latter half of the twentieth century that ratio was to be reversed. For the most part these early arrivals remain nameless to us, with occasional exceptions such as one Hajj Ali (rendered by Americans as "Hi Jolly"), brought by the U.S. cavalry to the deserts of Arizona and California in 1856 to help breed camels. This experiment failing, Ali is said to have stayed in California to look for gold.

The second wave came at the end of World War I, after the demise of the Ottoman Empire, which had controlled most of the Muslim Middle East. It also coincided with Western colonial rule under the mandate system in the Middle East. Many people coming to America at that time were relatives of Muslims who had already emigrated and established themselves to some degree in this country. U.S. immigration laws passed in 1921 and 1924 imposed quota systems for particular nations, which significantly curtailed the numbers of Muslims who were allowed to enter the country.

During the third period, which lasted through most of the 1930s, immigration was open specifically and only to relatives of people already living in America. The actual numbers of Muslims allowed to settle here were limited and did not rise until after World War II.

The fourth wave, which lasted from 1947 to 1960, saw considerable expansion in the sources of immigration. The Nationality Act of 1953 gave each country an annual quota of immigrants. Because it was based on population percentages in the United States at the end of the nineteenth century, however, most of the immigrants allowed to enter the country were from Europe. Still, the trickle of Muslims continued, coming now not only from the Middle East but also from many parts of the world including India and Pakistan (after the partitioning of the subcontinent in 1947), Eastern Europe (mainly from Albania and Yugoslavia), and the Soviet Union. Most of these arrivals settled in large cities such as Chicago and New York. Unlike their earlier counterparts, many of these immigrants were urban in background and well educated, and some were members of the families of former ruling elites. Often already quite Westernized in their attitudes, they came to the United States in hopes of continuing their education or receiving advanced technical training.

The last and final wave was related both to decisions internal to the United States and to events taking place in several parts of the Islamic world. In 1965 President Lyndon Johnson signed an immigration act repealing the quotas based on national diversity within the United States. For the first time since the early part of the century one's right to enter the country was not specifically dependent on his or her national or ethnic origin. Immigration from Europe thus declined, while that from the Middle East and Asia increased dramatically, more than half of the newcomers Muslim.

Over the last several decades, political turmoil in many countries of the Muslim world has occasioned increased emigration. In 1967 came what for Muslims was the disastrous and humiliating defeat of Arab troops at the hands of Israel, beginning an exodus of Palestinians headed for the West that has continued until the present time. The 1979 revolution in Iran and the ascent to power of Ayatollah Khomeini forced many Iranians to flee their country, a number of whom decided to come to America. Civil strife in Pakistan and the breaking away of East Pakistan to form Bangladesh, anti-Muslim pogroms in India, the military coup in Afghanistan, and the Lebanese civil war have all contributed to the Muslim presence in America. The Iraqi occupation of Kuwait led to the flight of a large number of Kurds to America, while the civil wars in Somalia and Afghanistan, the tightening of the military regime in Sudan, and ethnic cleansing in Bosnia also swelled the numbers of immigrant Muslims.

Most now come from the subcontinent of South Asia, including Pakistanis, Indians, and Bangladeshis. They first began to arrive as early as 1895 and over the century have been important in the development of Muslim political groups in America. Today this group probably numbers more than one million. Increasingly, they are being joined by sizable groups coming from Indonesia and Malaysia.

Some estimates place the Iranians in this country at close to a million, with representatives of Arab countries of the Middle East, Turks, and Eastern Europeans close behind. Muslims come from a large number of African nations, including Ghana, Kenya, Senegal, Uganda, Cameroon, Guinea, Sierra Leone, Liberia, Tanzania, and many others. Naturally, these immigrants represent a great range of Islamic movements and ideologies. They are Sunnis and Shi'ites, Sufis and members of sectarian groups, religious and secular people, political Islamists and those who espouse no religious or political agenda. Many have come from circumstances in which Islam is the majority religion and find their new minority status in America difficult to adjust to. Others already know what it means to be a member of a minority religious group and come with their coping skills well honed. With each new arrival the picture of Islam in America becomes increasingly complex.

Let us return, then, to the America of the late nineteenth century. The 1860s to the 1880s saw the first significant movement of young, relatively unskilled Muslim men, primarily from Syria and Lebanon in the Middle East. Some were fleeing conscription into the Turkish army, which they saw as little connected to their own national identities. Others had seen Christians from their homeland return from the United States with considerable wealth, and despite their reluctance to go to a setting in which they would be surrounded by non-Muslims, they were tempted to try their luck. World War I brought such devastation to Lebanon that many people were forced to flee to survive. Generally single, or at least traveling without their wives, they looked upon their time in America as only temporary, hoping that they could earn money to return and establish homes and families. Their dreams were hard to realize, however, as jobs were not easy to find in America, and often they were not able to compete for those that were available because of insufficient knowledge of English or inadequate educational preparation. Many were forced into menial work such as migrant labor, petty merchandizing, or mining. One of the most common occupations was peddling, which required little capital, language skills, or training. Working at first along the Atlantic seacoast, peddlers traveled into the South and West, often facing severe weather, thievery, and local hostility. Other Muslim immigrants served as cheap laborers on work gangs, as, for example, those contributing to the construction of railroads in the Seattle area. Women sometimes found employment in mills and factories, where they worked long hours under extremely difficult conditions. The lack of language skills, poverty, loneliness, and the absence of coreligionists all contributed to a sense of isolation and unhappiness. Compounding these difficulties was the fact that Americans of those decades certainly had little enthusiasm for foreigners, especially those whose customs seemed strange and whose religion was not Christian.

These early groups of Muslim immigrants tried to maintain a community of believers in an alien context, without institutional support. The religious training available to their children and grandchildren was minimal. They recalled that in their home countries, young people grew up with their religion in the air all around them, with holidays, festivals, prayers, and observances a constant part of the environment. America presented a different context, in which maintaining even an awareness, let alone regular observance, of the faith was obviously difficult. Neither schools nor businesses had any facilities for, nor interest in, providing opportunities for daily prayer. Those who wanted to fast during the month of Ramadan could expect no special accommodation in the workplace. Extended families to provide support and instruction were not available, and economic circumstances generally did not allow families to visit home for reinforcement of the larger familial context. Since so much of the practice of Islam is communal as well as personal, it was difficult to observe the prayers, holidays, and other Islamic occasions. The pioneer families thus had to struggle to maintain their religion and identity in a society that had been built on the backs of immigrants but that, paradoxically, had never appreciated the differences in culture that the immigrants brought with them.

Muslim Communities Across the American Continent

As the immigrants' visions of becoming rich quickly began to fade, so did their hopes of an imminent return to homes and relatives overseas. Inevitably, they were forced to adapt to a new life in their adopted land. Young men, eager to marry and establish families, found it difficult if not impossible to locate available young Muslim women in this country. Some went back home for brief visits to take a bride; others had their relatives arrange marriages with girls from their home countries. In any case, traditional patterns of courtship gave way to speed and expediency. Others married outside the faith, sometimes Arab Christian women, although the pressures from other Muslims not to succumb to marriage with "nonbelievers" was great.

Immigrants looked for more permanent kinds of employment, often successfully establishing their own small businesses. Many turned to their native cuisine as a source of revenue, founding coffeehouses, restaurants, bakeries, and small grocery stores. Initially, these were for their compatriots so that Muslims could at least enjoy their own food in a culture in which so much was alien to their tastes and traditions. Gradually, other Americans learned to appreciate Arab cooking, and in most cities today one can enjoy Arab cooking at everything from gourmet restaurants to fast-food joints featuring such treats as *shawarma* (spicy meat cooked on a rotating spit and stuffed into Syrian bread), *hummoz* (chickpea dip), and *tabouli* (chopped salad with tomatoes, onions, and parsley).

In the first part of this century many Muslim families found themselves drifting away from the faith, especially the young people, and attempting to hide or do away with those things that marked them as different from their American colleagues. Those whose skin was darker than that of the average American, especially in the South, found that they were treated as "colored" by local populations and were refused access to public facilities reserved for "Whites only." Stereotypes of Arab Muslims as people with large black eyes, big noses and mustaches, and ill-fitting clothes became commonplace. It became very difficult to maintain the use of Arabic as the youth resisted speaking a tongue that sounded strange to their peers. Their refusal to even learn the mother language was doubly painful for their families, as Arabic was not only their cultural but their liturgical language. Gradually, Muslims began to choose American names for their children or to allow the use of nicknames. Muhammad became Mike, Ya'qub was changed to Jack, Nasreen to Nancy. Arab and, to some extent, Muslim identity began to be something of the past rather than the present and the future as new generations of young people struggled to be part of the culture of their current homeland rather than of their heritage. When these young people matured and began to look to marriage, they turned increasingly to non-Muslim partners, intermarriage rates rising with each generation.

At the same time, however, and to some extent in response to concerns about acculturation and secularization, in a number of places across America Muslims began to organize into communities in which they affirmed their identity.

Midwest America

Among the first of these groupings were those located in the Midwest. North Dakota was home to several of the earliest documented Muslim groups in America, and in the small town of Ross, Muslims organized for prayers in the very early 1900s. They began building a mosque in 1920 but later had to abandon it as many of its members had converted to Christianity.

In Michigan City, Indiana, an Islamic Center of sorts was established as early as 1914, its members primarily Syrians and Lebanese who worked in the mercantile trade. They soon began to attract other Muslims from around the area and in 1924 reorganized under the name The Modern Age Arabian Islamic Society.

Cedar Rapids, Iowa has had a long history of housing a Muslim community. Its members were peddlers turned shopkeepers, providing goods needed for daily life among the farmers of the region. The first continuing mosque in America was begun there in 1920 in a rented hall, and a mosque building was completed in 1934. It has periodically been refurbished and extended, with a minaret added in 1980. Because it is the oldest mosque still in use today, it is often called the "Mother Mosque of America."

New York

Islam has been a presence in the New York City area from the late nineteenth century on, and its history there has been rich and complex. Always a hub of immigrant activity, the city was home to a variety of different racial-ethnic groups, and its Muslim population included merchant seamen, itinerant tradesmen, and those who chose to settle and establish businesses. The American Mohammedan Society was founded in Brooklyn in 1907 by immigrants from Poland, Russia, and Lithuania, who finally purchased a building to use for a mosque in the early 1930s. By the 1950s the society claimed to have some four hundred members. It has struggled but remains alive today as the Moslem Mosque, a name adopted in the 1960s.

In the 1930s a Moroccan immigrant began New York's second real mosque, called the Islamic Mission of America for the Propagation of Islam and the Defense of the Faith and the Faithful. Located near a significant settlement of Middle Eastern Muslims, the Mission is still an important institution in the city.

Over the past several decades, as the population of greater New York City has mushroomed, so has the construction of mosques and Islamic centers. Some are rebuilt houses, others refurbished office buildings and plants, and still others newly built structures. "Internally driven by the desire to obey and observe Islamic law and externally motivated by what many of them perceive to be a hostile environment, New York City's Muslims have labored to ensure that Islam will evolve into a significant social force within the five boroughs."[2]

Because of the size and heterogeneity of its population, New York City provides perhaps a unique locus for the gathering of Muslims from virtually all parts of the world. While many of the Islamic associations of the city are characterized by particular ethnic identities, others are consciously attempting to use this very diversity to emphasize the potential unity of the Muslim *umma* and are making particular efforts to bring together immigrant and indigenous Muslims as well as Sunnis and Shi'ites. One such group is the Islamic Cultural Center of New York, the first mosque to be built in Manhattan, and it is noticeably Islamic in style, with a traditional minaret and dome. The Islamic Center has made significant efforts to attract both immigrant and African American Muslims. National Islamic organizations find the city a particularly fruitful place to extend their activities, and a large number of elementary and upper-level Islamic schools, as well as Muslim stores and businesses, are springing up all over the city.

Chicago

Another of the major cities of America to become home quickly to immigrant Muslims was Chicago. The first Muslims arrived before the turn of the century, primarily from Syria and Palestine. Some claim that Chicago had more Muslims than any other American city in the early 1900s. Like other early arrivals, they had intended not to stay but to earn as much money as possible before returning to their home countries. When they did settle,

they did so generally in the south side of Chicago near the African American district. They too found that their associations with other Muslims were
more for cultural identity and support than religious interaction. Yet as they
became concerned about the possibility of their children's becoming Christian, they gradually began to take steps to provide some kind of Islamic
education for them. After World War I, following the pattern of immigrant
waves, more Muslims came to settle in Chicago, especially Arabs holding
Turkish passports. The Communist revolution in Russia brought some Muslims from Central Asia to the Chicago area, as did the later partition of the
subcontinent of India.

As in other major American cities, Chicago's Muslim population is comprised of people from a great range of cultural, racial-ethnic, and socio-eco-
nomic backgrounds. Chicago boasts the largest group of Muslims from India,
including Hyderabad, Gujarat, and Maharashtra, and it is the home of the
African American civic and religious leader Warith Deen Mohammed's
organization.

Muslims in Chicago are active in promoting their faith, in providing a
range of services to the Islamic community, and in interacting with one
another and non-Muslims in fostering good interfaith relations. More than
forty Islamic centers have been established to work with the different Muslim groups in greater Chicago, the oldest and largest being the Muslim Community Center established in 1969. Other mosques, centers, and schools are
now located in the outlying suburban areas. "It is fair to say that the Muslim
community of Chicago is religiously vibrant, financially sound, educated,
and active," said a recent commentator. "It plays a significant role in the
development and prosperity of the city of Chicago."[3]

California

Moving westward, we find that as early as 1895 Muslims from the Indian
subcontinent began to arrive in the coastal area. Mainly farm laborers and
unskilled workers from the Punjab, they settled in California, Oregon,
Washington, and western Canada. Because the early Punjabi immigrants
included both Muslims and Sikhs, Americans tended to lump them into the
only category they knew appropriate for India and simply called them Hindus.[4] Soon California became a destination for other Muslim immigrants,
with significant numbers from the subcontinent of India arriving after the
partition of 1947. California today is a center for Muslims from most areas
of the world, especially the Middle East, Iran, and South Asia. Recently,

significant numbers of Afghanis have arrived, along with refugees from Somalia and other areas of Africa.

California as a whole has experienced a notable rise in its Islamic population in the 1990s, and areas such as Los Angeles and San Francisco have become vibrant centers of Muslim life, providing much of the leadership of national Muslim organizations. The Islamic Center of Southern California in Los Angeles, for example, is one of the largest Muslim entities in the United States. It has a well-trained staff led by two Egyptian brothers widely known for their writings and community leadership, and a physical plant with a mosque, media center, school, publications office, and numerous meeting rooms. More than a thousand people normally attend Friday prayers, representing a wide range of racial-ethnic backgrounds. The center provides a range of services, including counseling on anything from divorce to drugs, to teens, young adults, and families.

Dearborn, Michigan

Originally home to small numbers of Sunni Ottoman Turks in the early years of the twentieth century, Dearborn, Michigan has continued to attract both Muslim and Christian Arab immigrants. Today it has one of the largest concentrations of Islamic communities in the nation, with sizable groups of Lebanese, Yemeni, and Palestinian Muslims.

In 1919 a Sunni mosque was built in nearby Highland Park, but it enjoyed only a short life. However, when the Ford Motor Company moved its plant to Dearborn in the late 1920s, providing sustainable and sometimes even lucrative sources of revenue for immigrant workers as well as for blacks from the South, a significant Arab community began to form. The pay was only five dollars a day, and working conditions were bad, but English was not required, and many Muslim immigrants welcomed the steady employment. Palestinian Muslims augmented the early Lebanese immigrant group in the late 1940s. A few Yemenis came down from the St. Lawrence Seaway to the Detroit area as early as 1910, but for the most part Yemenis have arrived since the middle of the century, mainly from Sana. Most recent arrivals have been Arabs fleeing the wars in south Lebanon and Beirut, as well as from other towns and villages in Lebanon and Palestine. In 1938 the Sunnis built a mosque, followed by the construction of the Shi'i Hashemite Hall in 1940.

Today the Arab Muslim community, Sunnis and Shi'a together, are a close-knit group with numbers of coffeehouses, stores, and businesses that continue to attract immigrants. One can walk for blocks in some areas and find only Arabic signs in grocery and other stores. Five active mosques or Islamic centers in the Dearborn area, two Sunni and three Shi'i, summon worshipers to prayer five times each day.

Quincy, Massachusetts

The Islamic community in Quincy, Massachusetts provides another interesting look at the establishment and development of a continuing Islamic presence in America. Its location too was determined by the availability of jobs, in this case in the well-established ship-building industry of New England.

The group began to assemble sometime after 1875 with the settlement of the first generation of Muslims primarily from Lebanon. The current Islamic Center of New England was the dream of some seven families (both Sunni and Shi'i) who had settled in the area by the early 1900s. In 1934 Muslim groups from the greater Boston area affiliated with the Muslims of Quincy to form the Arab American Banner Society. Reorganized in 1952, it effectively functioned as a Muslim organization, with affiliated charities allowing the members to perform the obligatory almsgiving. Both men and women in the Quincy community found themselves participating in community activities and even taking leadership roles. They were businessmen, teachers, and professionals as well as merchants and blue-collar workers. Not surprisingly, with this degree of establishment they began to think about building a mosque, which they supported by a wide range of fundraising activities. The building was completed in 1963, at which time it became officially known as the Islamic Center of New England.[5] Recently, under the direction of Imam Talal Eid (see "Profiles") the community has moved from Quincy to larger accommodations in Sharon, Massachusetts.

Shi'ite Islam in America

From the middle to late nineteenth century on, Muslim immigrants to the United States and Canada have included both Sunnis and Shi'ites, as well as members of other smaller sectarian groups. Of the more than one billion Muslims in the world today, approximately one tenth are Shi'ite. They constitute almost all of the population of Iran and more than half that of Iraq and are present in various communities in Africa, India, and Pakistan.

Precise information as to the earliest movements of Shi'ites to this country is difficult to come by. We do know that soon after the arrival of Lebanese Shi'ites in the late nineteenth and early twentieth centuries, others from India came to settle here. Later they were joined by Shi'ites from Iraq and Iran. By the 1950s small groupings of Shi'i families were beginning to be found in some of the major cities of America. While in recent years the community has been represented by well-educated professionals and members of the middle and upper middle classes, such was not true of the earlier immigrants. Shi'ites have always been among the less advantaged, both economically and educationally, and early Lebanese Shi'ite immigrants to America reflected this disadvantage.

It is estimated that today approximately one fifth of American Muslims belong to Shi'a sects. Many are from Iran, coming originally as students during the reign of the Shah and returning after the revolution of 1979. The second largest group of Shi'ites comes from Iraq, with smatterings of others from different global areas such as Lebanon, India, and Pakistan. In the larger urban centers they tend to have separate centers and places of worship, although in smaller cities and towns they often participate in already established Sunni mosques.

For the most part, when it is possible, Twelvers from Iran and those from the Indian subcontinent choose to keep their communities separate in America because of both language and cultural differences.[6] The latter are eager not to be associated with the Iranians, partly to avoid sharing in the American prejudices concerning Iranian Shi'ite "fundamentalists." The notoriety of events in places like Iran and Lebanon, in fact, has had a double influence on Shi'ites in America. On the one hand, it has heightened feelings of distrust on the part of other Americans. On the other, it has served to encourage greater efforts on the part of Shi'is to promote understanding of their faith as a distinguishable entity within the complex of American Islam. Shi'ites in America, like other immigrant Muslims, are in the process of determining how to adapt their own Islamic practice, often heavily associated with particular cultural expressions, to the new environment. In this process they need to consider where their highest priorities lie—with Islam as a whole, with Shi'ism in general, or with their own particular sectarian affiliation.

Ithna 'Ashari (Twelver) Shi'ites

In the absence of a living Imam within the Shi'ite community, leadership for Iranian Twelvers has come from men designated as *mujtahids*, educated deputies of the hidden Imam. They are organized into a central authority, independent of government control, that is supported by the payment of a religious tax called *al-khums*, a 20 percent levy required of all Twelvers and often paid in addition to their *zakat*. This system has extended to the United States, where *khums* money has provided for the building of Islamic centers and for the salaries of religious teachers and leaders. Shi'i scholars report considerable competition for *khums* money among the different Shi'i groups in America. The Kho'i Foundation in New York, despite the death of the Iranian Imam Kho'i, still continues to collect monies from a number of Shi'ites in the United States. Thus American Ithna 'Asharis, while still looking to Iran for leadership and guidance, are able to maintain an essentially autonomous position as they struggle to preserve and redefine their identity in this country.[7]

Returning to Dearborn, Michigan, we find an interesting example of Shi'ism in America. In the middle of the century the community was in serious danger of being absorbed into the more dominant Sunnism of the area. The Shi'ites lacked trained leadership, and many Muslims were unwilling to acknowledge significant differences between the two branches of Islam. With the arrival in succeeding years of *shaykhs* who were prepared to teach the Shi'i community about its own history and practices, distinctions became clearer. More lenient practices in relation to the mosque, such as holding parties and dances, gave way to the stricter and more classical customs of using the mosque only for worship and religious instruction.

The civil war in Lebanon brought a large number of Shi'ite refugees to Dearborn. That event and the Iranian Revolution have had a significant effect on the lives of these Shi'ites, who have had to defend themselves against the prejudice of the American public. This, too, has added to their sense of solidarity and identity apart from the Sunnis of the area.

The Shi'i mosques in Dearborn, which loosely reflect ethnic particularities, differ primarily in the degree to which they adhere to Islamic law. Those that are stricter require women to be properly covered, follow Islamic dietary laws with care, and are in general reluctant to make any compromises with American society. Others argue, through their leaders, that to be too strict is to run the risk of alienating members, especially the youth, and that new times and new places do indeed encourage new understandings and interpretations. Linda Walbridge tells the story of a woman asking one of the Muslim leaders if wearing makeup is permissible for women. "Knowing full well that it was hopeless to ask this woman to throw away her mascara and eyeliner completely," she says, "he instead opted to encourage her to pray and to follow the rules that forbid wearing makeup while at prayer. In this way he did not alienate her, yet gave her sound religious advice."[8]

Like many American Muslims, Shi'ites in Dearborn have had to make accommodations to their new environment. While Friday mosque services continue to be held, they are attended only by men. On Sundays, however, far more people come to the Islamic Center of America, including women and children, where they hear sermons that traditionally would have been delivered only on Fridays.

Isma'ili (Sevener) Shi'ites

The two main groups of Seveners are known generally as the Nizaris and the Mustalis, or Boharas. In the United States the Boharas are the smaller of these groups, with centers in major urban areas such as Chicago, New York, San Francisco, and Detroit. Boharas in America, while concerned for the unity of Islam, place a high priority on community preservation and generally associate both religiously and socially only with members of their own group. Intermarriage among these groups and others within the Muslim community is rare.

Nizari Isma'ili Shi'ites are a larger and faster growing segment of American Islam. While firm about maintaining their distinct identity, they are much more assimilated than the Boharas. Nizaris are united in allegiance to their religious leader, Imam Prince Karim Aga Khan, who is considered a direct descendant of the Prophet Muhammad and 'Ali. The Imam gives both spiritual guidance and advice as to the general welfare of his community.

When the first Nizaris came to America, they were small in number and had to gather informally for prayer, with their religious life taking place primarily at home. Since the increased immigration of Nizaris after 1972, worship life has become much more organized, with prayer halls and centers springing up in many cities. They are the loci of particular commemorative days, such as the birthday of the Prophet and the Imamate Day honoring the time when the present Imam assumed his position.

Members of the community select the religious leader of the local mosque, and the Imam confirms the selection. The leader is generally not paid for his services, and he does not serve as a spiritual guide to the other members. He performs certain ceremonial functions at the prayer hall and on public occasions.

As always, it is difficult to determine exact percentages, but estimates are that Nizari Isma'ilis comprise some 10 percent of the American Shi'ite community. Since the middle of the century the Aga Khan has made strong efforts to reconcile and integrate his followers into the Muslim community as a whole. The current Aga Khan is a well-known public figure who in America often addresses academic audiences, as in his 1996 commencement address at Brown University.

The Druze Community in America

Another faction of Fatimid Shi'is splintered in the eleventh century, forming what we now know as the Druze community. By tradition the Druze, living primarily in the mountainous regions of Lebanon and in some parts of Syria, have kept their beliefs hidden from outsiders. Druze faith and practice have been passed on only to progeny, with marriages outside of their tradition strongly discouraged. Whether the Druze are considered Muslim, or even consider themselves Muslim, has been the subject of much controversy. In any case, their presence, though small, has been a significant part of the Lebanese migration over the last century to both North and South America, as well as to parts of Australia and West Africa. In the first several decades of this century, many immigrants to America identified as Muslim were Druze settling in regions such as Virginia, Kentucky, and Tennessee in the South and up to Washington in the West.

Like others from the Middle East, for some time Druze in America chose to deemphasize their identity and to try to become more American. Many officially converted to Christianity, becoming members of Presbyterian or other Protestant denominations. In more recent times, however, there have been notable movements within the U.S. Druze community not only to claim their identity as Druze but also to include in that identity their affiliation to Islam. Emphasizing the importance of what is sometimes called "Tawhid Faith," they acknowledge not only their Islamic roots but also their continuing allegiance to mainstream Islam.

After a century in America the community, while still small, is growing and struggling with how to be true to their Druze culture and heritage, their role as Arab Americans, and the tradition of Islam. As Abdallah E. Najjar, spokesperson for the Druze community in America, said at a national Druze convention, "We do not deny our history and native culture as we blend the old and the new into an integrated reality possessing hybrid vigor."[9] Many immigrant Muslim communities in America might claim such a goal.

Converts to Islam

Anglo Converts

While the great majority of Muslims in America are either African American or part of the immigrant population, a growing but significant number of other Americans are choosing to adopt Islam as their religion and way of life. Estimates of the number of Anglo Muslims in the United States range from twenty to fifty thousand, but as always it is difficult to determine anything close to exact figures. Some of these are Anglo women who have married Muslim men. Islamic law, as we have seen, permits Muslim males to marry women from among the People of the Book, namely Christians or Jews. While there is no compulsion for such women to convert, because the children will be raised according to the religion of the father, a number of them do choose to adopt Islam. Their conversions may occur because a women's husband is eager for her to accept Islam, or she is persuaded that Islam is the right religion for her, or she wants her children raised in a monolithic home. Probably more than half of the marriages between immigrant Muslim males and non-Muslim American females end in the wife's conversion to Islam, although it should be noted that surveys of female converts indicate that in many cases their adoption of Islam came before marriage to a Muslim man. Children are also raised in the religion of the father if a Muslim woman should marry a Christian or Jewish man. Although such marriages are not legally condoned, they do happen occasionally, putting great pressure on the husband to convert.

Other Anglo Americans choose to convert to Islam for a variety of reasons. Some find the intellectual appeal of a great civilization of scholarly, scientific, and cultural achievements a refreshing antidote to the often anti-intellectual and secularist climate of the contemporary West. One of the reasons for the spread of Islam in various parts of the world over the centuries has been the straightforward simplicity of the declaration of faith and the five pillars that an observant Muslim is obliged to follow. For some Americans this directness is an appealing alternative to what they may find to be confusing Christological doctrines and Trinitarian affirmations espoused by the Christian Church. As Islam in one form or another has attracted many blacks as an antidote to the continuing white racism of American society, other Americans have found its egalitarian platform a viable alternative to a Christianity that sometimes seems inextricably bound to prejudicial practices. Some Anglos without intimate personal relationships or close family connections hope that in a religion so explicitly community oriented they may find solace from loneliness. Unfortunately, that is not always the result, as Muslims orient their communities not only to the commonality of Islam but also and often to the particularity of national and ethnic identities.

The zeal of the new convert to any faith or ideology is notoriously high and certainly not less so in the case of Americans who decide to adopt Islam. Generally religiously conservative in belief and in dress, for reasons of personal conviction, with perhaps the desire to persuade themselves and their families of the rightness of their decision, converts are articulate and enthusiastic spokespeople for a clear and sometimes rather inflexible interpretation of their new faith. Some of the current literature discusses the loneliness Anglo converts may feel after their conversion, especially those not married to Muslims. They share neither in the specific cultures represented by immigrants nor in the ethnic identity of African Americans. Some resent what they feel to be the unnecessary monitoring of their progress as Muslims by conservative immigrants. "Sometimes the questions can become pretty intimidating," writes one convert. "For example, if you are approached by a salafi [conservative] group, Beware! They will test your knowledge of Islam. . . . Don't get nervous. Don't panic. Remain calm. . . ."[10] Some Anglo converts have formed support groups to help one another in the transition to a new faith and identity.

Hispanic and Native American Converts

A good deal of attention is currently being given to the importance of making more converts from the Latin American community in America. Enthusiasts are quick to point to the natural affiliation of Islam with many parts of Hispanic culture, begun with its movement into the Iberian Peninsula in 711. Throughout the years of Muslim presence in Spain until its expulsion after 1492, Islam and Spanish culture were deeply intertwined. Whether such historic affiliation really influences the decision of some Hispanic Americans to adopt Islam may be questionable, especially given the fact that many who convert prefer to ignore their Hispanic heritage and refrain from speaking Spanish in the attempt to be part of the American Muslim "scene."

Islam first appeared in the barrios of the American Northeast in the early 1970s. Mainly first-generation Puerto Ricans from New York, many of these converts entered Islam by affiliating with African American mosques. Since then, immigrant Muslims have tried to organize missionary movements among the Latino populations, with the end of integrating them into established Sunni mosque communities. Hispanics have found much in Islamic culture that is akin to their own cultural heritage, especially the importance of the family structure and specifically defined roles for men and women. Divorce, which has been growing in American Hispanic communities, is noticeably much lower among Latino Muslim couples.

Muslims are slowly waking to the reality that the Hispanic community in America is a ripe source for new converts. "Olé to Allah!" reads the cover page of an issue of *The Message* devoted to articles about American Latino Muslims.[11] Increasing attention is being paid in Muslim journals to the fact that American Hispanics have been virtually ignored as a community in need of *da'wa*, and many are arguing for increased efforts at providing basic Islamic instruction in Spanish. A particular need has been identified for accurate Spanish translations of the Qur'an. The few Hispanic Muslims who actively teach members of their communities about Islam lament that so little is available on the history, traditions, doctrines, and practices of the faith for those whose first language is Spanish. Some works suffer from having been written first in an Asian language, then translated into English, and finally rendered in Spanish.

One illustration of the growth of Latino Islam is a missionary effort in New York City entitled PIEDAD (Propagación Islámica para la Educación y Devoción de Ala'el Divino). A Puerto Rican convert began PIEDAD in 1987, and it has focused particularly on Latinas who are married to Muslims as well as Latinos who are incarcerated. Another Islamic Latino organization in the El Barrio area of New York City, called the Alianza Islámica, began some fifteen years ago as an outgrowth of the Darul Islam movement, illustrating the close association between Hispanic converts and African American Islam. Operating out of a small storefront, it provides a number of social services for the surrounding community as part of its outreach program. Members do after-school tutoring, plan summer recreation, offer drug and alcohol as well as marriage counseling, and provide diploma instruction for kids who have dropped out of school. The Alianza has served to bring wayward Muslims back into the fold, as well as to attract new members from the Hispanic community.

In California the recently formed Asociación Latina de Musulmanes en las Américas (ALMA) seeks to spread Islam among Spanish-speaking people, educating them about the contribution of Islam to their society and culture, with the hope of bringing them back to their ancestors' way of life. ALMA is currently planning to begin publication of the first Spanish Islamic magazine for distribution in the United States, Canada, and Latin America.

While their numbers are still very small, a few Native Americans are also becoming more vocal about their identification with Islam and are reminding other Muslims of the long association of Indians and Muslims on the North American continent. Seminoles in Florida claim that some of their number are descended from African slaves who before emancipation managed to escape and mingle in their ranks, even converting some of the Seminoles to Islam. The Algonquian and Pima languages are said to contain words with Arabic roots. Cherokees claim that a number of Muslims joined their ranks and say that the chief of the Cherokees in 1866 was a Muslim named Ramadhan Ibn Wati.

Some Muslims are now recognizing significant commonalities between Native American and Qur'anic world views, such as a deep reverence for nature and obedience to God's laws for the created world and the acknowledgment that people of all races and colors must be treated equally. Native American understanding of a kind of original divine instruction for humankind parallels the Qur'anic concept of the *din al-fitra*, or natural inherent religious response basic to all people. Native American awareness of divine presence in all the four directions is compared with the Qur'anic assurance that wherever one should turn, there is the face of God. Native American traditions pay much attention to the importance of sacred sites and pilgrimage, which balances the Islamic duty of *hajj* to Mecca and pilgrimages to the tombs of saints. The current concern of American Muslims for what they see as the excesses of modernism and secularism in the West resonates in much of Native American tradition. As Muslims and Native Americans both struggle to clarify and maintain their identities in the American context, it may well be that their ties, both historical and philosophical, will be strengthened.

American Converts to Sufism

Another reason for a number of Americans to consider themselves Muslim is their association with Sufi groups in this country. As indicated in the previous chapter, Sufism is a complex part of the history of Islam, sometimes greatly appreciated and at other times rejected as a deviation from the true faith. To the extent to which Sufi groups in America associate themselves with one of the established and recognized Sufi orders, they must be counted as part of what has emerged as a genuine American Islam. Again, the lines are often blurred, and who is or is not a "real" Sufi may be anyone's call. Some U.S. groups that choose to adopt the name Sufi as part of the

New Age movement do little more than combine body movements with stylistic meditative practices and have no Islamic theological understanding of Sufism.

Particularly attractive to some Americans are forms of Sufi dancing. Normally, these dances are done with a leader in the center, along with a musician, the participants grouped in a circle or circles moving in rhythm. Sometimes the movements are accompanied by group chanting. Such chanting and dancing have often been suspect to orthodox Islam but in some cases, such as the "whirling dervishes," have become a recognized and honored part of the tradition.

Muslims associated with long-established and internationally recognized orders have little patience for the "silliness" of Americans eager to adopt new fads of so-called spirituality, and they are quick to point out that pseudo-Islamic Sufi groups have no legitimate role in American Islam. Reflecting the tensions of Sufism with mainline Islam over the centuries, many immigrant Muslims of a traditional orientation find it difficult to acknowledge the legitimacy of any American Sufi groups. Muslim organizations that are supported financially by Saudi Arabia refuse to allow the participation of Sufi groups. While those who actually "convert" to Islam via Sufism are relatively few, there seems to be a growing interest in Sufism as both a spiritual/psychological discipline and, in the American orders, a locus of fellowship and communal identification. In general, Americans find Sufi movements open, accessible, tolerant, and supportive of individual needs and concerns.

Interestingly, two of the most popular Sufi personages in the West in this century, Hazrat Inayat Khan and Idries Shah, have both seen Sufism as a phenomenon distinguishable from the formal religious structure of Islam. The writings of these two teachers, with their emphasis on the inner life over the outer forms of religion, have been voluminous and influential, especially on young American "seekers."

Hazrat Inayat Khan, who was initiated into the Nizami branch of the Chistiyya Order in India, studied with both Muslim and Hindu masters. His philosophy blended Advaita Vedanta and the "unity of being" philosophy of the school of the Andalusian mystic Ibn 'Arabi. Commissioned by his teacher to bring harmony to East and West, he devoted his life to introducing Sufism to America. He was one of the first to teach Sufi doctrines in the West, lecturing and traveling across America from 1910 to 1927, initiating a number of disciples, and founding the Sufi Order in the West. Many of his teachings are contained in a multivolume series titled *The Sufi Message of Hazrat Inayat Khan*.[12]

When Inayat died in 1927, his son Vilayat Khan, still a boy, inherited leadership of the order. Severe tensions arose in the group, and some turned to the well-known Sufi leader Meher Baba for direction. One of those whose personal claims would not sit well with orthodox Muslims, Baba, who was born in India in 1894, believed himself to have realized Godhood. After 1925 he never spoke, communicating with his disciples by hand gestures or in writing. A number of his many books were "dictated" in this manner.

In the 1960s, a time of growing appeal of Sufism in America, the European-educated Pir Vilayat Khan emerged as effective leader of the Sufi Order in the West, and the movement grew rapidly. The classically trained Pir is said to have felt somewhat distanced by some of his new hippie followers. He was particularly distressed when his disciples wanted to use drugs to induce a spiritual state.

The Sufi Order in the West is still under Vilayat's guidance, although it has expanded to include a variety of teaching and experiential modes. The order continues to stress spiritual awakening, but it also does work in social services, education, and health. It is active in a number of major cities and sponsors retreats, psychotherapy and healing seminars, work camps, and musical presentations. Most Muslim groups in America look on the activities of the Sufi Order in the West, however, with suspicion and even disapproval, disclaiming it as a truly Islamic movement.

Idries Shah, a popular writer and teacher who emphasizes the psychological aspects of Sufism, has been influential in America since the 1960s. An Indian of Afghani lineage, Shah spent most of his time in the West in England, although his writings have been on the shelves of American bookstores from the beginning. Particularly popular are his folktales imparting Sufi wisdom through anecdote and example. Shah, whose followers constitute the Society for Sufi Studies, has been especially critical of those who perpetuate old forms and practices of Sufism that are not relevant to the modern Western world. Shah's works, such as the early and still popular *The Sufis*, conspicuously lack terminology that would specifically identify his interpretation of Sufism with traditional Islam. His writings especially appeal to Westerners of a more intellectual orientation.

Since the 1970s, Sufi groups that have clearly been formed and adapted to fit American culture and demand have been joined by others whose members are immigrants well familiar with Sufi lineage and the practices of a specific *tariqa*, or path, of which they were members in their home countries. These people tend to be more traditional than the earlier practitioners of Sufism in America and more committed to stressing the continuity of Sufism with Islam. Americans are increasingly drawn to these teachers, attracted by the mystical and pietistic form of Islam represented by their orders.

One group that illustrates a blend of New Age influences with the more institutional tradition-based Islamic orders is the Bawa Muhaiyaddeen Fellowship, located in Philadelphia. Its members are both immigrants and American converts from a range of ethnic and religious backgrounds. The experience of Bawa's followers serves as a good illustration of the blending of East and West, immigrant and indigenous experience, and traditional Sufism with new adaptations. The Sri Lankan-born Bawa, a member of the Qadiriyya order, first arrived in America at the invitation of a young Philadelphia woman who had corresponded with him for several years. He quickly drew a number of devotees and decided to remain to fulfill his mission in America. Many of those who found his message appealing were young Americans whose lives had been troubled and lacked a spiritual base. Only gradually were they made to realize that his teachings were grounded in Islam and that he was part of a long and venerated Sufi lineage. He is said to have so embodied the principles of love and charity in his own person and life that simply being in his presence was spiritually uplifting. He considered himself, and was considered by his followers, to be their *shaykh*, or spiritual leader.

Bawa was eager to keep abreast of the latest technological developments, and his use of television and video equipment in the propagation of his message added to the sense that, despite his lineage, the Bawa Muhaiyaddeen Fellowship was a genuine American order constantly adapting to new developments. Bawa's death in 1986 did not mean the dissolution of the Fellowship, and in fact the group has member branches in several other cities, such as Boston. It did, however, raise the question of what it means to be an American Sufi group. By what means can another *shaykh* emerge to guide the community, and will such a person come from overseas or be an American-born convert to Islam? Because of the training prerequisites of a Sufi leader in a traditional order such as the Qadiriyya, the question of what constitutes American Islam may be sharper for Sufis than for other Muslims. The Bawa Muhaiyaddeen Fellowship is only one such Sufi group to face these questions.[13]

Some Sufi groups combine holistic health, music, dance, poetry, and other aesthetic forms with traditional Sufi meditation. Many have become active in the *da'wa*, or missionary activity, of Islam in America. Members of the new generation of Muslims born in America to immigrant parents are joining white converts to Sufi movements. For many men and women,

Sufism seems to breathe the possibility of life and activity into religion in a way that they have not known before, at the same time that one's relationship both to the *shaykh* and to God gives new meaning to the very word *islam*, submission. Sufism also seems to provide a way of cutting across the racial, ethnic, and cultural definitions of so many American Muslim groups, which despite the egalitarian appeal of Islam often continue to segregate themselves along lines of particular identity. In recent years Americans who have studied with Sufi masters abroad have returned and written numerous works to distill the Sufi message into a distinctly Western idiom.

Sufism particularly interests some American women, who find in it an appealing alternative to the Christianity or Judaism, or the agnostic environment, in which they may have been raised. Particularly attractive are those orders more lenient in their restrictions on, for example, the mixing of women and men during the worship time. Sometimes practitioners may be seated in a circle, with men forming one half and women the other. Those Sufi groups unconcerned about separation of the sexes generally pay little attention to any affiliation with the tradition of Islam. As in the Muslim community as a whole, there is both considerable discussion about the appropriateness of women's assuming leadership roles in Sufi organizations and increasing examples of such leadership. The Naqshbandiyya, a "sober" order founded in the Indian subcontinent in the fourteenth century by Baha' al-Din al-Naqshbandi, is particularly popular in the United States and Canada and has provided a context in which significant numbers of women have felt comfortable participating.

Several Shi'i Sufi orders exist in America, one of the most evident being the Nimatullahi Order of Sufis founded and led by Dr. Javad Nurbakhsh, former head of the department of psychiatry at Tehran University in Iran. The order was established in America with his arrival in the 1970s. Located first in California, it maintains centers in a number of American cities, including San Francisco, New York, Washington, D.C., and Boston. Nurbakhsh, who himself now lives in England, stresses a Sufism concerned with doing and seeing rather than thinking and talking, one whose aim is the realization of Truth through love and devotion. The writings of this prolific leader include works on Sufi poetry, psychology, and spiritualism, Jesus in the eyes of Sufis, and Sufi women. He is perhaps best known for *In the Paradise of the Sufis*.[14] Other Iranian Shi'i Sufi orders have grown up across the country in the past several decades. Generally, they emphasize the connection of Sufis with the mystical movements of Islam above the beliefs and practices that would set these groups off as distinctively Shi'i.

Among the numerous groups loosely associated with Sufism, or at least inspired by Islam, is the Indonesian spiritual movement of Subud. Begun around the middle of the century and now with branches in a number of countries, Subud became part of the American scene in the 1970s at the time that so many new movements were taking root. Reported to have once had more than seventy North American centers, Subud continues to attract small numbers of American adherents who, while certainly not seeing themselves as converts to Islam, are drawn by the appeal of participating in social welfare projects on an international scale.

One interesting American communal-living experiment cast in a decidedly Sufi mold has been the establishment of the Dar al-Islam community located in Abiquiu, New Mexico. Distinct from the African American Darul Islam movement described above, this first Islamic village in America was begun in 1980, with the support of Saudi Muslims, as an attempt to model the piety of the early Islamic community of Prophet Muhammad. Located on more than eight thousand acres of land northwest of Albuquerque, the community is home to an adobe brick mosque and school designed by the late and famed Egyptian architect Hassan Fathi. With the goal of bringing together Muslims of all backgrounds from across America as well as from Europe and the Middle East, the community stresses the interracial and interethnic nature of Islam assured by God in the Qur'an: "We have made you tribes and nations so that you might know one another" (Sura 49:13). Members, who dress in a variety of styles appropriate to Southwest existence and to a modest understanding of Islamic requirements, try as much as possible to live a life of quiet piety exemplifying the virtues of Islamic life. At present, it must be acknowledged that the Abiquiu experiment is far from reaching its goal of becoming a large and Islamically organized living community. Never more than twenty-five families in all, membership in residence has dwindled, and much of the original land has been sold. The Dar al-Islam, nonetheless, performs an important service for American Islam through its Institute of Traditional Islamic Studies.

The Ahmadiyya Community of North America

While the classification of Islamic individuals and associations in America into immigrant, African American, and convert is generally useful, some groups do not fall neatly into these categories. Immigrants who are converting to classical Sufism in the United States are one such exception. Another is the Ahmadiyya community, originally a Pakistani missionary movement, which has been a presence in North America for many decades. Its members have worked since the early part of the twentieth century for the conversion of Americans to Islam. Many, but certainly not all, of those converts have been African American. This group is one of the most active within the Islamic fold (if, indeed, it is within, an identity challenged by many Muslims) in the work of *da'wa*, calling or recruiting new members to its understanding of the faith of Islam. Ahmadis have worked particularly on translating and providing copies of the Qur'an to Muslim communities around the world. Claiming more than ten million followers in more than one hundred countries, they have recruited many thousands in North America.

The founder of the Ahmadiyya movement, Hazrat Mirza Ghulam Ahmad, was born in 1835 in Qadian in India's Punjab. An enormously prolific writer, he claims to have received divine revelations or signs legitimating his role as an Islamic leader. Then in 1889 he announced that he was the *mahdi* whose coming Muslims have long expected. Critics have charged that he actually appropriated the status of prophet, an accusation that his followers have explicitly denied. Around the turn of the century the movement began to move beyond India. Of its two branches, only the group called the Qadiani Jamaat has been influential on the American scene. Sunni Muslims have denounced the Ahmadiyya movement as a deviation from the true teachings of Islam, both because of its founder's claims about his own status and because Ahmadis believe that Jesus was not taken up to heaven at the crucifixion but continued his work on earth, ending up in Kashmir, in India. When statistics about the number of Muslims in America are cited, other Muslims are adamant that Ahmadis not be included. Ahmadis, however, claim vigorously that the movement does not depart from Islam at all and see the Ahmadiyya movement as an active and effective organ for the recruitment of new Muslims in America and across the world.

The first Ahmadi missionary to the United States was Mufti Muhammad Sadiq in 1920. He began a society for the preservation of American Islam and in 1921 started publication of the periodical *Moslem Sunrise* (changed in 1959 to *Muslim Sunrise*). Chicago became the official headquarters of the American Ahmadiyya movement and the site of its first mosque. Ahmadi missionaries played a significant role in the early decades of the century in attacking what they saw as the blatant racism of American society. By 1940 there were said to be between five and ten thousand converts in the United States. In 1950 the Ahmadiyya headquarters moved to the American Fazl Mosque in northwest Washington, D.C. This continues to serve as the center for the educational and propaganda mission of the movement.

Copies of its publications are distributed to members of Congress and other government officials, foreign diplomats, the press, and so on. At present Ahmadi centers can be found in more than fifty cities in the United States and Canada.

In their Western missionary work, Ahmadis have been particularly attuned to the necessity of maintaining a strict Islamic faith in the face of Western secularism and materialism. Ahmadi women, who generally dress more conservatively than women in other Muslim or pseudo-Muslim movements, have played and continue to play important roles in the American Ahmadi mission. Like many other Muslims, Ahmadis worry about appropriate education for their children, especially girls, and often opt to develop their own schools. Members of the community bear the special burden of affirming their Islamic identity both within a culture that does not appreciate it and as part of Sunni Islam, which does not accept it.

Clearly, the picture of American Islam is growing increasingly complex. Stories of immigrant and African American Islam in this country for a long time were quite distinct and separate, and relations between blacks and immigrants were generally quite rare. Now, however, those stories are coming to be interrelated. Added to this fascinating mix are the conversions of whites, Hispanics, and Native Americans to Islam. These groups are still small but are significant both for their actual presence and for the impetus they give to the *da'wa*, or mission movement, within Islam. They are also of great importance to those who want to gain political capital out of the fact that American Islam is multiracial, multi-ethnic, and growing. Let us turn now to the story of African Americans and the many ways in which they have played and continue to play a crucial role in the development of American Islam.

CHAPTER FOUR

Islam in the African American Community

Students of black religion in America are now increasingly aware that voluntary immigration was only one of the ways in which Muslims arrived on the shores of "the promised land." Others came against their will, finding America a land not of promise but of bondage. These were the Muslims brought in the slave trade of colonial and post-colonial America. It is now a well-established fact that a significant number of black Africans brought to North America during the antebellum slave trade were Muslim. Numbers are impossible to determine, but there may have been several thousand. Some have even postulated that as many as 20 percent of African slaves were Muslim, but that estimate is probably high. These men and women seized into slavery came from a variety of areas in sub-Saharan Africa from Senegal to Nigeria. Some were highly literate and educated in their religion, while others were more humble practitioners. A few, such as the well-documented Prince Ayub Ibn Sulayman Diallo, who was abducted in 1731, even came from the ruling elements of their societies.

Most of these African Muslims had never had any contact with whites before being taken into slavery. The account of one of them, Kunta Kinte of Senegambia, is documented in Alex Haley's popular novel *Roots*,[1] also broadcast in a series specially made for television. The novel sets the scene of Kinte's Islamic heritage from page 1, on which Haley describes the Muslim early morning call to prayer, which, as he says, had been offered up as long as any living person there could remember. Haley records other occasions attesting to Kinte's faith, as when he prays to Allah while chained in the bottom of a "Christian" slave ship.

Unfortunately for those who would have wished to practice their Muslim faith during the harsh circumstances of slavery in America, their Christian overlords rarely permitted it. Just as Muslims who remained in Spain after 1492 had been forced to convert to Christianity, so American slaves were required to become Christians also. "When I was a Mohammedan I prayed thus: 'Thanks be to God, Lord of all [the] Worlds, the Merciful the Gracious. . . .' But now I pray for 'Our Father. . .' in the words of our Lord Jesus the Messiah."[2] Slaves in America, however, did not have the option available to the Moors of leaving the country, although a very few did manage to escape and return to Africa. While most of these black Africans did indeed become Christian, documents indicate that at least a few managed to maintain their Islamic faith, continuing as practicing Muslims until the early part of this century. Generally, they had to maintain their practice in secret. Some records indicate that a few even risked ridicule and harsh punishment by continuing to pray publicly, as they understood it to be their Qur'anic obligation to do. According to one account, a Muslim slave while pretending to write the Lord's Prayer in Arabic was actually writing out the Fatiha, the first chapter of the Qur'an. Those who could write left behind a few documents that have added greatly to our understanding of who these people really were, their experiences recording more than a century of trade in human life.

A number of families now living on the coast of Georgia are said to be descendants of slaves, some of them reportedly Muslim. Best known, perhaps, is one Bilali Mahomet, who was probably taken into slavery around 1725. His *Bilali Diary*, written in a West African Arabic script, is now located in the rare books library of the University of Georgia. Grant records from South Carolina contain reports of slaves who refused to eat pork and who prayed to a god named Allah. For many African American Muslims today, the presence of these Muslims in early American history, and their achievements both before being taken into slavery and while in bondage, have added a great deal to the sense of pride in being Muslim and of sharing in the long struggle for freedom that has characterized the black experience in America from its earliest days. "The Afro-American people have Islam in their hearts," says a recent convert. "We have it on our tongues as we struggle to pronounce the Arabic which we have forgotten, but with which perhaps we came as slaves. This was the culture that was stripped from us, along with the language and religion. Most critically, the religion of Islam was taken from us through slavery."[3]

As we have already seen, the question of who is and who is not a Muslim in the American context is sometimes straightforward and other times difficult to ascertain. While some individuals and groups consider themselves to be under the umbrella of Islam, or at least identify with elements of Islamic faith and practice, those very individuals and groups may be denied Islamic affiliation by others who accuse them of marginality, sectarianism, or even heresy. The history of African American groups who have looked to Islam for their identity is replete with illustrations of this kind of disputed identity. One of the earliest examples is that of the Moorish Americans at the beginning of the twentieth century.

Noble Drew Ali and the Moorish Science Temple of America

Most emancipated slaves, having had their original identity—whatever it might have been—taken away by white masters, found themselves in a desperate quest for a place in American society. It was an extremely difficult time for blacks in an overwhelmingly white culture, with economic and social problems compounded by the desperation of having no sense of belonging. Immigrants from Europe resented blacks migrating North who competed for the same jobs. Those blacks remaining in the South occasionally found themselves victims of lynchings and even burnings.

Not surprisingly, a series of movements arose geared to helping blacks find their identity. Among them were those that sought an identity outside of the American context, like Marcus Garvey's Universal Negro Improvement Association (UNIA), which advocated a return to Liberia in the African motherland. Garvey's movement strongly influenced several black leaders who, in the early decades of this century, associated themselves with Islam. One was Noble Drew Ali, among the first to adopt certain symbols of the Islamic faith. Unlike Garvey, Ali looked to another continent not as a home to which black Americans should retreat but as a source of roots that could be transplanted into American soil. He wanted to unite a people who had been oppressed, to provide a means for them to contribute both individually to their own well-being and collectively to the larger American society. To do so, he said that Americans of African descent were by their heritage Asiatic, or Moorish. Thus the community he founded was originally known as the Moorish National and Divine Movement, later changed to the Moorish Science Temple of America.

Noble Drew Ali was born Timothy Drew in 1886 in North Carolina. Working his way north, he settled in New Jersey and began to preach a message that was to develop into the five principles of his community, namely, love, truth, peace, freedom, and justice. The scripture he provided for Moorish Americans was titled *The Holy Koran of the Moorish Science Temple of America* but in fact has nothing in common with the Holy Qur'an of Islam. Drew reported that while on a trip to Morocco the king gave him the mandate to instruct African Americans in the Islamic faith. Drew Ali was convinced that he was a prophet of Allah, the last in a long line, and that it was his destiny to serve as a warner to the Asiatics of America, as Muhammad had been a warner to the Arabs of his day. The primary message of his teachings was that salvation can be achieved only if blacks discard the various identities forced on them by whites in America, such as Negro or colored person, and understand that their true origin is Asiatic. Slave names should be dropped and new names adopted to reflect the pride and dignity of their heritage. Ali's message was appealing to little-educated blacks who were suffering from economic deprivation, bitter about their lot in American society, and desperate to find an identity that separated them from white oppression.

The first Moorish temple was established in Newark in 1913. By 1916 the community was divided into two groups. One remained in New Jersey, with its name changed to the Holy Moabite Temple; and the other moved with Noble Drew Ali to Chicago. By 1928, the year of the first Moorish National Convention, temples had also been established in Pittsburgh and Detroit. The various communities focused on achieving economic independence by setting up grocery stores, restaurants, and other small businesses. "We shall be secure in nothing until we have economic power," said Noble Drew Ali. "A beggar people cannot develop the highest in them, nor can they attain to a genuine enjoyment of the spiritualities of life."[4] Harmonious race relations were encouraged but not always possible. As pride in their black identity grew, so did tensions between members and the white community. In 1929 Ali was arrested and jailed, and shortly after being released he mysteriously died. Various claimants immediately arose to challenge one another for leadership, but as is so often the case, none was ever able to capture the admiration and devotion accorded to their original leader. Despite problems, however, the Moorish American movement has continued in a number of urban areas of the eastern and midwestern United States. Both W. D. Fard and Elijah Muhammad of the Nation of Islam are said to have been Moorish Temple members.

The Moorish Science Temple, now a small association, is open to any people who consider themselves Asiatic, although its membership is essentially

African American. The national office is currently located in Chicago, and meetings are held annually, although some local temples operate independently. Leaders are known as grand sheikhs or sheikhesses, members as brothers and sisters. Affiliates generally assume the name "El" or "Bey" after their given names. The education of children is given extremely high priority. "A field of grass will grow on its own," says a pamphlet advertising a parent/child development seminar in Newark, conducted by the Moorish Institute in 1984, "but a garden of flowers requires cultivation. And if our children are to bloom and grow, deliberate educational stimulations must be introduced early into each child's home." Appropriate dress is considered important, with men traditionally wearing fezzes and women turbans and long dresses, particularly in the temple. Members are strongly encouraged to avoid alcohol or drugs, sometimes even caffeine. The Moorish Science Temple community has received civic recognition for its achievements in promoting the social, economic, and moral advancement of Americans of African descent.

Elijah Muhammad and the Nation of Islam

The early decades of this century continued for American blacks to be a time of social displacement, economic deprivation, and yearning for some kind of national identity. Marcus Garvey was sent into exile in 1927, after which his movement was effectively dead, and the Moorish American Temple, while continuing, had lost much of its earlier appeal. While each in its time had significant numbers of followers, neither Garvey nor Drew Ali was able to capture the imagination of "Negroes" in America as did one small black man from Detroit, with his emblematic cap of stars and crescents. That man was Elijah Poole, later to be called Elijah Muhammad, first prophet of the first indigenous American movement claiming an affiliation with Islam to gain the attention of the country, namely the Nation of Islam, or NOI. (It should be noted that the name black Muslims, popular because of C. Eric Lincoln's sociological study of that title, has never been one by which the Nation of Islam has called itself.[5]) Malcolm X and Louis Farrakhan, both recipients of continuing publicity, were products of the NOI movement. Warith Deen Mohammed, son of Elijah and friend of Malcolm, has made his own name as one of the most important leaders of Islam in North America.

In part because of director Spike Lee's popular film about Malcolm X, the story of the rise of the NOI is one with which most people are quite familiar. It bears repeating, however, as a fascinating example of a truly indigenous socioreligious, even political, movement that played a unique role in meeting the needs of significant numbers of African Americans. The very inclusion of the word *nation* in its title set forth the ideal of a political as well as an ethical and religious entity, grounded at least nominally in a faith whose roots are far from the racist society of America. That it advocated a doctrine of human origin far from the ideals of an egalitarian Islam mattered little and, in fact, was scarcely realized by those who found in it a means of recapturing personal identity through a standard of performance that was strict, clean, and economically viable.

The precise beginnings of the movement remain hazy, despite the exacting scholarship that has tried to peel back the layers of mythology surrounding the appearance to African Americans in Detroit of a stranger named Wallace D. Fard. Among Fard's most ardent followers was Elijah Poole, son of a poor itinerant Baptist preacher. Poole was ripe for the kind of encouraging message that Fard was to dispense. According to Poole's own account, Fard made his first appearance in Detroit on July 4, 1930, identifying himself as having come from the holy Muslim city of Mecca. He proclaimed a message that was specifically directed to the blacks of America, who were identified as members of the lost, and now found, ancient tribe of Shabazz. Poole believed that Fard's mission was to redeem and restore this lost tribe. Through one of Fard's early lectures, Poole came to understand that Fard was the personification of the promised *mahdi*, the guided one whose return is expected to initiate the final period before the Day of Resurrection and Judgment. Poole understood this identity actually to accord Fard a form of divinity, an idea that, of course, is anathema to orthodox Islam. Later, in an apparently syncretistic blending of Islam and Christianity, he said that Fard was the one for whom the world has been waiting for two thousand years. Fard himself encouraged the interpretation that he was indeed a Christ-figure, to displace the white Christ that Christians tried to give to blacks.

The real identity of W. D. Fard has been the subject of much ongoing debate. Reluctantly, he was acknowledged as having been Caucasian, although later it was said that he actually embodied both black and white so that he could move with ease among both groups. Followers found the obscured identity a source of mystery and appeal rather than suspicion.

Fard first preached while traveling around peddling silks and artifacts. Initially meeting in private homes, his followers were soon sufficiently organized that they rented a meeting hall, which they called a temple. At this point, the Lost-Found Nation of Islam in the Wilderness of North America came officially into being, to be shortened simply to the Nation of Islam. Fard's ministry lasted only a little more than three years, during which he was able to develop an organization with educational resources for men, women, and children, as well as the still existing private security force known as the Fruit of Islam.

His was, however, a ministry marked with some serious and unfortunate incidents. Fard was accused of inciting violence with his racist teachings and was several times arrested. He was finally expelled from Detroit on May 4, 1933. Soon afterward, Fard disappeared as mysteriously as he had first come, seen no more after 1934.

Elijah Poole found Fard's message compelling. As he himself began to pass on the message, he was accorded the status of minister and given the Muslim name of Elijah Muhammad. He quickly assumed a position of leadership in the movement and was eventually named Chief Minister of Islam. In 1932 he moved to Chicago, where he established what was known as Temple Number Two, the main headquarters for the NOI after the disappearance of W. D. Fard. A tough taskmaster, Elijah Muhammad ran the Nation with authority. He established a hierarchy with himself at the head, and under him were ministers, supreme captains, captains, and lieutenants. Those who wished to join the NOI had to submit a letter of application to the Chief Minister, who soon adopted the role of messenger of Allah. When accepted for membership, a new convert dropped his or her "slave," or last, name and adopted simply an X to signify an unknown African ancestry. Like Moorish Americans, NOI members referred to themselves not as blacks or Negroes but as Asiatics. They identified specifically with the Tribe of Shabazz, people of African descent who were said to have discovered the Nile Valley of Egypt and the holy city of Mecca.

Many of the teachings of the NOI as developed by Elijah Muhammad are irreconcilable with the tradition of Islam. Mainstream Muslims today actively dissociate themselves from the current Nation under the leadership of Louis Farrakhan for a number of reasons, not the least the extent to which he continues to preach what to them can only be understood as heresy or blasphemy. As we have seen, the *shahada* attests in its two articles that only God is divine and that Muhammad is God's Prophet, and the Qur'an affirms that Muhammad is the seal and the last in a long line of prophets. Elijah

Muhammad's belief that Fard claimed for himself some kind of divine status belies the first part of the *shahada* and thus constitutes an act of *shirk*, or association with God, the greatest sin one can commit in orthodox Muslim understanding. NOI insistence that Elijah was the last messenger of W. D. Fard, which contradicts the second article, is abhorrent to most Muslims. When Steven Barboza in *American Jihad* asked Louis Farrakhan, current NOI leader, whether Elijah really was a prophet, he denied that Elijah ever made such a claim, saying, "We do not believe that there is any prophet after Prophet Muhammad. But we see that the Qur'an teaches us that every nation has received a messenger."[6] Elijah Muhammad's son Warith Deen, leader of those who broke from the NOI after 1975, has said his father knew that some of his teachings were not in accord with true Islam. They were essential at the time he gave them, however, in order for blacks to pull themselves up from the circumstances of genuine degradation in which many found themselves to a station of pride and self-respect, thrift and discipline, and economic stability.

Islam also prides itself on the recognition fostered since the days of Prophet Muhammad that all people and all races are equal before God. The NOI teaching that whites are descended from the devil obviously contradicts this essential Muslim egalitarianism. An elaborate NOI mythology supports the identification of whites as evil and blacks as the chosen people of Allah. Briefly put, a scientist named Yacub, descendant of the Shabazz tribe, after being exiled from Mecca, devised a plot to enslave the other members of the tribe. By clever genetics and cross-breeding he is said gradually to have developed the white race by matching recessive genes with recessive. The lightest in color of the races to have ensued is the most inferior and, correspondingly, the most evil. Elijah Muhammad identified the process of coming to a knowledge of these realities and of the splendor of original black civilization, and thus to the place where whites can be overthrown, as a kind of resurrection for African Americans. This affirmation of the strength and goodness of blackness and the weakness and moral degeneration of whiteness was a powerful message for blacks who had been weaned in the culture of white supremacy. A member of Masjid Muhammad in Hartford tells about her father, who had been raised a Baptist in the South and experienced prejudice and persecution, including seeing his family's house burned down by whites. When he came north and heard the message of Elijah Muhammad, he especially listened to the part about the white man being the devil. "There is a connection between the devil and fire," she says with a smile.[7]

Elijah Muhammad, Chief Minister of the Nation of Islam until
1975. AGENCE FRANCE PRESSE/ARCHIVE PHOTOS

Elijah Muhammad preached that blacks are not American citizens
because they are not Americans by race, and he was imprisoned during
World War II for telling his followers that they should not participate in a
war that was not their concern. The Nation, therefore, represented itself as
a black entity within the United States, its members citizens of Mecca and
its flag the emblem of Mecca. It considered the fall of America as a white
society to be imminent. The key for Elijah Muhammad was not integration
into American society but separation and the establishment of a political
and social unit in which whites would have no role. If a separate state were
not achievable—and Elijah Muhammad was under no illusions about the
difficulty of such an attainment—the goal remained justice and equal
opportunity for blacks. Like Noble Drew Ali, he, therefore, advocated the
establishment of black-owned businesses and other means of self-provision.
To foster economic independence and security, essential for the goal of

political independence, Elijah Muhammad encouraged members to think black, invest black, buy black. Economics and ethics were combined into a structure in which NOI members were required to be personally abstemious and professionally industrious.

In addition to prayer five times a day—one of the most obvious borrowings from traditional Islam—he enjoined members not to eat more than one meal a day and to avoid pork, alcohol, gambling, undue emphasis on athletics, laziness, and excessive sleeping. Intermarriage was strictly forbidden to maintain the purity of the black race. Following the Islamic duty of *zakat*, or almsgiving, he also asked members to give a regular part of their income to the Nation, whatever it was possible for them to afford. Education was extremely important to Elijah Muhammad, who himself never went past the fourth grade, and he fully supported the establishment of Muslim schools. Already in the 1930s the University of Islam, really a set of parochial schools, had begun in association with the Muslim temples to educate children through high school. This institution operated under the name of the Clara Muhammad School, after Elijah's wife, with a highly organized curriculum and strict discipline for students.

Malcolm X

Among those most persuaded of the imminent fall of America's white leadership was Malcolm Little. Apparently addicted to the fast and unsavory life of the inner city in Boston, Hartford, and New York, Malcolm tells in his autobiography an intricate and compelling story of his family (whose home was burned by the Ku Klux Klan when Malcolm was six), his friends, his temptations as he grew through early manhood, and especially his bitter anger with the white society that had so demoralized and devalued blacks.[8] "Do you mean to tell me that in a powerful country like this, a so-called *Christian* country, that a handful of men from the South can prevent the North, the West, the Central States and the East from giving Negroes the rights the Constitution says they already have?" demanded Malcolm years later in an address at Boston University. "No! I don't believe that and neither do you. No white man really wants the black Man to have his rights, or he'd have them."[9]

Having spent much of his young adulthood indulging in various forms of vice and crime, including bootlegging, pimping, and selling drugs, Malcolm was serving a seven-year sentence in the maximum security Massachusetts Norfolk Prison when he first became aware of the Nation of Islam and its teaching through his brother Reginald. He was absolutely ripe for the message of black liberation preached by Elijah Muhammad, and in 1947, at the age of twenty-two, he became an ardent member of the NOI.

Malcolm X's role in the propagation of Nation of Islam ideology in the years succeeding his release from prison in 1952 is a well-known and much discussed part of recent American history. A highly intelligent man, Malcolm submitted himself wholeheartedly to the discipline as well as the advocacy of the movement. He was to become the National Representative of the Honorable Elijah Muhammad for the next twelve years, speaking nationally and internationally about the circumstance of blacks in American society and about the opportunity presented by the NOI to alter those circumstances. He became a public figure and in 1959 was interviewed by Mike Wallace for a controversial television documentary on the Nation titled *The Hate That Hate Produced*. Major news magazines and journals vied for coverage of Malcolm and his inflammatory messages about white bigotry. His autobiography and other records attest to his friendship with Elijah's son Wallace, later to be known as Imam Warith Deen, a deeply spiritual and well-trained Muslim who even in the early years had questions about some of his father's doctrines and interpretations. Many have speculated that this relationship was significant to Malcolm's eventual change from the hatred-of-whites mentality of his earlier years, consonant with NOI ideology, to an appreciation and advocacy of orthodox Islam's racial tolerance and inclusiveness.

Meanwhile, the FBI was stepping up its systematic efforts, begun in the 1950s and 1960s, to monitor the Nation, changing from simple surveillance to active intelligence. "The Holy Qur'an warns the Muslims that the devils see you," said Louis Farrakhan in 1974. "The United States Government has paid enemies and informers in every temple, among every society of Muslims. Whenever you meet, the devil meets with us. Whenever you pick up the phone to talk, the devil is listening."[10] The FBI has been accused of trying to destroy the Nation not only through the gathering of information "leaked" by informants but by actually creating disputes between the members of the NOI and other movements for black liberation, such as the black Panthers. The tactics did not work, partly because they reinforced the ideology that whites really *are* devils.

Malcolm's presence as a spokesman for the Nation of Islam influenced numbers of African Americans, including some public figures. In February

Malcolm X, later to become El Hajj Malik el-Shabazz.
ARCHIVE PHOTOS

of 1964, immediately after his heavyweight fight against Sonny Liston, boxer Cassius Clay, whom Malcolm had befriended, became one of the first of a significant number of athletes to become a Muslim, known thereafter as Muhammad Ali (see "Profiles").

In the meantime, however, other events led to Malcolm's deep disappointment and eventual disenchantment with Elijah Muhammad, whom he professed to have loved and respected deeply for more than twelve years. "I have sat at our Messenger's feet, hearing the truth from his own mouth! I have pledged on my knees to Allah to tell the white man about his crimes and the black man the true teachings of our Honorable Elijah Muhammad," he had said earlier. "I don't care if it costs my life. . . ."[11] In the early 1960s it appeared that with Elijah's declining health the leadership of the NOI would go directly to Malcolm. Jealousy on the part of other members, however, led to discrediting rumors. Malcolm began to receive less frequent coverage in Nation organs, such as its newspaper *Muhammad Speaks* (which Malcolm himself founded in 1961), and he was discouraged from being such a public spokesman. This coincided with rumors concerning illicit relations on the part of Elijah Muhammad with two of his former secretaries, rumors that Malcolm felt he could confirm. Probably influenced by Wallace, Malcolm also began to question more seriously some of the doctrines and beliefs of the Nation. His disillusionment with Elijah, the jealousy of his fellow Nation members, and his questioning of basic NOI doctrines, along with his increasingly vocal opposition to American policy in the Vietnam War, were a combination that ultimately would prove deadly to Malcolm. Responding to charges that he was a dangerous extremist, Malcolm affirmed that only a radical stance could address the extremely bad conditions in which blacks found themselves in racist America. Malcolm's widely quoted comment that John F. Kennedy's assassination was a case of chickens coming home to roost, the natural outcome of the violence prevalent in America, was interpreted as his somehow sanctioning the president's death. Elijah silenced Malcolm for three months. The rift grew deeper. In January of 1964 Malcolm was removed as a minister of New York's Temple Number Seven, and at the same time Wallace was excommunicated for his association with Malcolm. The scene was set for a dramatic change.

Three months later, Malcolm X set out for Mecca to participate in the pilgrimage that is required of all Muslims at least once in a lifetime. It was, indeed, to be the experience of a lifetime for Malcolm. His autobiography describes his deep sense of shame as he realized that while he called himself a minister of Islam, he did not know the ritual for prayer or some of the basic requirements of living an Islamic life. The realization of the inadequacy of his training, as well as the quite overwhelming recognition that people of all races can and do participate together without rancor or prejudice in the great ceremonial pilgrimage, shocked and humbled Malcolm. His ensuing speaking tour through Africa after the *hajj*, in which he outlined his ideas for an international black liberation movement, included visits to a number of African Muslim heads of state. Conversations with these leaders opened his eyes further to the incongruity of separatist Nation of Islam doctrines with the inclusiveness of worldwide Islam.

The die was cast for Malcolm's break with the Nation. On March 8, 1964, he left his once-beloved association and organized a new group called the Muslim Mosque, Inc., with its political wing the Organization of Afro-American Unity (OAAU). In recognition of his pilgrimage and his new identity as an orthodox Muslim, he changed his name to El Hajj Malik el-Shabazz. He was attacked severely from within the Nation, and even his brother Philbert X was persuaded to denounce Malcolm publicly as a false prophet.

On February 21, 1965, the former Malcolm Little was shot and killed while addressing his newly formed OAAU in New York City, leaving his wife of seven years, Betty Shabazz, a widow (see "Profiles"). The U.S. government also had its reasons for a strong critique of el-Shabazz's words and actions, and some have accused the FBI of arranging Malcolm's murder. The actual assailant was never determined, though many might have wished for his death, and the world lost one of the most compelling political and religious leaders of the twentieth century.

By the 1960s, turbulent days for black Americans, many who saw themselves as political activists had affiliated with some kind of Islam. This was particularly true of those who worked in the arts, such as writers, poets, musicians, and others who in their public presentations were symbolizing their break with white society and their encouragement of other African Americans to look on Islam as a vehicle for personal achievement as well as communal advancement. Some black intellectuals such as LeRoi Jones (Amiri Baraka) were analyzing the social and political issues current in the black community and advocating Islam as a solution to societal ills. For many African Americans, adopting Islam served to set them apart from white society, Muslim or not. Since that time, and particularly after the death of Elijah Muhammad, others have moved consciously to look for the unity of all American Muslims, regardless of color or cultural background. One of those who has pioneered the effort to bring African American and immigrant Islam closer together is Elijah Muhammad's son Wallace.

Wallace Muhammad (Warith Deen Mohammed)

As we have seen, Wallace had difficulties all along with his father's separatist and racially based doctrines. To understand the importance of his efforts, it is necessary to look again at the Nation of Islam. Elijah Muhammad was quick to blame Malcolm X's death on his denunciation of NOI doctrines, although Elijah denied that the members of his organization had actually fired the deadly shots. Meanwhile, Wallace was in continual trouble with the Nation for questioning some basic doctrines. Finally, he regained his status as Minister of Islam in the Chicago Mosque in 1974. The organization was continuing to grow, and by the middle of the 1970s it claimed a million members. It was active in farming and sheep and cattle ranching, various kinds of industries, and many small businesses across America. Some seventy-five temples were in operation in the United States, as well as outside the country.

Then, early in 1975, the Nation of Islam was stunned to hear of the death of its long-time leader, the Honorable Elijah Muhammad, of congestive heart failure. For some ardent followers of Elijah, this was a staggering event, sorely testing their faith, as they had believed that their leader would never succumb to the throes of mortality. At the annual Savior's Day Rally the day after the death, the public announcement was made that Wallace was to succeed his father as Supreme Minister of the NOI. While many were shocked because of the checkered history of Wallace's relationship with his father, and because of his lack of public exposure, those on the inside knew that Elijah wanted leadership to stay within the family. For the time being, most of the more visible leaders of the Nation, including Louis Farrakhan, gave their allegiance to Wallace. With his succession were to come momentous changes within the movement itself in the following years as the political millenarianism of the earlier Nation gave way to a visible move toward orthodox Islam.

Wallace, born in 1933, was the seventh of Elijah and Clara Muhammad's eight children. From an early age interested in the academic and spiritual disciplines of Islam, Wallace immersed himself in the study of Arabic and the Qur'an. As we have seen, he soon critically assessed those teachings of his father that did not concur with what he was learning of orthodox Islam. Wallace made his own first pilgrimage to Mecca in 1967, three years after Malcolm's momentous journey. Immediately upon assuming leadership of the NOI after the death of Elijah Muhammad, Wallace began to rethink publicly the ideology that had characterized the Nation in its earlier days. While always careful to credit his father with wise and skilled leadership, he made it clear that as Fard was not divine, so Elijah was not the pure and unblemished messenger of Allah that so many of his followers believed him to be but only a gifted but also very human man. Wallace's communications about Fard were delicate, and early on he tried to persuade his followers that Fard was still alive and in communication with him. Only in the early 1990s did he announce Fard's actual death.

Central to Wallace Muhammad's early preaching was the rebuttal of the doctrine of black superiority, a keystone of Fard's and Elijah Muhammad's teachings. Only a few months after his father's death, Wallace announced that whites were to be considered fully human and even encouraged to become members of the Nation of Islam. He also posthumously brought Malcolm X back within the fold. Wallace evidenced his obvious interest in Islam as a spiritual force rather than a political tool in his de-emphasis of the nationalism that in different ways had characterized the preaching of both his father and Malcolm. His message also appealed to a broader base of people, although still directed primarily to African Americans. With the end of the demand for a separate state came his call for acknowledgment of citizenship within the United States of America and respect for the U.S. Constitution.

Among the many organizational changes Wallace effected was the abolition of the men's Islamic security force, the notorious Fruit of Islam. This ban was probably a strategic action, as the FOI was the only unit within the Nation that could offer organized opposition to the direction in which he was taking the movement. Wallace also moved to separate business from the practice of religion. He basically began to take apart the huge but unwieldy and unsound business empire his father had tried so hard to build, leasing some small businesses to non-Muslims and liquidating large long-term debts by selling off those that were not profitable.

Much of the community's evolution under Wallace Muhammad's leadership reveals itself in the succession of name changes he introduced. Moving the locus of identity from Asiatic to Islam in its more global connotation, he also emphasized the link with black Africa. In recognition of Prophet Muhammad's original choice of a black Ethiopian named Bilal to give the first call to prayer, Wallace referred to his members as Bilalians. He changed the name of the NOI journal *Muhammad Speaks* to *Bilalian News*, and its content became much less political and more inclusive. "Bilalian" continues to be a general identification for black American Muslims. Initially, he saw the former Nation members as continuing to have their own group identity, which he called "The World Community of Al-Islam in the West" (WCIW).

Other external changes signaled the community's adoption of a new identity. Mosques were referred to by their Arabic name *masjid* (literally, "the place of prostration"), Arabic symbols formed the decor instead of the former slogans that denounced America and Christianity, Islamic prayers were broadcast, and seats were replaced with carpets so that all could sit on the floor as in a traditional mosque. Savior's Day, one of the most important observances of the Nation, became Ethnic Survival Week, to celebrate the achievements of black Americans. While the importance of cleanliness and honest upright behavior has continued from the old NOI days, Wallace relaxed the strict dress code. The subordinate role assigned to women under Elijah Muhammad gave way to an equality of participation and function for men and women, with equal educational opportunities.

In 1978 Wallace began restructuring and decentralizing, resigning his own direct leadership in favor of an elected council of six people serving as imams. Two years later he announced that he had officially changed his name to Warith Deen Mohammed, which in Arabic means "the inheritor of the religion of (Prophet) Muhammad." At the same time, to emphasize the significance of a specifically American Islam, he changed the name of the organization from the World Community of Islam in the West to the American Muslim Mission. The journal received yet another title, changing from *Bilalian News* to the *American Muslim Journal*. In the mid-1980s, to signal the movement's identification with worldwide orthodox Islam, the periodical was called simply *Muslim Journal*, a title it retains today. Still published out of Chicago, it contains articles primarily but not exclusively about African American Muslims, highlighting their community achievements and recognition, and in virtually every issue features several prominent spreads about the activities of Warith Deen Mohammed. It also includes basic Arabic

Warith Deen Mohammed, Imam of the Muslim American Society. © Ted Gray

lessons, as well as listings of literary and technological resources available for the study of Islam and Arabic.

In 1985 Warith Deen felt that the decentralization he had begun some years earlier was complete, and he declared that his followers were no longer to be characterized by any distinguishing name. We are simply Muslims, he affirmed, members of the worldwide body of Sunni Islam. Recently, however, apparently by request of those in the community he represents, he has decided to refer to them as the Muslim American Society.

Warith Deen emerged from this long process as a significant, recognized, and respected leader of American Islam, one whose vision highly influences American blacks, both Muslim and non-Muslim. He has been called the contemporary *mujaddid*, the renewer of the religion of Islam for his age. Accepted by the World Mission Council of Imam Administrators as leader of the Muslim community in the United States, he is responsible for certifying all Muslim Americans who wish to undertake the *hajj* to Mecca. In 1990 Imam Warith Deen was the first Muslim to be asked to open the U.S. Senate with prayer, and later he participated in President Bill Clinton's inaugural celebration. About his own status, he said: "I hope what I leave behind is enough evidence of my sincerity as a Muslim for people to say, well, maybe he had ups and downs, maybe he didn't do a lot of things we thought he should do, but one thing we have no doubts about: he was a sincere believer in his religion."[12]

Louis Farrakhan

The former Nation of Islam, in the meantime, has been resuscitated under the leadership of the fiery Louis Farrakhan, generally following the ideology of Elijah Muhammad. Despite his earlier assurances of allegiance to Wallace, Farrakhan soon felt that Elijah's son was leading the group in a direction that would neglect the immediate task of addressing the still unfortunate circumstances of American blacks. In 1978 he publicly stated that he no longer felt welcome within the World Community of Islam in the West and was cutting off all ties with Wallace. "When I could not agree with him any longer," he said, "I separated myself from him. Not to take up stones to throw them at him but because I honestly could not abide his criticism of his father, who had laid the basis for our development Islamically in America."[13]

His plan, Farrakhan said, was to rebuild the old Nation of Islam. Wallace was exceedingly cautious in his response to Farrakhan, urging that he still had a home and a place within the WCIW. But Farrakhan again affirmed the ideology of black supremacy, along with the vision of the imminent fall of white America. For the most part, Farrakhan's followers are not former Nation members, most of whom stayed with Wallace, but new converts from within the African American community.

The current NOI is basically a black-power movement dedicated to the old separatist ideal of establishing an independent nation. It continues to proclaim the injustices visited on the black community by racist white American society. Farrakhan insists that integration simply cannot solve the problems of blacks who have not achieved at least middle-class status. *The Final Call* newspaper resumed publication in 1979, featuring Farrakhan's speeches and activities, the involvements of other current NOI members, and a regular replay of the writings and talks of Elijah Muhammad. Farrakhan spearheads efforts by NOI members to work for the betterment of the black community. While still a small organization, the Nation continues to engage the attention of the American public because of its community efforts to clean up drug-infested areas and otherwise work to improve the lives of inner-city blacks. In 1997 Farrakhan's call for a "million man march" in Washington, D.C., brought together African Americans from across the nation.

Who is this figure who continues to capture the imagination of significant, if small, numbers of African Americans with his message of black supremacy and separatism, to elicit other Muslims' constant insistence that the Nation is not part of their fold, and to intrigue and sometimes frighten others who listen to his rhetoric and experience his charisma? Born Louis Eugene Wolcott in 1933, the same year in which Wallace Muhammad was born, he pursued a musical career as a violinist and calypso singer. He gave this vocation up in 1955, however, after hearing the preaching of Elijah Muhammad and vowing his commitment to the NOI. He professes to have been strongly influenced by Malcolm X, whom he heard and knew in Boston, but says that it was Elijah who really brought him around. When Malcolm was killed, the former Louis Wolcott became Minister Louis Farrakhan of the New York Temple and acted as the national representative for the Honorable Elijah Muhammad.

For the most part, tensions between Imam Warith Deen Mohammed and his followers and Farrakhan's NOI have been controlled, perhaps because there has been little interaction. Certainly, mutual resentments have been far from absent, and Warith Deen has indicated that his followers should not acknowledge Farrakhan at all. Farrakhan has periodically erupted into national prominence by making inflammatory statements, as during Jesse Jackson's 1984 candidacy for President of the United States, when he was quoted as calling Zionism a "gutter religion" and hailing Adolf Hitler as a "great man." Despite his attempts to distinguish between Zionism and Judaism, the charge of anti-Semitism has stuck. Subsequent statements by some of Farrakhan's followers have served to substantiate the charge. While Warith Deen has continually affirmed the egalitarian nature of true Islam, Farrakhan has identified what he sees as strong color prejudice among some immigrant Muslims, supporting his efforts to affirm the importance of black consciousness.

In the late 1980s Louis Farrakhan began to redefine the mission of the NOI. Still preaching the basic doctrines that had long characterized the Nation, he began also to stress elements of the Islamic faith such as prayer and fasting, seemingly wishing to align the NOI more closely with traditional Islam. Friday prayers are strongly encouraged, particularly in Mosque Maryam, which serves as the national headquarters, on the south side of

Louis Farrakhan, current leader of the Nation of Islam. Mike Theiler/Archive Photos

Chicago. Farrakhan has always attempted to affirm his allegiance to Elijah Muhammad and his teachings, but more recently he seems to have reinterpreted these teachings a bit. He continues to affirm his own succession from Elijah, implicitly denying that of Warith Deen.

In the apparent effort to "Islamicize" his movement, Farrakhan has affirmed the importance of closer ties with other Muslim communities in the Middle East and Africa. Thus he has become a frequent and highly visible international visitor. For a number of years Islamic countries overseas contributed significant funding to the NOI movement, which they saw as helping propagate the religion of Islam in America. Sunni Muslims wait to see whether Farrakhan is serious about his desire to bring the NOI more fully in line with orthodox Islam, but they are skeptical. In 1990, at the Palmer House in Chicago, he moved his listeners with an inspiring profession of the two elements of the *shahada*, faith in one God and belief in Muhammad ibn Abdullah as his Prophet. ISNA General Secretary Sayyid M. Syeed, however, in a 1997 letter to Farrakhan published in the journal *Islamic Horizons*, expressed his personal disappointment, and that of other Sunni Muslims, that the NOI leader nonetheless has continued to affirm many of the original tenets of Elijah Muhammad.

NOI members are generally quite strict in their dress code (women do not wear makeup and must cover their hair), in their observance of dietary laws, and in their disavowal of tobacco, narcotics, and such habits as overeating and oversleeping. They do not, however, pray five times a day; and unlike orthodox Muslims, they believe in a resurrection of the mind in which people are freed, rather than in the classic doctrine of the resurrection of the body on the Day of Judgment. Members tithe to the organization— which, along with sale of *Final Call*, provides the major source of income.

The Nation under Louis Farrakhan, while obviously controversial, has unquestionably provided important social and community services. The U.S. government supports its drug and AIDS programs and security efforts in crime- and drug-infested federal housing units. Members of the reconstituted Fruit of Islam serve as patrols in a number of large urban areas, wearing their recognizable uniforms of pressed shirts, ties, and dark suits. The Nation has had notable success working with gangs and drug dealers, especially young blacks and Hispanics, in an effort that has few parallels. While most Muslims in America, black and immigrant, continue to say that the Nation is not to be considered part of the community of Islam, some like Warith Deen himself are less willing to be so dismissive, urging that the changes gradually introduced in the Nation may perhaps indicate steady, if slow, movement in the right direction.

African American Sunni Movements

Followers of Warith Deen Mohammed and Louis Farrakhan, of course, are not the only African Americans to associate themselves with Islam. A number of others serve as examples of Islam's appeal to blacks, especially in the urban American context. Some of these identify themselves specifically as Sunni and attempt to follow the teachings of orthodox Islam with diligence, often in opposition to Nation of Islam teachings.

The Hanafi Madhhab movement, for example, was first begun fairly early in the century by a Pakistani immigrant. His follower Khalifa Hammas Abdul Khaalis tried unsuccessfully to infiltrate the NOI and change its direction. Failing that objective, he established the Hanafi Madhhab Center in Washington, D.C., in the late 1950s. Its members express their public commitment to America, a stand that has sometimes made it unpopular with other black groups and especially with the Nation. In an ugly incident in 1973, unknown assailants killed seven Hanafis, four children among them. Three years later Hanafis themselves, in protest against the showing of a film titled *Mohammad, Messenger of God*, which they felt to be blasphemous, raided office buildings in Washington, D.C. and took hostages. A man was killed, and ambassadors from several Muslim countries were called in to resolve the matter. The Hanafis have since stayed well out of the public eye. The most prominent Hanafi member has been basketball star Kareem Abdul-Jabbar (see "Profiles").

Another group self-identified as Sunni is the Darul Islam Movement[14] (also rendered as the Dar ul-Islam), begun in Brooklyn in the early 1960s. The first converts were men who had been associated with the black power movement and who, despite their pledge to follow the Prophet Muhammad and the *shari'a*, or Islamic law, in the beginning adopted an agenda of racial separatism. From its earliest days, the group suffered from internal conflicts and several times disbanded and then reassembled. A new association was formed in the late 1960s, meeting in a small flat in Brooklyn that served as a house of prayer, instruction, and even communal living for those who chose it. The movement solidified, grew, and began to establish branches in many major U.S. cities. Various ministries were set up, including one for self-defense training required of all young men. By the time of Elijah Muhammad's death in 1975, the Dar claimed more than thirty mosque-based Sunni Muslim communities. At that point, before Warith Deen began to move former NOI members toward orthodox Islam, the Dar was the largest black Sunni Muslim organization in the country, with mosques as far west as Colorado and in the West Indies, Ontario, and Alaska. While each chapter had its own imam, the leader was Imam Yahya Abdul-Kareem of the Brooklyn mosque. The various branches were joined in a federation modeled on the treaty of Medina fashioned by Prophet Muhammad.

The Darul Islam Movement at its height took its Islam seriously. Members were asked upon entry to take a pledge that amounted to a lifetime commitment. They were challenged to follow a rigorous course of religious teaching, including classical training in Arabic, the Qur'an, and Sunna. Gradually, they were also introduced to elements of the Sufi tradition of Islam, as Imam Yahya understood these from his study with a Pakistani Sufi *shaykh* of the Qadiriyya Order.

As the Dar developed, it moved away from its earlier agenda of separatism, although the theme of racism and the belief that Islam could be the liberating force was always present. Unwilling to advocate some of the theories that have made the Nation so unpalatable to orthodox Islam, the Dar has actually held more strictly to the tenets and practices of Islam than many other Muslims might feel necessary. Members have been encouraged to dress in Muslim fashion and to avoid contact with non-Muslims. At times, strong enmities have arisen between the strict observers of the Dar movement and other Muslims, especially immigrants, who seemed to Dar members to be buying into the American system. In the 1970s some members again broke off to establish a separate and ultraconservative group, identifying themselves as the Fuqra.

By 1980 Imam Yahya, under the influence of his Sufi master, announced the end of the Dar as a separate movement—much as Warith Deen was to do with his followers—and its assimilation into Sufi Islam. He gave up his own leadership role, and the Ya-Sin mosque in Brooklyn ceased functioning and was sold.

One Atlanta Darul Islam member who opposed the absorption into Sufism and led the attempts to reaffiliate Dar members was former chairman of the Student Nonviolent Coordinating Committee (SNCC) H. Rap Brown. In his new identity as Imam Jamil Abdullah al-Amin, Brown helped form and lead another much smaller federation now called the National Community. The Community, along with the Islamic Society of North America, the Islamic Circle of North America, and Warith Deen Mohammed's Muslim American Society, currently constitutes the National Shura Council in America. Imam Jamil al-Amin's movement has some thirty branches in various parts of America as well as in the Caribbean.

Among the Sunni African American Muslim groups who reacted against NOI teachings, two others deserve brief mention. Shaykh Khalid Ahmad

Tawfiq began the Mosque of Islamic Brotherhood (MIB) in 1970 in Harlem. Tawfiq, former member of the Moorish Science Temple, became a follower of Malcolm X. He never accepted the racist doctrines of the Nation, and under Malcolm's sponsorship left to study at al-Azhar in Cairo, bastion of Islamic orthodoxy. On his return to Harlem, he began the MIB in the attempt to adapt what he understood to be true Islamic teachings to the specific needs of African Americans. He tried to blend the teachings of Marcus Garvey's UNIA with those of Hasan al-Banna and the Egyptian Muslim Brotherhood. Tawfiq died in 1988, and the MIB has continued as a relatively small movement in Harlem.

Another group that arose during the same period is the Islamic Party, begun by jazz musician D. C. Muzzafruddin in 1971. Also influenced by Malcolm, like Tawfiq he traveled in the Middle East to learn more about Islam. In addition to the Muslim Brotherhood, he was influenced by the teachings of Pakistani leader Maulana Mawdudi. He began the Islamic Party in Washington, D.C., to spread a better understanding of Islam and to counter what Muzzafruddin saw as the apathy of immigrant Muslims in not attending appropriately to the task of spreading the faith. Branches were later established in other major American cities such as Chicago, New York, and Houston. During the 1970s the movement gained considerable strength, and numbers of students at Howard University joined the *da'wa* effort. Many saw the Party as a substitute for the flagging civil-rights effort. In 1975 the Islamic Party received a significant gift from Libya's Colonel Qadaffi. The group's decision in the late 1970s to move to Georgia to live in a rural context proved its undoing. It suffered a series of splits, offices in other major cities were forced to close, and a surviving faction moved to Trinidad and finally to the Dominican Republic. Muzzafruddin returned to America, where he died in 1983, but the movement was effectively finished. A few of his followers, attracted by the Iranian Revolution, became affiliated with Shi'ism.

African American Sectarian Movements

Meanwhile, a number of other African American groups have spun off from the ideology of the Nation of Islam, manifesting themselves as quasi-Islamic as they borrow some elements from orthodox Islam and disregard others. The extent to which these sectarian groups are accepted by Muslims as part of the fabric of Islam is often difficult to gauge, although they are increasingly accused by Sunni African Americans, as well as those in the immigrant community, of being beyond the boundaries of what is Islamically acceptable. Looking to Asia and/or Africa as the source of identity continues to be a common theme for black sectarian movements in the last part of this century as it was for people such as Noble Drew Ali and Elijah Muhammad. Two examples can serve to illustrate the nature of some of these groups.

The Ansar Allah community is a black sect founded almost thirty years ago by Isa Muhammad, who was familiar with the teachings of both the Moorish Science Temple and the Nation of Islam. Like those groups, the Ansar have consistently emphasized the importance of American blacks' breaking free of the inferior status to which whites have consigned them, striving to attain dignity and self-worth by a black rather than a white definition. Isa Muhammad, however, rejected the claims of both Drew Ali (whose version of the Qur'an he ridicules) and Elijah Muhammad to prophethood. In what is clearly an effort to position himself within the range of competing "Islamic" messages to African Americans, he proclaims his own message to supersede theirs and others. Isa Muhammad's origins seem deliberately to have been obscured, though he says he was born in 1945 in the Sudan, exactly a century after his grandfather the Sudanese *mahdi* Muhammad Ahmad ibn Abdullah. He claims to have written more than 365 books and pamphlets by the power of Allah speaking through him, and indeed many of these are available. Since 1990 all of his written works have appeared under the name As Sayyid Isa al Haadi al-Mahdi.

Originally called the Ansar Pure Sufi in the late 1960s, with the Star of David and an Egyptian ankh part of its symbolism, the group changed its name to Nubians and then Nubian Islamic Hebrews. The mahdist Islamic crescent was added to its symbols, and its members were requested to wear long African robes. Soon they began to publish a newspaper and several journals, and Isa himself went to Trinidad in the West Indies to establish more branches. In 1973 he traveled to Egypt and the Sudan, where he says he was visited by the figure of Khidr, the so-called "green man" who is said to be a spiritual guide of Muslim mystics. From that point, his teachings began to sound much more specifically Islamic, and he portrayed himself as responsible for propagation of the Qur'anic message in the West. When Elijah Muhammad died in 1975, Isa Muhammad lost no time in identifying himself as Elijah's legitimate heir. His affirmation of the importance of being black carried the corresponding condemnation of the "pale-skinned" race in a series of attacks on whites that rivaled even early NOI ideology. The "Nubian Islamic Hebrews" terminology was dropped, and the community was officially named the Ansar Allah, from Sura 61:14 of the Qur'an, which refers to the "helpers (*ansar*) of Allah." In 1981 Isa seemed to proclaim himself the promised messiah of Islam, and by 1988 he was able to trace his descent through the Prophet Muhammad's grandson Husayn directly to the Prophet himself.

By the beginning of the 1990s, Isa Muhammad began to sound more orthodox in his preaching and teaching, modifying earlier attacks on whites. Nonetheless, he continued to refer to black Americans as Sudanese or Nubians and to his own task of raising up these sole surviving members of the tribe of Israel. Much of the more recent literature shows him proclaiming that the Ansaru Allah follow the teachings of the Qur'an more closely than any other Muslims, especially those of Saudi Arabia.

Ansaru Allah communities are now located in many cities of the United States, as well as in a number of countries in Africa, the Caribbean, and even Europe. Their headquarters is in Brooklyn, New York, in a mosque called Masjidu'l-Mukhlasina. It includes a school offering classes on a range of Islamic sciences, with lectures halls, playground facilities, a library, and a museum of ancient Islamic relics.

The verbal contest between some Saudi Muslims and Isa Muhammad became sharper over the years. Isa accused Arabs, among other things, of Westernizing and modernizing, equating that with coming under the influence of Christianity. Although he officially retired as imam of the Ansaru Allah community in 1988, giving way to new leadership, heightened attacks against him by certain Saudi intellectuals have caused him to come out of retirement for the express purpose of defending himself and his community, as well as launching counterattacks.

The community, still small, continues to be redefined and, after moving toward Sunni Islam, now seems to be reversing itself. Isa Muhammad indicated that a real Muslim is also really a Christian and that the Ansar are followers of Jesus awaiting his second coming. Since 1974 the Ansar has again changed significantly, and is now known as the Holy Tabernacle Ministries, with increasing attention to such things as the extraterrestrial beginnings of the Nubian peoples. Its leader now assumes the name of Dr. Malachi Z. York. The Ansar thus serve as a fascinating example of the mixture of Islam, black nationalism and identity, and a number of the traditions making up the fabric of American religion.

Another spin-off from the Nation of Islam is a group called Allah's Nation of the Five Percenters.[15] This group's message is transmitted in a variety of ways, as for example through the staccato lyrics of rap music.

The movement, founded in Harlem in 1964 by former NOI member Clarence "Pudding" 13X, has spread across urban America and is now found in major cities from New York to Los Angeles. Its direct appeal affirms even more immediately than the NOI doctrine the value of being black, and it especially attracts African American youth. An enthusiastic Nation advocate for some years, Clarence began openly to question the NOI's teaching that W. D. Fard was God. Since the NOI itself taught that the original black man was God, and clearly Fard was not black, he could, therefore, only be human. Indeed, Clarence came to believe and teach that not only is God black but, by extension, that all blacks are themselves God. After being reprimanded by the Nation, Clarence 13X left with some of his associates to begin preaching to black street youth.

Always a smooth and articulate speaker, Clarence first developed what has become the popular fast rap message of the Five Percenters. Each youth who learns the ideology is charged to pass it on to someone even younger. For more than two decades the movement was headquartered at the "Allah School in Mecca" in Harlem.

In June of 1969 Clarence met the fate of Malcolm and others, shot by unidentified gunmen. Some blamed the NOI for avenging his departure, although Farrakhan, who was then head of Harlem's Temple Number 7, strongly denied it. Like Malcolm's, Clarence 13X's murderer was never caught.

Five Percenter ideology is a complex combination of vaguely Islamic symbolism, black supremacy theory, and popular culture. To NOI teachings about the original black man, Clarence added a classification of people according to percentages. The largest group is the 85 percent of the world's population who do not know God, ultimately work to destroy themselves and others, and are incapable of salvation. The next 10 percent have knowledge and power but are the oppressors and teach that God is a "spook" who cannot be physically seen. This group includes both orthodox Muslims and white Christians. Finally come the 5 percent of righteous people who understand that the Living God is the black man and who teach freedom, justice, and equality. The 5 percent are thus to be the righteous teachers of all others.

For the Five Percenters, Islam is less a religion than a way of life. It borrows from Sufism the science of interpreting the meaning of letters of the Arabic alphabet, which it develops into an elaborate system called the Supreme Alphabet. This science is balanced by the Supreme Mathematics, a kind of esoteric system of numerology that also relates to similar interpretations in parts of Islamic Sufism. The numbers also have particular moral messages about how members are to understand and comport themselves. The Five Percenters acknowledge the status of males as Gods by teaching that the proper name for the black man is Allah, which stands for the physical members of *a*rm, *l*eg, *l*eg, *a*rm, and *h*ead. black men often adopt names that reflect their divine status, such as "Allah Supreme" or "God Allah Mind."

The group is also called "The Nation of Gods and Earths." In this classification, men are the Gods and women the Earths, or sometimes men are the Suns and women the Moons reflecting their light. What makes a woman a Muslim, in fact, is her testimony that her man is actually "Allah." Earthly productivity is stressed, with a premium put on bearing the child of a "God." Earths are required to cover their hair and wear full-length dresses and are thus sometimes taken for Sunnis. This is not pleasing to the latter, who greatly object to the Five Percenters' use of any terminology that would identify them as Muslims. For the Nation of Gods and Earths, Sunni Muslims, who are part of the 10 percent, are as guilty as Christians of perpetuating the false idea of a "spook" God.

While the exact membership of the Five Percenter movement is difficult to determine, there is no question of their popularity among young African Americans. The medium of rap music is an effective tool for propagating a message based on fast talk and tricky reinterpretations, and several popular rap recording artists have consciously identified with and propagated Five Percenter ideology. The rap never stales because it keeps incorporating the latest in slang expressions and developing new and fresh interpretations to fit the conditions of each new set of possible recruits.

Immigrants, African Americans, and converts from other groups all combine to illustrate the many ways in which it is possible to be Muslim in America. Just as many characteristics distinguish them from one another, so too they share many concerns. In the following chapters we will look at some of the issues members of all of these communities face as they try to define who is Muslim and who is not, to assess what roles are appropriate and necessary in a Western context, and to determine what as Americans they share as they attempt to forge an Islamic *umma* in the West.

CHAPTER FIVE

Women and the Muslim American Family

Some observers of Islam in the international arena have predicted that issues involving Muslim women's roles and identities will be near the top of the concerns to which contemporary Muslims must pay serious attention in the coming decades. Certainly, movements for women's rights and for reform of traditional family laws are taking place in many parts of the world. In this as in other areas of Islamic change, America may well prove to be a place both of experimentation and of affirmation of many traditional values. Women and men in the United States are turning their attention increasingly to the ways in which women contribute to the formulation of American Islam as they participate in the public as well as private spheres of Muslim life and are active in academia, various aspects of professional life, and the American workplace.

Many of the arenas that traditionally have been open only to men are now considered legitimate for female involvement. In the same way, those fields of operation that classically have been seen as women's domain, such as the home and family, are in many cases being seen in America to provide opportunities for shared participation and responsibility. In this chapter we will look at a range of concerns that both deal specifically with women's rights and roles and illustrate what seems to be a growing American movement toward cooperation and co-involvement as men and women raise families that reflect as much as possible of traditional Islamic values at the same time that they are viable in the new American environment.

In the interconnected set of concerns daily facing American Muslims, few issues are more central than those dealing with the family. For immigrants and African Americans alike, maintaining strong family ties is of such crucial importance that much else is, of necessity, secondary. The question of whether women should work, for example, either in full-time professional positions or in part-time jobs to help with family finances, is often framed in terms of how such employment can be balanced with family responsibilities. Child-care issues greatly concern other women who must work simply to keep the family afloat financially, particularly those from a culture in which the extended family assures that children are always in the company of adult relatives.

For some African American or Anglo convert Muslims, family issues may have a different focus. Those coming originally from Christian families, for example, often find their decision to adopt Islam extremely hard for their parents and other relatives to accept. They may even be virtually cut off from the support of loved ones. While estrangement certainly does not always occur, it is reported with sufficient frequency that it must be taken seriously as yet one more difficulty facing the new convert. To the extent to which African Americans or others may find it hard to enter into a Muslim community predominantly composed of immigrant families, the sense of isolation can be even sharper. While this may foster a sense of community among African American Muslims, it may also work against the easy creation of an interracial and intercultural *umma*, or community.

Roles and Responsibilities of Women

Educated American Muslim women are increasingly vocal in their insistence that Islam provides for equal rights and opportunities for women and men, although their roles are to be seen as complementary rather than identical. In some cases, this complementarity may also involve separation of the sexes in the public sphere. It is evident, for example, in the fairly common practice of men and women being separated in worship, meetings, and other public gatherings. While maintaining different space is certainly not mandatory, and many Muslims do not observe it, for others it signifies that women have as much right to define their own space as do men and that they are comfortable sitting and interacting with one another. For many women, it certainly does not curtail their vocal participation in public forums and discussions. "This is not forced segregation," commented a participant in a regional conference on women in New England in 1997. "Often we just feel more comfortable being able to relax with our friends, not worry if our knees happen to touch those of the man next to us, and enjoy a time of comradeship and even a little friendly gossip. Besides, if we object to what is being said we can do it as a block, or in small groups." Many other Muslim women and men, while supporting the complementarity of roles, see little point in not having a free mixing of men and women in most public arenas, although not in worship.

American Muslim women often invoke the "mothers of the faithful," as Muhammad's wives were referred to, as models for their own behavior and professional involvement. Khadija, first wife of the Prophet and the owner of a successful camel caravan business, is cited as the earliest Muslim "businesswoman." 'A'isha, his beloved wife, is said to have been the first female politician because of her role in opposing the leadership of 'Ali, as well as a great religious and spiritual authority and the most important collector of traditions about the Prophet. Attempts to relegate women to the private sphere, keep them from active professional and public involvement, and remove them from positions of religious authority are vigorously opposed as antithetical to the intentions of the Prophet and the way in which his early community functioned. The Qur'an is cited as being fully egalitarian in its treatment of men and women, insisting that both have the same religious responsibilities in this life and affirming that both will be called to exactly the same accountability on the day of resurrection. Muslims generally insist that this equality represents a great improvement over the circumstance of women before Islam and that the Qur'an is a remarkably equitable document in comparison with the sacred scriptures of other religious traditions.

Muslims generally defend the few verses in the Qur'an that non-Muslims (especially, perhaps, Western feminists) say indicate the inferior status of women as needing to be seen in context. Women inherit only half of what men inherit, for example, and the testimony of two women is required to equal that of one man in a court of law. These injunctions are interpreted as viable because of the Muslim man's responsibility to take care of and provide for the woman. Many Muslim men and women argue that equity is probably a better term than equality in comparing expectations for men and women and that the distinctions between men's and women's roles and the resulting differences in some of the responsibilities do not mean that one is better or more privileged than the other. Some more progressive voices can be heard saying that some of these passages suggesting what appears to be an inferior status for women must be reinterpreted in the light of new contexts and new roles for women. The one male prerogative that is generally not challenged is that of serving as imam, or religious leader, of a worshiping Muslim congregation. The reason classically cited, and still supported, for women's disqualification is menstruation, which renders her impure and thus unfit to lead the prayer. Women normally do not participate in religious activities, including fasting during the month of Ramadan, while menstruating.

Increasingly, both women and men are insisting that women play a dynamic part in shaping American Islam. Even women with families are encouraged to find ways to participate and not use the excuse of responsibilities in the home, which of course must not be ignored, to avoid their communal obligations. While there is little disagreement that Muslim women are allowed to have full professional lives (most American Muslims acknowledge and lament that women in some Muslim countries are still denied these opportunities), there is much discussion about what kinds of professions are appropriate and what family sacrifices, if any, should be made to allow a woman to maintain a full-time job. Many immigrant women note how much more difficult it is to work full-time in the United States because here they do not have an extended family to help care for children. Reluctant to leave their children at a day-care center, many women choose to stay home with them while they are young to provide the family environment and support they feel is crucial in their developing years. When asked if they would be more willing to use day care if it were run by Muslims "in an Islamic way," many say yes, while others still feel that being at home with their young children is essential. Some professional women are willing to risk becoming dated in their fields of expertise, even jeopardizing their professional reentry, rather than leave their children to the care of nonfamily members.

Other women, however, argue strongly that this willingness on the part of some to sacrifice their careers for the sake of their children is a kind of capitulation to the traditional roles that will keep American Muslims from being full participants in society. What they need to work for, they insist, is the development of cooperative resources among Muslims to provide for child care and the recognition that survival in American society means not retreat but courageous participation. Others disagree strongly. "It seems to me that we can well learn from other American women who have tried the highly professional route and found it just doesn't work with family responsibilities," says a young Egyptian woman. "Divorce rates rise, children get into trouble, and the model of an alternative family structure that true Islam provides gets shattered."[1]

There is little disagreement among American Muslims about the importance of adequate education for girls and women. As they often cite, that the first word revealed by God to Prophet Muhammad was *read* (or *recite*) indicates that all Muslims, women as well as men, must be as well educated as possible. One argument is that part of a woman's religious responsibility is to accept the challenge to expand her knowledge, and God will ask her on the day of judgment why she did not take advantage of all the opportunities available to learn. Another is that if women do not educate themselves, un-Islamic sexist and repressive customs will be allowed to continue. Implied is the assumption that what men will not do for women in terms of reform must come from their own initiative. Both women and men insist that a mother be able to educate her own children intelligently, that an educated woman is necessary for *da'wa*, or calling others to follow Islam (many underscore their conviction that the best person to give the message of Islam to a non-Muslim woman is a woman), and that women be able to participate intelligently in the mutual consultation that is the ideal Islamic way of governing the community. Arguments about what subjects may be appropriate for women to study are still occurring in many parts of the world but do not seem to be a high priority among American Muslims.

One of the most controversial subjects in the American Islamic community is that of appropriate dress for women. Clearly, this is a topic about which many women feel strongly, one way or the other, and about which they are interested in coming to their own determination, apart from the discourse of Western feminism or secular critique. On two important points there is agreement. First, that it is appropriate for both men and women, as the Qur'an itself makes clear, to dress modestly. The issue, of course, is what constitutes modesty. (The Qur'an, despite what some Muslim women seem to think, does not actually specify exactly how much of the body has to be covered.) Second, that the choice of how to dress is completely the woman's and cannot, or at least should not, be forced on her by her father, husband, or any other male relative. For Muslims in many parts of the world, and especially those in America, what is referred to as "Islamic dress" is not necessarily the same as the traditional dress that women from other cultures may have worn. What is now being called appropriately conservative clothing really began to appear after 1967, the time of the Arab-Israeli War, which was seen as so devastating to the Muslim cause. Political observers have noted that defeat brought about much Muslim introspection as to what it means to live Islamically, to assure victory and success under God's guidance. Many women began to wear the *hijab* (head covering) after that time as a sign of their allegiance to Islam, and it soon became one of the manifestations of the Islamic revival that has occurred in so many parts of the world.

The main issue for American Muslims is whether all women must dress conservatively, or Islamically, to be considered good Muslims, and what, in fact, exactly constitutes such dress. African Americans and some Anglo converts are often the most consistent in wearing clothing that covers everything except their hands and face, as well as some kind of head covering. A few choose to wear the full face veil. That there is now a burgeoning number of stores and retail houses specializing in Islamic dress, including robes (sometimes called *jilbabs*), scarves, and other kinds of fancier headgear and even matching shoes, is a joy for many women and a worry for others. When the dress business begins to sound more like high fashion, some feel due cause for concern.

Many Muslim circles engage in a quite lively discussion about the role of Islamic dress in the success, or lack of it, of women in the workplace. Many women insist that having adopted conservative clothing, they now feel free to enter fully into public life, secure in the knowledge that people will respect them as women of faith and piety. Some even argue that dressing Islamically makes it easier to move up in one's professional field. Many, however, cite the opposite experience. "When I was up for promotion," says a middle-aged Palestinian woman, "my boss called me in and said candidly that because of the public relations aspects of the new position it would be much better if I did not have to wear what he called 'that hat' all the time. I replied that the 'hat' was more important to me than the promotion, and I was not surprised when I didn't get it."[2] Some cite more blatant examples of prejudice, such as women wearing *hijab* to work being called "ragheads" or "mops." If such incidents give pause to some professional Muslim women, they seem to energize others to be even more intentional about their dress. Clearly, the main issue concerning dress has not to do with long sleeves or having one's legs more or less covered. It centers on the headdress that ensures no hair is showing. Hair traditionally has been considered a woman's most alluring aspect, to be revealed only to her husband or immediate family.

Much of the discussion clearly supports the woman's right of free choice in matters of dress, although many feel that the choice is *when* rather than *whether* to adopt the *hijab*. An African American Muslim woman cites examples of female Muslim acquaintances who were not dressed Islamically and who met prospective husbands in social clubs and even bars, places she would never go herself. "In the meantime," she laments, "women like me who express our Islam in our dress maybe threaten men who think they can't live up to the standard. So I am still not married."[3] Others insist that their husbands chose them *because* their dress seemed to reflect a genuine piety. Many Muslim women in America, of course, completely reject the notion that they should have to wear long sleeves and a scarf or *hijab*. Acknowledging that dressing as revealingly as some Western women is inappropriate, they argue that modesty is a matter of judgment and that the mark of a good Muslim should be her behavior and not her appearance. An Egyptian woman who has lived in America for several decades expresses the feeling of a number of American Muslims about wearing the veil: "At home," she says, "no woman in my family has worn a veil or head covering since the early part of this century. I find it very painful to come to this country and feel so much pressure to adopt a form of dress that feels just like that which it took so much courage for Muslim feminists to get rid of so many years ago."[4]

The role of women in the mosques is another issue that has received much attention from American Muslims. Without doubt, women have been deeply involved in the activities related to organizing and establishing mosques for decades, and both men and women are listed as founders of some of the early institutions. Women often have played strong organizing roles and, not surprisingly, have been involved in the social side of mosque activities such as dinners, bake sales, and other occasions to bring people together. In the immigrant community, however, the roles that women play institutionally to a large extent are still circumscribed by the cultural expectations of the countries from which they or their families originally came. Muslims strongly oriented toward the traditions of their country of origin may find it difficult to be flexible in their understanding of leadership roles for both men and women in the mosque. Additionally, some of the mosque communities that have been operating since fairly early in the century, and in whose activities many women have actively participated, have found those opportunities somewhat curtailed with the arrival of new immigrants and leaders from countries in which fewer opportunities for women in public life have traditionally been available. In other cases, stronger and more visible roles for women have accompanied the movement of some mosques toward more diverse constituencies and greater involvement in various kinds of outreach. Occasionally, although not often, a woman serves as president of the congregation.

Whether women should even attend the mosque is an issue for some Muslims. As we have seen, while the Prophet Muhammad did encourage the full participation of women in the worship life of his young community, soon afterward women by and large came to be removed from public life. The mosque, as the locus for the public expression of faith, in most places became the province of men. Women, if they prayed at all, were relegated to doing so primarily at home. In many areas of the world today, this model is being seriously challenged, and certainly this is so in the United States. The mosque and Islamic center is increasingly the locus of activity for the entire family.

Muslims deal with issues of appropriate dress and location during the prayer service itself in a variety of different ways, according to the constituency and orientation of the mosque and the direction of its leadership. Generally, both immigrant and African American women dress conservatively when participating in mosque activities, being particularly careful to cover their hair as well as their arms and legs. Many of the newly constructed mosques have separate entrances for women. Where women sit during the prayer is related to tradition, the inclination of the imam or other mosque leaders, and the mosque facility itself. Buildings converted to *masjids* may well not offer the possibility of having women located in a separate space during the prayer. A number of different models are currently used in American mosques, although the general rule is that men and women do not sit together in mixed groupings for worship. No matter what the configuration, the rationale is that the very physical nature of the prayer prostrations, with one's forehead sometimes touching the floor and one's rear parts elevated, necessitates the separation of men and women to avoid distraction from attention to God.

In more "liberal" *masjids*, men may be located on one side of the prayer hall and women on the other, equidistant from the front and perhaps separated by a low partition. Another possibility, based on what is understood to have been the practice in the Prophet's Medinan community, is for men to worship at the front of the prayer hall and women in the back. In a number of mosques, particularly those constructed more recently and according to traditional specifications, women move through their private entrance directly to facilities for performing ablutions and then to a second-floor balcony, where they gather with their children. Generally, there is a railing of some sort over or through which they are able to look down on the imam and men assembled below. In more conservative mosques, women may be located in a completely separate room with no visual access to the main prayer hall. In these places, the actual prayer service is often broadcast on closed-circuit TV or over a loudspeaker so that the women can watch or listen and participate as they are able.

Which of these models is most appropriate for worship in America is under continuing discussion, and certainly refinements will continue. While some Muslim women may object if they are completely segregated from men and are thus unable to see the imam during worship, few would argue for the kind of complete mixing common during most Christian services.

Marriage and Divorce

Marriage is of great importance in Islam, so much so that traditional societies have not had a place for the unmarried man or woman. Muslim families have given great importance to the preparation of daughters for marriage. That importance is naturally changing a bit in the West, although the concern for marriage and family remains paramount.

By Islamic legal stipulation, Muslim men are free to marry Jews and Christians, on the understanding that the male head of the household determines the religion in which the children will be brought up. Muslim women, on the other hand, are not permitted by law and custom to marry anyone but another Muslim, even though the Qur'an does not specify it in quite that way. This freedom of choice for men and not for women has caused some difficulties in American culture, in which Muslims are so much the minority. When young men have chosen to marry outside the faith, women have sometimes found their choice of a marriage partner to be seriously curtailed. In some circumstances, families of eligible young Muslim women have had to look to their home countries to find suitable husbands.

While in America it is not unusual for a Muslim to marry a non-Muslim, pressures are strong for both men and women to choose a partner from within the Islamic community. The conviction of many families that they do not want their daughters to date stems not only from a desire to protect them but from the fear that dating will inevitably lead to greater instances of intermarriage. Often, the additional desire that young people marry within their particular ethnic or cultural group further complicates the marriage issue. Some Anglo Americans who have converted to Islam, for example, are frustrated in their attempts to marry immigrant Muslim women because their families will not permit it. On the whole, African American, Hispanic, and other ethnic minority Muslims tend to marry within their own groups.

It is not unusual for a non-Muslim woman who has married into a Muslim family to feel some pressure to convert, even though it is not legally necessary for her to do so. Sometimes a woman adopts Islam with the hope

A young Muslim couple gets married. © JOLIE STAHL

of relating more easily to her husband's family. Or for her own personal reasons she may choose to become Muslim. The problems are significant no matter what choice a young wife makes and contribute to feelings on the part of both Muslims and non-Muslims that interfaith marriages should probably be avoided if possible and entered into only with the greatest of caution and forethought.

Muslim families are concerned about their young people, especially daughters, marrying outside of the faith. In the same way, parents who are not Muslim are often alarmed when their children declare their intentions to marry a Muslim. Carol Anway, who has written of her own experiences to help other parents in situations like hers, records her initial pain when her own daughter's interfaith marriage led to her adopting the faith.

> "Mom, I need to talk to you."
> I turned my back and headed for the kitchen. Tears were welling up in my eyes. No, I wouldn't talk with her. I couldn't stand what I thought she had to say. "Not now," I answered without looking at her. . . .
> "I don't want to hear it."
> "You've got to hear it, Mom, please," I finally gave in, and we sat down.
> "Mom, I've converted to Islam. . . ."[5]

Some parents are concerned that a prospective Muslim son-in-law may after marriage want to return to his country of origin, where circumstances for the non-Muslim wife could be considerably more difficult. Their fears are not allayed by such films as *Not Without My Daughter*, a Sally Fields rendering in which a Muslim man from Iran literally kidnaps his own child and takes her back to his family and away from her real mother. Such stories, while unfortunately sometimes true, are often exaggerated for their shock value, causing a great deal of pain for American Muslims who find such episodes deeply disturbing and certainly un-Islamic.

In actual fact, of course, marriages between Muslim men and Christian women often do encounter serious problems, despite the best intentions of the two parties and sometimes even when they have their families' support. One of the most difficult realities is that marriage in the American context generally means a union of two individuals, with the families somewhat incidentally and rather uncertainly joined only for family occasions. For Muslims, however, marriage is still seen as the union of families, with parents or other relatives traditionally making all of the arrangements. While these so-called arranged marriages are now less common in many urban areas of Islamic countries, many immigrant families bring expectations that hamper the contracting of marriage in the American scene between Muslims and non-Muslims. The joining of two families rather than simply two individuals is still very much the common understanding, and it is being adapted but not completely discarded in America.

Muslim counselors working on college campuses and in Islamic centers advising on marriage in general, and also on interfaith marriage, warn prospective partners of other potential problems. Many young Muslim men are absolutely convinced that they want a marriage of equality in which both partners share responsibility for home and family and both contribute financially to the family budget. Then they begin to feel pressure from other Muslim immigrants in the mosque or in their community who may not agree with these contemporary American "liberal" standards. Or these men may return home for an extended visit, wherever home originally was, and without realizing what is happening slip back into the old ways of doing things. Such occurrences are not inevitable but happen often enough to warrant some serious forethought. There have been some attempts to establish a network of Muslim chaplains at the national level who can advise young interfaith couples when such problems arise, and some Christian pastors have been working with Muslim leaders to see how they might cooperate in these consultations.

Traditional relationships between men and women in the family structure are under a great deal of scrutiny in America. One of the most highly
debated verses in the Qur'an is Sura 4:34, often cited to affirm male authority: "Men have authority over women, because God made the one of them
to excel the other, and because they spend of their property [for the support
of women]. So good women are obedient. . . . As for those from whom you
fear insubordination, admonish them and banish them to beds apart, and
beat them."

As the verse makes clear, Muslim men have traditionally been financially responsible for women. Thus, either her husband or some other male relative must take care of a woman's needs. At least in theory, this custom
assures that a woman will always be taken care of, and Muslims are eager to
point out that the American reality of so many single women, and single
mothers, living below the poverty level with no men to support them would
be inconceivable in a true Islamic system. The rub is, this financial responsibility means that final decision-making lies with the man. Many Muslim
women who think about the matter seriously, even in the American context,
consider that this is a small price to pay for security. A young Egyptian
woman was asked by an American friend, "Doesn't it really annoy you to
think that your future husband will have the last word?" "Yes," said the
Muslim girl, "it is frustrating. But I honestly think that if you don't make it
a big deal, it is finally the only system that works." But many contemporary
Muslims, especially those raised or educated in the American context, are
challenging the question of final authority. "Muslims are simply having to
figure out new kinds of interpretations that respect the intention of the
Qur'anic text but allow for the kind of give and take that Western women
generally insist on. And the fact is that in most Muslim marriages today,
whatever lip service is given to male authority, the woman knows exactly
how to exert power, as she has always known."[6]

It must be said that although "beating" seems to be allowable in the last
part of this Qur'anic passage, no reputable Muslim interpreters would suggest that it should involve anything more than the lightest of taps as a
reminder to the wife of her conjugal responsibilities. Never can this legiti-
mately be cited as justification for wife-beating, although Muslim men, like
Christian and other men, have on occasion resorted to such measures.
Domestic violence has been very little discussed in the American Muslim
community until recently. Now there is more public recognition that domes-
tic violence in Muslim families is on the rise, although Muslims profess that
they are less culpable than their non-Muslim neighbors. Articles in Muslim

journals encourage their readers to face the reality of increasing violence, understand the stress factors that contribute to it, and work for its elimination. "Only a strong Islamic character, that condemns anger and emphasizes tolerance and compassion," writes one journalist pleading for Muslim attention to this potential problem, "can reduce the tendency toward violence."[7]

Americans who are not Muslim have always had difficulty understanding the justification for what they understand to be the Islamic sanction of polygamy, or more technically polygyny (the taking of more than one wife). Muslims explain that, indeed, the Qur'an does specify that under certain conditions a man may marry up to four wives. It stipulates, however, that the husband must treat each of his wives as equal to all the others. Many modern commentators on the Qur'an have interpreted that requirement to mean that God really does not want a man to marry more than once or he would not have levied such a difficult stipulation on multiple marriages. Others point out that at the time when the Qur'an was being revealed, women were losing their husbands in the many battles and skirmishes occurring in the young Muslim *umma*. The injunction to take up to four wives, they argue, was out of charity to these husbandless women. In any case, few Muslim men anywhere in the world can afford financially to marry more than one woman at a time, although in some poorer countries an additional wife may actually serve to ease the financial burden by adding to income earned outside the home. Some American Muslim women, as is true of their educated counterparts in other countries, understand that it is their prerogative to stipulate in the marriage contract that the husband may not take a second wife. Over the centuries, the taking of multiple wives has often created difficult circumstances for the first wife, and even the threat of a husband's taking another wife has served as an effective tool of male control.

Multiple marriages are generally not an issue in America for the simple reason that they are prohibited by law, although they are also not unknown. Nonetheless, the matter is not irrelevant in this Western context, and some women still express fear that they may find themselves one of several wives. "Dear [Islamic counselor]," writes one worried wife in an advice column. "My husband has confided in me that he would like to take a second wife . . . that he would like for us to help a widowed woman and her sons by his getting married to her." The writer confesses that she feels guilty because she is sorry for the other woman but does not want to share her husband. What, she asks, should she do? The counselor responds that because polygamy is illegal in the United States, the husband cannot take a second wife, and the husband's concern for the divorcee's welfare must be balanced by concern for the mental well-being of his own wife.[8] Muslims sometimes counter Western ridicule of polygyny with the accusation that more Americans have multiple wives than Muslims. The difference, they say, is that Americans take their wives in serial order, through divorce and remarriage, rather than all together.

The potential problems men and women face in marriage can often be avoided, say advisers and counselors to young Muslims, if proper attention is paid to the business of selecting an appropriate mate. Islamic organizations at the local and national level function in some ways as "matchmakers" or as a kind of extended family assisting people to find the right marriage partner. Many Islamic journals and other media, including the Internet, contain matrimonial sections in which both men and women describe themselves, their characteristics, and their interests and indicate their hope to find a like-minded mate. "Most Muslims with access to the Internet maintain friendships with students that they would otherwise have never met. I have heard several stories about Muslim youth meeting, courting, and deciding to marry all through e-mail contacts, perhaps the ultimate in Islamically appropriate interaction."[9] Usually high on the list of desired qualifications is the intention to live a good and respectable Islamic life.

In a typical scenario, a man or woman may answer an advertisement placed in a journal or other listing source. Before meeting, they exchange more detailed information and then go through the process of checking out each other's references. When they do meet, it will probably be in the presence of friends or family rather than alone. If both parties agree, and often if the attending families also feel that prospects are good, the courtship begins in earnest.

Some Muslims believe that a woman who desires to get married should designate some member of her family to serve as a *wakeel*, or representative, to handle premarital negotiations. She and the *wakeel* should research as thoroughly as possible the background of the Muslim to whom she is to be engaged, on the understanding that commonality of religious belief and commitment is the most important ingredient in a successful marriage. Appropriate questions for the prospective groom can be asked either in person by the *wakeel* or in writing. His piety ascertained, the task is then to investigate his personal life, including his financial resources for maintaining a wife and his willingness to have children. Following such precautions will go far, many believe, to assure that a marriage does not end in divorce, as seems to happen so often in America. Even this, warn some advisers, may not be sufficient to guarantee a successful marriage. "It is not haram [forbidden] for Sisters to investigate the brother's background themselves," suggests one journalist. "At the top of the list of things that a Sister needs to know is: Can he maintain you?"[10] He assures his readers that there is no perfect marriage but that with appropriate care and attention, one can have the best marriage possible.

Increasing numbers of Muslim couples are spelling out the conditions of marriage and divorce in detailed premarital agreements. Marriage is a legal arrangement in Islam, not a sacrament as in the Christian sense, and is secured with a written contract. While some more conservative Muslims oppose the practice of prenuptial arrangements, others argue that by facing potential problems before they arise, couples will be more able to address the everyday concerns of marriage. These agreements are considered by some to be especially important when couples come from different countries and social backgrounds and can go a long way in anticipating problems that might otherwise lead too easily to divorce.

American Muslims are also paying more attention to the matter of divorce. They are quick to note that while Muslims are often accused of "easy divorce," in fact, statistics among Muslims worldwide show a much lower rate than among Western Christians. Nonetheless, the fact that many men in the history of Islam have rid themselves of unwanted marriages by uttering what is called the triple *talaq*, or divorce, has without question been an affliction for many women. While considered a reprehensible practice, it has been possible for a husband simply to say three times in a row, "I divorce you, I divorce you, I divorce you." According to Islamic law, practices are not just required or forbidden but fall into grades of acceptability and nonacceptability. This "triple divorce," while historically common, is legally barely acceptable. American Muslims are quick to point out that Prophet Muhammad deemed divorce in any case to be the worst of solutions, to be avoided at almost any cost. If one absolutely must divorce, the process should be carried out over a three-month period according to the more acceptable Islamic legal determination. This is both to make sure that the woman is not pregnant and, giving the man a chance to reconsider his decision, to avoid the possibility of severing a marriage because of the anger of the moment.

The question is often asked whether the husband must initiate the divorce or if a wife, who for whatever reason cannot stand living with her husband anymore, can initiate divorce proceedings. While the system may seem to favor the man, who can divorce at will although certainly not with license, a woman does have recourse in the termination of a marriage if there is good reason. The problem for many women, especially those who are not educated, is that they simply do not know their rights. In many Muslim countries, helping women understand their legal prerogatives has been identified as an important task. Another deeply problematic matter for divorced women in many cultures has been the fate of children of divorced couples. The four major schools of Islamic law, while differing on the age of the child, give custody of both sons and daughters to the father. Like everything else, however, these stipulations are subject to the modifications of American civil law and are often interpreted differently in the Western context.

Children and Youth

As is true of Muslim cultures across the world, having children is a matter of great importance to Muslims living in America. While certain realities, such as the employment of the wife, may place constraints on the number of children a couple will decide to have, to be childless or even to have only one child is often considered a deep disappointment to the larger family. Children are very much a part of the family activities from birth and accompany their parents outside as well as inside the home as often as possible. At most social occasions, in the women's section of the mosque, or even in group meetings and conferences, children are present and occupy themselves playing around their mothers. Muslims use babysitters only when they absolutely have to, believing that the more children are with them the better they will understand, and feel a part of, community events. The occasional disruptions caused by children's squabbling, crying, or making demands on their parents are generally seen as normal and perfectly acceptable. On the whole, Muslim children are well behaved and learn at an early age how to amuse themselves in public and social gatherings that may keep them up past their usual bedtime.

How to raise children in American society and culture is an ongoing concern to all Muslim parents. Deeply worried about the influences of American television, for example, many families have strict rules for the number and kind of shows their children may watch and try to find acceptable alternatives. Many parents take advantage of the huge amount of material that is now available through various Muslim agencies for helping children focus on wholesome issues in the context of an Islamic identity. They buy videos in which puppet characters like Adam, dressed in Muslim garb, talk to young children about how happy he is to be a Muslim, how lovely a trip to the Ka'ba in Mecca can be, and how Allah should be thanked for all the good things of life. An Arabic Playhouse video teaches children the stories of the Qur'an. Muslim Scouts Adventures substitute for the often violence-filled cartoons of American TV, and heroes of Islamic history such as Fatih, in the story of Sultan Muhammad II, capture their imagination. Tapes like "Alif [the first letter in the Arabic alphabet] is for Asad [lion]" provide early lessons in Arabic. Designed for young readers, *Young Muslim* magazine (published by Sound Vision) features stories, puzzles, comics, and interviews with well-known Muslims such as Muhammad Ali and Hakeem Olajuwon.

Many Muslim parents discuss with one another ways to reinforce Islamic identity in their young children and teenagers. Interaction with non-Muslim children and youth is both inevitable and, in the view of most Muslims, a good thing. But it can lead to difficulties if the young people of the community do not possess the tools to help them understand their differences and see them as a matter of personal pride and significance. As children reach the teenage years, issues of identity often become more complicated

Illustration from the children's section of *The Muslim Magazine.*
SELIM DJEBILI/COURTESY *The Muslim Magazine*

for young Muslims. Sometimes they may feel some pressure to live double lives. Comfortable with their Muslim identity at home, and at least reasonably willing to conform to the expectations of their elders while with relatives, they may find it tempting to drop that identity in the more public aspects of their lives, especially as they socialize with friends who are not Muslim. Some girls may even leave home wearing Islamic head covering with the intention of removing it later. Muslim journals are eager to report the testimonies of young women who insist that they find the *hijab* a source of pride and distinction when they do wear it to school.

Sometimes the different expectations of private and public come into direct conflict, as, for example, when Muslim young people want to date and attend social functions sponsored by their schools or private parties given by non-Muslim friends. Muslim parents struggle with how to respond to these issues, and again the answers range widely. Some simply refuse to allow either boys or girls to socialize outside the home or mosque community, with varying results. Their fears may be fueled by articles in Islamic journals expressing concern over what is sometimes called "dunya-itis," or infatuation with the things of this world (*dunya* in Arabic), characterized as a malady of many young Muslim Americans.[11] Families who advocate separation want their children to be educated in Muslim schools, to socialize only with the children of other Muslim families and then always with adult chaperones, in general trying to inoculate them against the problems inherent in American public schools and youth culture. They are concerned about both boys and girls, but most obviously and particularly with the latter. Many articles in Muslim journals are devoted to urging Muslims to unite against the ills of America. "As Muslims, let us work hand-in-hand, forgetting our ethnic diversity or language differences, and help our children stay away from the aberrations of this society. Let us help them stand proudly as good Muslims."[12]

Others, more willing to accommodate the American social system, hope that the Islamic values they have instilled in their children will shield them against inevitable temptations. They espouse a more moderate view of social interaction for boys and girls, in which they would be sent to public schools but would not be allowed to date or in general to participate in outside-of-school activities. Some young people, however, rebel against this, feeling that it is prejudicial in favor of boys. "Most of the Muslim girls I know are like me and not allowed to date or even to go to social activities at school like dances or parties," complains a Pakistani teenager. "Our parents don't seem to notice when the boys go out, but the door gets locked even when a group of girls wants to go to the mall together or something."[13] That girls in Islamic society have always been highly protected is a legacy that has both positive and negative angles for young American Muslims. The greatest fear of Muslim families, of course, is the horror and shame of a daughter's becoming pregnant outside of marriage, and they adopt a great variety of measures to prevent this from happening.

Still other parents take an even more "integrationist" view, questioning why they should have come to this country at all if they are simply going to hide from it. They argue that Muslims simply have to learn how to live *in* America and to deal with it as it is, rather than trying to find ways to circumvent it. Children should be given as solid a training in Islamic morality in the home and the mosque school as possible, they say, and then they should be trusted to use their good judgment when interacting with friends in the public school. Some even insist that girls should be allowed to date after a certain age, although this remains a highly controversial topic among American Muslims.

Organizations such as MYNA (Muslim Youth of North America), sponsored by The Islamic Society of North America (ISNA), play an important role in providing conferences and activities with an Islamic focus. MYNA is divided into four zones covering Canada and the eastern, central, and western United States. Each summer young people from across the United States and Canada gather to meet one another, hear speakers of prominence, and talk about issues of common concern. These meetings provide an opportunity for young Muslims to socialize in "an Islamic environment." Many of the activities planned for Muslim young people are designed to provide opportunities for them to meet eligible marriage partners. Often, the youth stress the things they have in common, affirming the importance of being Muslim together in the American *umma* and rejecting their families' attempts to focus on immigrant and ethnic identities. MYNA emphasizes the benefits of recreation, and youth are instructed in the appropriate activities for girls and boys, young men and women. The organization also sponsors seminars and retreats throughout the year, as well as winter conferences during Thanksgiving and Christmas breaks.

Numerous other opportunities fill the time of young Muslim Americans. Some high schools are providing for Islamic clubs as part of after-school activities. "I am a high school sophomore and we have an Islamic Club that was formed a few years ago," writes a young Muslima. "The Club is really an advantage because we help each other to stay strong and are there when someone needs support."[14] The Islamic Assembly of North America provides summer interns with travel, lodging, and expenses to give them the opportunity to work with the IANA staff in Michigan learning professional and organizational skills. Muslim Boy and Girl Scout troops organizing across America are particularly attractive to young African Americans, especially those from the inner city. Young Muslims (YM), an organization of the Islamic Circle of North America based in Jamaica, New York, provides a network for youth across North America who are active in the propagation of Islam among their peers. In a slick brochure featuring a canoe and paddles, the organizers of YM urge prospective participants to "get in the boat and grab the oars as you make the journey through the currents of life. . . . One must gather the oars of Al-Qur'an & Sunnah to maneuver past the dangers and reach the harbor of Jannah [heaven]." Organizations such the Muslim Arab Youth Association (MAYA), affiliated with the ISNA, sponsor regional meetings and annually bring together Muslim youth to talk about Islamic law and its implications for their lives, issues of marriage and social life, Islamic culture, and many other topics related to participation in the *umma* of Islam.

Behind all these efforts is the hope that Muslim youth can see Islam in positive, enlightened ways rather than as something shameful or as something that keeps them from enjoying their teen years as they see other young people apparently enjoying theirs.

"Rather than constantly telling teenagers what is haraam [forbidden] and what they cannot do because of Islam," writes one adviser, "it is important to show them how much fun they can have while still adhering to the Deen [religion]. Keeping teenagers busy with worthwhile yet entertaining activities will eliminate their boredom and counteract American culture's pull toward un-Islamic activities. It will also keep them from resenting Islam for stifling their fun."[15]

Care of the Elderly

Like other Americans, Muslims are keenly aware of the concerns facing their families in terms of care for the elderly. Living in a different situation from the extended family in which they were raised, many immigrants do not have the support of large numbers of relatives nearby. If husband and wife are both working, an elderly parent may find himself or herself alone for long periods and may become exceedingly lonely. This isolation, of course, is exacerbated when elderly immigrants speak little English and thus do not find much comfort even in watching television. Many of America's older immigrants have come originally from situations in which they were actively employed, but in their new life they do not work outside the home and feel isolated and often quite useless. If they cannot drive, they may feel trapped in the house.

Mosques and Islamic centers recognize the need for special services for the elderly. Some organize activities to bring together members of the older generation to socialize and feel welcome in an Islamically defined space. This effort may involve providing special transportation. It is often the elderly, particularly those more recently arrived in America, who feel the sharpest pain at the anti-Muslim prejudice they experience through the press and media. Participation in the mosque offers them at least a temporary refuge from loneliness and social isolation. Imams, increasingly having to assume roles similar to those of Christian pastors, sometimes make "house calls" on the parents of persons active in their mosque congregations. Individuals and programs also focus on advising the elderly about such matters as health care, finances, and nutrition.

Elderly parents, certainly those still following the norms of their home cultures, expect to live with their adult children, most normally with the son and his family. And whenever possible, Muslim families try to meet that expectation. There are, however, obvious problems. Often families with limited incomes have very little extra space in their homes. The traditional role of the mother-in-law as "boss" of her son and especially of her daughter-in-law meets with scant approval in most American-oriented families. In many cases, however, grandparents in the home provide a wonderful source of support and identification for children. Many adults busy outside the home rely on elderly parents not only to provide babysitting services but also to give foundational instruction in what it means to be Muslim. On the other hand, the elderly are sometimes so baffled by aspects of American culture that they appear disapproving of the dress, activities, and world views of the younger generation. The pressure not to "Americanize" that teenagers especially may feel from their grandparents can lead to tensions between the generations and even greater feelings of loneliness on the part of the elderly.

The initial response of most Muslims to the growing American custom of moving elderly relations into retirement or even nursing homes is annoyance, skepticism, and even anger. It is not the Islamic way, they insist, to isolate older people and deprive them of the fellowship of the family. "I would never dream of putting an elderly relative in a nursing home," says a first-generation immigrant. "I do not believe, whether you are Muslim or not, you should put your parents in a nursing home—unless, God forbid, they are seriously ill and need the care of a professional person."[16] Still, as families face the realities of two working adults away from the home for a long period each day or of their inability to meet the health care needs of the aging to which they are inadequate to respond, as well as the simple reality that people are living much longer than previously, Muslim groups are trying to find Islamic solutions. A few of the larger centers are constructing special housing for older Muslims near the mosque so that residents can experience greater community support.

The literature coming from national organizations and publications reminds Muslim individuals, families, and communities that just as children must have constant care, so too older people need as much love and attention as can possibly be given. "Just as helpless infants need parents, older people need their children to give constant loving care," says one health care expert. "An infant cannot explain its needs in words. Elders also experience many moments when they find it difficult to express their needs. It is up to the care-giver to search out the real needs of those he serves. Elders need love and compassion; therefore, it is important that the community adopt older citizens who do not have willing adult children."[17]

These, then, are some of the concerns that face Muslims in America as they ponder the rights and roles of women, work for the establishment and maintenance of sound family structures, and struggle to raise and support their children and provide for the needs of those who are reaching the end of their more productive days. We turn next to consider some of the extrafamilial issues with which Muslims living in the West must contend. For some, such concerns are neither pressing nor terribly significant. For increasing numbers, however, they present a complex set of questions that must be addressed on a daily basis.

CHAPTER SIX

Living a Muslim Life in American Society

Education

One of the most important concerns for American Muslims is the education of members of the community, stretching from conversations about Islamic parochial education for children, to mosque instruction, to forms of continuing adult education. The acquisition of knowledge has always been a prime consideration in Islam, and American Muslims refer frequently to the Prophet's affirmation that every Muslim attain as much knowledge as possible, even if one must go as far as China to get it. Such encouragement strengthens the educational resolve of Muslims of all ages, from young people to elderly immigrants, who may need simply to improve their English. Current conversations among Muslims in the United States focus on better training for youth in history, technology, the sciences, and many other subjects that will allow them to find personal and professional success. Learning about elements of Islamic faith and law that are relevant to life in this society is given high priority for all age groups, and the study of Arabic is strongly encouraged whenever possible.

Many Muslim families are increasingly concerned about their children's experiences in the public schools. "In 'the good old days,' " writes one critic of public school education, "certainly it was easier to trust the public school system was going to do the job. Life has gotten increasingly complex, and [parents'] responsibilities now include involvement in the educational environment and curriculum of our children."[1] Parents worry about the quality of education provided to their children, particularly in some of the larger metropolitan areas. As we have seen, they are troubled about the influences to which their children are exposed, from societal ills such as drugs and crime to the pressures on young people to become more "Americanized." Some see the problems of American schools as an abdication on the part of Christian (and Jewish) America of its basic religious values. Believing that an Islamic system of education would serve better in terms of both academic content and value training, many wonder whether to work for the establishment of private Islamic educational institutions.

Alternatively, some Muslim families choose to educate their sons and daughters at home. Muslims who advocate home schooling are writing articles about what they call the "S" word, meaning socialization and its dangers. Countering others who say that keeping children at home will prevent them from knowing how to interact with children of other faiths and backgrounds, they contend that "that level of socialization can be harmful to children."[2] They also debate whether single-sex schools are desirable or unrealistic in American culture, some citing studies by educators that claim girls learn better when segregated from boys. A few families who are sufficiently concerned about American education, and with appropriate contacts and financial resources, choose to send their children abroad for their education. Other families, however, even though they may have concerns about American schools, argue for not removing children from the public arena. Worried that the isolation of private or home schooling will not prepare them for their eventual transition into American public life, these parents hope that proper Islamic training in the home and the mosque or Islamic center will sufficiently "arm" their children to make wise decisions.

No matter what form of education is chosen, educators enjoin Muslim parents to provide the resources and environment in the home that will help the child learn not only more effectively but also "more Islamically." In an article titled "Muslim Parents' Recipe for Children's Success in School," the director of the Council of Islamic Schools in North America (CISNA) urges parents to have children do homework for a full hour before prayer. Then washing for and performing the prayer will seem like a form of recess. He also suggests that studies should be correlated with Islamic teachings: "Parents should keep a copy of the Qur'an, Seerah [life of the Prophet] and Hadith available. When the child is studying history, geography, science or social science, they should look up in the index of the Qur'an and Hadith for comparable subject matter and show the parallel ideas from the Islamic point of view."[3]

Meanwhile, as the question of appropriate education continues to be addressed, the number of Islamic schools is growing. Advertisements for teachers and administrators fill Muslim journals. Staff are expected to be well trained, with the appropriate academic and teaching credentials, and to be committed to educating within an Islamic ethos. Most of these institutions are geared to provide education from kindergarten through the sixth or eighth grades, with some encompassing high school also. According to the director of the CISNA, one of four Islamic school organizations in place in the United States and Canada, more than one hundred Islamic schools now provide education in an environment based on the Qur'an and Sunna. Although most states currently do not require accreditation for private educational institutions, the CISNA argues that the situation is changing and that accreditation of Islamic schools will signify high performance. Some Muslims are working actively for the promotion of a voucher system that would provide private Islamic schools with financial assistance from the government. Muslims are encouraged to make the funding of Islamic education a mainstay of their charitable giving.

A large and growing body of materials is available for those who wish to begin training youth at home or in private institutions. "Don't let valuable time slip away," urges an ad in a prominent Islamic journal. "Take the

Youth at an Islamic school in Queens, New York. © JOLIE STAHL

first step toward getting the assistance you need." Various Muslim organizations provide correspondence courses, suggestions for new literature and curricula, handbooks for educators, and other useful tools and information. The annual conventions of these organizations occasionally offer special sessions on home schooling, which is becoming increasingly popular as electronic services provide access to significant educational materials.

Some parents choose to supplement their children's public school education with special training sessions after school and on weekends in their homes, where copies of the Qur'an and Hadith are readily available and other symbols of Muslim culture and ethos create suitable surroundings for Islamic education. Other groups work for the improvement of American public education. The International Institute of Islamic Thought (IIIT) in Herndon, Virginia, for example, publishes "Social Studies Supplementary Teaching Units," prepared for different grades in the standard social studies curriculum. While many American public school social studies courses present a Eurocentric account of Western history, these materials provide a broader perspective and are designed to instill Islamic identity and values throughout the curriculum. Much of this training material promotes the Islamization of knowledge on the model originally proposed by Isma'il al Faruqi (see "Profiles"). If education of Muslim youth does not rest firmly on Islamic principles, say proponents of this model, it cannot be fully satisfactory in the context of a secular pluralistic society such as North America.

Increasing efforts are being made to help non-Muslim public school teachers present the religion of Islam with better understanding and more accuracy. The Council of Islamic Education (CIE) is a national scholar-based organization that works with K–12 textbook publishers to produce more comprehensive and balanced textbooks with respect to world religions, conducts in-service workshops for teachers at national social studies conferences, and produces teaching units that shed light on various aspects of Muslim civilization. Among the resources available from CIE is a handbook for educators titled *Teaching About Islam and Muslims in the Public School Classroom*. It includes information on beliefs and practices, a section on issues about which Muslim students in the public school classroom may be particularly sensitive, activity sheets for students learning about Islam, and up-to-date information on books, videotapes, and other educational materials. CIE brings together representatives of all the many cultural groupings of American Muslims (immigrant, African American, Hispanic, Native American) to talk about the ways in which American history textbooks represent

TEACHER'S GUIDE

Answer Key

Comparison of Islam, Judaism and Christianity

Item	Judaism	Christianity	Islam
Belief in how many deities?	One (monotheism)	One (monotheism)	One (monotheism)
Name of Supreme Being	Jehovah (Yahweh)	God	Allah
Central Prophet/Figure	Moses	Jesus Christ	Muhammad
Holy City	Jerusalem	Jerusalem	Makkah, Madinah and Jerusalem
Ordained Religious Leader	rabbi	priest or minister	none, but imam leads worship
Sacred Writings	Hebrew Bible (Old Testament)	Bible (Old and New Testaments)	Qur'an
Name for Believers	Jews	Christians	Muslims
Worship and Use of Idols or Images	images and statues forbidden	statues allowed but not worshipped	images and statues forbidden
Symbol of Faith	Star of David	cross	none
House of Worship	synagogue	cathedral or church	masjid
Special Events	Passover, Yom Kippur	Christmas, Easter	Eid al-Fitr, Eid al-Adha
Beliefs concerning "the good life."	complete obedience to Mosaic law	love God and fellow humans	adherence to "Five Pillars" of faith
Beliefs concerning life after death.	Day of Judgment	Day of Judgment	Day of Judgment

Activity sheet from an instructional book on Islam from the Council on Islamic Education.
COURTESY COUNCIL ON ISLAMIC EDUCATION

different cultures. Members work with a number of publishers to encourage broader and more representative coverage, as well as the correction of errors and misperceptions about Islam and Muslim peoples. Muslims and others in the educational community join them in the effort to eliminate stereotyping and prejudicial presentations in the materials used in the public schools.

Meanwhile, some Muslims are joining forces with conservative Christian groups and others who are lobbying for prayer in the public schools. "The pro-school prayer coalition is changing," says a commentator on education for Muslim children. "Today, it includes Muslims, black urban leaders, and Christian clergy. Even liberal politicians are joining hands with religious conservatives. The increase in heinous crimes among youth and promiscuous sex has sounded the alarm and led to the broadening of the prayer lobby's base. It's important for young people to have a moment to reflect."[4]

The Islamic educational program in America also provides training for youth and adults in the mosques and weekend schools of Islamic centers. Again, journals and organizations make a great deal of material and assistance available. Instruction ranges from the Qur'an, Sunna, and Islamic history to issues of appropriate dress and behavior for Muslims in different circumstances. Realistic about the possible reasons their youth may have for not wanting to attend after-school or weekend instruction in the mosque, adults are working out strategies to make such activities more fun. Some of the larger Islamic centers, for example, offer athletic facilities such as basketball and volleyball courts to balance the classroom instruction. The study of Arabic is particularly encouraged for those who are not from Arabic-speaking families, and mosques may hold contests for youth and adults in recitation and knowledge of the Qur'an. A number of well-organized efforts currently support the Islamic education of American Muslims. Plans for an Islamic Institute of Religious and Social Sciences in Georgia (GIIRSS), for example, include a mosque, educational and recreational facilities, and opportunities for board and lodging. The GIIRSS represents itself as nonpolitical, nonsectarian, and nonprofit, intended purely as a way of providing religious and educational training for American Muslim youth. The Institute hopes that by

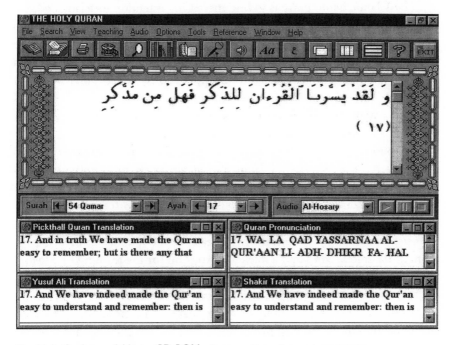

The Holy Qur'an available on CD-ROM. COURTESY MICRO SYSTEMS INTERNATIONAL

attracting young people from across the country, it can serve as a spiritual and intellectual link between youth and their parents.

One of the themes receiving particular attention among American Muslims as the twentieth century draws to a close is the importance of educating Muslims in Islamic ethics and equipping them to lead morally responsible lives. Reflecting concern for the perceived moral disintegration of American society, this stress on an Islamically defined morality serves both to provide a serious alternative for American Muslims and to show other Americans the great importance Muslims give to living morally and ethically. The Islamic Society of North America (ISNA) has recently published a twelve-volume *Encyclopedia on Moral Excellence* available on CD-ROM and translated into a number of languages. The theme of a recent Muslim Student Association annual meeting was "Pursuing Moral Excellence in the Quest for Change." Articles and books now appearing are stressing the integration of moral responsibility with academic training. "From the Islamic perspective," writes one educator, "the purpose of education in general is the upbringing of righteous Muslims. This righteousness instills in the Muslim child a set of fundamental values which in turn make him observe his obligations as well as the correct norms of conduct in society naturally."[5]

The Islamic community is giving increasing attention to Islamic education at the college and university level, although to date only a few specifically Muslim institutions exist, among them the American Islamic College established in Chicago in 1983. The first institution of its kind, the AIC is a bachelor of arts–granting institution approved by the Illinois Board of Higher Education and offers a range of studies in the social and physical sciences, computer science, economics, history, and other areas, as well as a number of courses in Arabic and Islamic studies.

In 1996 the first Muslim school of graduate study in America was established as the School of Islamic and Social Sciences in Leesburg, Virginia. The SISS, as it is known, provides an opportunity to study with an Islamic faculty in the traditions of Islam. Its goal is to train leaders dedicated to the establishment of Muslim culture and civilization in North America. Currently, SISS offers two areas of study, a master of arts program in Islamic Studies and a master's program for the training of Muslim imams, or prayer leaders. The school has already received permission from the Virginia Council for Higher Education to offer its graduate-level classes, although there is no established organization in the United States to authorize its imam-training program. There is also the Imam Ali Seminary in Medina, New York, a Shi'i school dedicated to providing training

The American Islamic College in Chicago, Illinois.
COURTESY AMERICAN ISLAMIC COLLEGE, CHICAGO, ILLINOIS

for teachers to assist in the personal and community growth of Muslims living in America.

Muslim students enrolled at other American colleges and universities are becoming increasingly vocal in their efforts to gain recognition for themselves and their community. These efforts, supported by national groups such as the Muslim Student Association (MSA), are bringing results. Syracuse University has recognized *'eid al-fitr* at the end of Ramadan as an official school holiday, and the entire university closes for the day. At Syracuse and Harvard Universities, Islamically permissible meat is available to students on demand. At Mount Holyoke College, Muslim and Jewish students may elect once a week to share a common meal prepared in a kitchen that is both Islamically acceptable and kosher. Meanwhile, Islamic periodicals and newspapers high-light the achievements of Muslim youth in colleges and universities, and many contain special sections devoted specifically to education, providing tips to prospective students on everything from filling out financial-aid applications to selecting an appropriate roommate. Muslim students themselves are start-ing to write articles in school newspapers and in national Muslim journals warning of the difficulties of living Islamically in college and emphasizing the importance of keeping company with other young Muslims. "I would like to say that the secret to keeping your Iman [faith] and strengthening your Deen [religion] when you are in college lies in brotherhood and sisterhood. Muslims on campus don't have the Taqwa [piety] to live as an individual in their kafir [unbeliever] society," writes a student at Rutgers University. "Strength is in our numbers because Shaitan [Satan] finds difficulty in deceiv-ing whole flocks as opposed to lone sheep."[6]

Economics

Among the many difficult issues facing Muslims who want to live accord-ing to the strictures of Islamic law is that of proper financial stewardship. This problem has a number of dimensions, of which perhaps the most com-plex is the Qur'anic prohibition on the accumulation of interest (*riba*). Many issues arise for American Muslims trying to be faithful to this injunc-tion. "Is the money a Muslim earns from working at a bank haram (unlaw-ful)?" writes a concerned reader to a national journal's *fatawa* (legal opin-ions) discussion forum. "Work at any bank that deals with ribaa (usury/ interest) is haram," comes the answer, "because it is from the act of helping one another in sin and transgression."[7] Interpreted strictly, the term can be understood to refer to usury, or interest in excess of the legal rate. Some Muslims, however, argue for a more flexible interpretation of the law that would allow for the accumulation of some reasonable interest on money invested. The detailed arguments require a subtle understanding of Islam-ic law and interpretation. The ramifications, however, are important for those Muslims who try conscientiously to adhere to the law. One of the obvious ways in which the prohibition on interest impinges on Muslims has to do with taking out mortgages on houses, mosques, and other long-term establishments. In some instances, communities in America simply collect all the money needed to build an Islamic institution, to avoid the necessity of having a mortgage and dealing with the matter of interest. The growth of Islamic banks across the world, and now also in America, helps provide some solutions.

Another financial issue attracting growing attention is whether capital gains on investments are Islamically acceptable. Some argue that capital gains should never be allowed, while others claim that they should be prohibited only when they would destabilize the smooth functioning of the economic order. More banks in America now work with "bank deposits" and "Islamic deposits," in which money is entrusted to the bank for safekeeping and later returned without interest, upon request or the satisfaction of certain conditions. Such deposits may be accessed through checking accounts or may be put in term-limit accounts such as certificates of deposit.

As American Muslims articulate their economic concerns more specifically, more opportunities present themselves through advertisements for counseling and assistance in Islamic investing. The North American Islamic Trust, for example, provides counseling for investors about the ways in which they can achieve long-term growth at the same time that they avoid both the accumulation of interest and the possibility that their money will be invested in businesses that trade in alcohol, tobacco, pornography, or gambling.

Such debates remain to be settled by those with extensive knowledge of economics as well as Islamic law. In the meantime, Muslims in the United States raise practical questions about finances, and increasing attention is being given in the popular literature to helping them think through Islamically acceptable responses. "Have you fallen into the debt trap yet?" reads the opening line of an article in the journal *Al Jumuah*, warning its readers of the importance of avoiding outstanding loans and the inevitable payment of interest on those loans. Specific examples illustrate the concrete ways in which the sayings of the Prophet and the injunctions of the law can inform everyday financial decisions. For families living close to the economic margin, difficult questions often arise, particularly if for reasons of religious conviction a husband feels it Islamically unacceptable for his wife to participate in the workplace and contribute to the family income. Letters to religious advisers in Muslim journals often ponder how to be responsible both to Islamic expectations and to the exigencies of providing for the economic stability of one's family in the American context.

One response increasingly advocated is to manage one's money through investment clubs. "Muslims seeking halal [permissible], safe and rewarding means of making their money grow have a choice in the shape of an 'investment club,' " suggests a Muslim economist.[8] These clubs function as low-risk structured partnership agreements in which members pool money and invest, meeting regularly to explore new opportunities. Management and brokering costs are lowered, and members have an opportunity to share in broad expertise working for maximized investment returns.

The issue of how finances affect mosque growth and maintenance exceeds questions of interest and mortgage. Traditionally, members of Islamic societies do not pledge to the support of a religious institution, as such support comes from the state. Muslims in other parts of the world attend the mosque according to their needs and interests but do not consider themselves "members." In the American context, the situation differs markedly. Mosques and Islamic centers generally function as self-supporting units, often dependent on the contributions of the local Muslim community and on fund-raising activities for maintenance and continuation of services. Those who attend sometimes react with annoyance if expected to "pledge" to the support of the mosque, claiming that is a Christian and not an Islamic custom. Muslims who are conscientious about paying the *zakat*, or Islamically required tax for the care of the needy, may feel doubly pressured at the expectation of also having to contribute to the mosque or Islamic Center. At the same time, they increasingly realize that such institutional support is crucial in America and needs to be thought about in new ways. Many mosques find themselves forced further to adopt American customs of seeking financial support, engaging in fund-raising activities such as dinners, rummage sales, special events, and direct-mail appeals. The matter of financing becomes even more complicated when foreign governments—Iran or Saudi Arabia, for example—offer support to communities in this country. While the infusion of monies may be welcome, the expectations that recipients assume certain social and political positions may not be.

National Islamic organizations make concerted efforts to help Muslims in America think creatively about their financial options. They put forth strategies to assist in economic advancement, such as better entry into the American mainstream economy, economic pan-Islamism (insofar as possible, attempting to buy from and sell to Muslims only), and even international Muslim economic solidarity. Some argue that the American *umma* must have its own treasury (*bait al-mal*) for the collection of *zakat* and other kinds of charitable donations on local, state, and national levels. The hope is that such a central agency could not only deploy charitable giving most effectively but could develop a surplus of its own resources to assist in financing Muslim projects.

The managing director of the first full-service Muslim-owned investment bank in America, located on Wall Street, argues for the importance of establishing a chair in Islamic finance at a major university. Acknowledging that many schools teach courses about Islam, he says, "Now, it is vitally important to take the next logical step, which is to establish a Chair on Islamic Finance to not only create and fulfill a demand in our youth (our future), but also explain why high profile conventional financial institutions . . . have established Islamic financial 'Windows' for business."[9]

Considerable debate in national and local forums examines such issues as whether Muslims should try to benefit from affirmative-action hiring programs as long as they exist. Some leaders urge Muslims to look more closely at the history of Jews in America for examples of how to succeed financially in the face of prejudice and minority status. Clearly, the many factors relating to economics will continue to be addressed with great seriousness in the coming years.

Nutrition and Health

American Muslims have long been concerned lest they be unable to observe the dietary restrictions of Islam. These, including the prohibition on pork products and alcohol, they understand both to be based on the commands of God in the Qur'an and to reflect concerns for health and hygiene. African American converts to the Nation of Islam from the middle of the century on were enjoined in the strongest terms to abandon completely all former customs of eating any parts of the pig. Books and pamphlets still available in Muslim bookstores warn of the disastrous effects of disregarding these rules, complete with graphic depictions of the one who succumbs to such temptation and then begins to assume porcine characteristics. Extensive efforts over the last several decades have determined the ingredients used in breads, pastries, and other products found in grocery stores, fast-food establishments, and other places where Muslims might buy their food. This endeavor has caused the discontinued use of a number of products, like lard, for example. The movement to focus public attention on the importance of proper diet in Islam is growing and includes warnings about the necessity of moderate and supervised consumption of any pharmaceutical products.

In recent years, more attention has also been given to the proper ritual slaughter of animals prepared for consumption. Earlier, those Muslims who wanted to ensure that their meat was permissible were forced to buy it from Jewish kosher delicatessens. Now many more places sell Islamically slaughtered meat, generally known as *halal* (from the Arabic word meaning "allowed" or "lawful") meat. The proper Islamic slaughtering of an animal has both health and ritual dimensions. The animal's throat should be slit cleanly with a sharp instrument, cutting through the windpipe, gullet, and jugular veins. After the throat is cut, the blood must be drained before the head is fully removed. This method contrasts with the typical American way of slaughter, in which the animal is stunned with an electric shock before being killed and the blood is not fully drained. Meat from which blood is removed is much less prone to fermentation and the accumulation of bacteria. In addition, while the animal is being slaughtered, the name of God is to be recited, as is indicated in Sura 6:118 of the Qur'an: "Eat of that over which the name of God has been mentioned." It is generally considered permissible to have a tape of Qur'an recitation running during the slaughter as an alternative to having someone speaking in person. The issue of *halal* meat includes the slaughter not only of beef and sheep but also of poultry. North Carolina, a large chicken-producing state, exports Islamically slaughtered birds to Muslim countries, especially in the Middle East. Groups such as the Islamic Food and Nutrition Council of America, located in Bedford Park, Illinois, are preparing information kits to assist Muslims employed in various parts of the American food industry.

An issue of particular interest to many Muslim Americans, and to which Islamic scholars give a number of answers, is whether Muslims should be allowed to eat food prepared by non-Muslims, specifically Christians and Jews. Some more conservative scholars argue that the answer is no because one cannot be sure that it has been prepared in the proper way. Others agree with the Egyptian reformer Rashid Rida, who early in this century argued that if the Qur'an allows a man to marry one of the People of the Book, surely it is not wrong to eat the food of Christians or Jews. Obviously, the increasing social interactions of Muslims and non-Muslims, through business and other contacts, makes it difficult to maintain the strictest dietary observance.

Some Muslims refuse to attend any occasion at which alcohol is served, while others simply abstain from drinking it themselves and leave their neighbors to make their own decisions. Some wonder whether it is necessary to serve alcohol to guests. "In our family . . . we used to serve liquor to our American guests," reports a Muslim from upstate New York. "We would just put it on the table and leave it there for them to help themselves. But we stopped doing this as a result of comments made by my older daughter— that when we don't drink, why do we serve drinks?" The issue of whether a

Muslim should work in a store or restaurant that sells alcohol has greatly concerned some Muslims, particularly when the job is essential for the support of their families, and the decisions have varied. Some question whether Muslims should be allowed to take any drugs possibly containing traces of forbidden substances such as alcohol. Again, responses differ, with most affirming such use if it is necessary for the patient's life and no substitute is available. The general rule is that substances that impair one's mind or cloud one's discernment are to be avoided at all costs short of life endangerment.

Also receiving considerable attention in the American Muslim community is the matter of proper health care opportunities. In some cases, organizations are planning for free care for the needy, such as that provided by the University Muslim Medical Association (UMMA) Free Health Clinic in Los Angeles, run by Muslim physicians and medical students. Located in the heart of gang-troubled South Central Los Angeles, the clinic focuses on issues of health care and social welfare. It runs on the charitable donations of money and supplies by hospitals, businesses, and other agencies and donations of time by medical and other staff. In other cases, efforts are being made to ensure that Muslims under medical care in public and private hospitals in America are treated in ways that accord with their beliefs.

Riverview Hospital in Detroit, Michigan, in collaboration with the Islamic Health and Human Services organization, recently made an unprecedented decision to provide for Islamic practices as a regular part of its hospital services. "*Al-Hamdilullah* [praise be to God]!" cried the Muslim reporter describing the consequences of this decision. "This is not a dream. You are not in a Muslim country. You are in Detroit. . . ."[10] The *adhan*, or call to prayer, is whispered in the ear of a newborn baby, *halal* food is prepared in the hospital kitchen, Muslim patients and caregivers do *salat* in the meditation room, Qur'ans are available by request, and female hospital personnel are allowed to go about their work in full *hijab* if they so choose. Lists of patients contain the reference "Muslim" by their names when appropriate. Riverview is the first to offer total Islamic care to Muslim patients, but it will certainly not be the last.

Holidays

As Muslims become more aware of their presence in North America as a definable religious entity, they are becoming clearer about the importance of distinguishing between their own holidays and festivals and those of

Christian, or secular, America. It is often difficult for some Muslim children to understand why they are not allowed to participate in the holidays their classmates enjoy. For more observant Muslims, the problem is exacerbated when many of their fellow Muslims enjoy all the holidays, taking what is fun and ignoring specifically religious implications. Other Muslim parents want to encourage their children to "own" their own holidays and to distance themselves from American observances that they feel are specific to Jews and Christians or are too secular to have a part in Islam.

Questions arise especially around Christmastime. Why not let our children have a Christmas tree and exchange gifts, some argue, especially since Muslims, along with Christians, honor the birth of Jesus? Others try to compromise or avoid any observance of the holiday at all. Still others decide that observing Christmas has some advantages. "We celebrate Christmas for two reasons," says one woman. "It is important to get involved with American society, and if you don't celebrate Christmas and if you don't celebrate Thanksgiving, to me really you are telling those people you are not part of American society. . . . The second reason is that we do believe in Jesus. We don't believe that he was a god, but we do believe he was a prophet."[11] Muslim parents who are not happy when their children come home singing Christmas carols may be even more startled when they hear songs about "Happy Hanukkah."

Other holidays present fewer immediate problems. Easter is so clearly an acknowledgment of a Christian belief denied by Islam, namely the resurrection of Jesus, that there is little at issue, aside from wondering whether to allow children to color eggs or have bunny baskets. Muslims may see the fourth of July as a time to affirm their participation in American civic life, Halloween for the most part is deemed rather harmless—although most parents do not want their children trick-or-treating—and Thanksgiving can easily be appreciated as a truly Islamic event insofar as it is a time to appreciate God's bounty with one's family and friends.

Nonetheless, occasions in the calendar in which the vast majority of Americans participate in some measure or another continue to raise questions. These may be compounded as Muslims develop friendships with other non-Muslims, to whose holiday celebrations they may be invited. Young people especially may find it difficult to understand why they cannot participate in holidays celebrated by non-Muslim friends, such as birthdays or other occasions. The conservative response, calling on the rulings of Muslim legists over the centuries, is a firm no, some insisting that one should not even congratulate Christians, Jews, or others at the time of their holidays.

The strictness of this decision will not appeal to all Muslims, even those trying hard to live Islamically acceptable lives. "Recently I was asked to organize the wedding of a Hindu friend of mine because most of his relatives were abroad," writes a concerned man to a Muslim adviser. "And I was the closest person he knew and could trust. I have similarly actively participated in other Hindu and Sikh births, deaths and even religious functions like Holi, Diwali and Baisakhi. Are there restrictions on how closely a Muslim can participate in such functions and rituals?"[12] More conservative than many would give, the response was that organizing and helping out on such occasions is fine because it helps foster good community relationships. But to actually participate in them, unfortunately, is totally prohibited. Many Muslims are trying modifications of strict Islamic regulations that can satisfy both their own consciences and their desire not to isolate themselves and their children unduly from the influences of a culture in which they are, in fact, citizens and participants.

One important element is the rethinking of how to observe the traditional Islamic holidays in the Western context. Although the *'eid al-fitr*, the breaking of the fast of Ramadan described in chapter 1, may be the most publicized and thus the most evident Islamic holiday to Americans who are not Muslims, in fact it is considered to be the minor, or lesser, *'eid*, or celebration. The major *'eid* is the *'eid al-adha*, the festival commemorating Abraham's attempted sacrifice of his son, whom Muslims believe to have been Ishmael rather than Isaac, occurring at the end of the pilgrimage to Mecca. Traditionally, Muslims sacrifice animals, or purchase *halal* meat, to distribute to the needy of the community. Muslims in America observe the holiday at the same time that pilgrims are completing their *hajj* in Mecca. Many Muslims choose to celebrate the birthday of the Prophet, *mulid al-nabi*, often as much as possible according to the particular customs of the country or society from which they originally came. One of the most important yearly observances for American Shi'ites is that known as Muharram, during which they recollect and reenact the events that took place at the time of the massacre of Prophet Muhammad's grandson Husayn at Karbala. The month itself is already sacred to all Muslims, as it was the time when Muhammad changed the direction in which Muslims were to face when performing the ritual prayer from Jerusalem to Mecca. "The Muharram majlis [lamentation assembly] provides each successive generation with the religious instruction necessary for the continuance of Shi'i identity. Throughout the year the verity of the emotional experience of Karbala that begins in childhood is repeatedly reaffirmed."[13] Shi'is are being creative both in carrying out this observation and in translating it to the better understanding of their non-Muslim neighbors.

Public schools in America are becoming more aware of all these holidays and often encourage Muslim students to tell the other members of the class what their celebrations mean. School calendars in more progressive institutions record the major Islamic holidays as well as those of Christians and Jews.

Islamic "Products"

Muslims who want to eat, dress, and comport themselves in recognizably Islamic ways have access to a great range of commodities designed to assist, enhance, and promote their identity. In most urban areas of America today one can find numerous products in markets and stores designed particularly for Muslim consumption. Many of these products are also available by mail order, evidenced in the growing number of advertisements in Islamic journals and newspapers as well as in other publications and through the media. Websites and home pages giving information on Islamic materials multiply daily, and one faces more information and products than can easily be imagined. Most obvious are the great numbers of books, videos, CDs, software packages, and instructional materials about Islam. Many of these educational materials are designed for pleasure at the same time that they instruct, such as videos with Islamic cartoons for children. Increasing numbers of games and puzzles attract families wishing to engage in wholesome group activity. A large and accurately proportioned three-dimensional scale model of Mecca with more than a thousand foam-backed pieces is available by phone order and at game stores. Fully assembled, it is more than two feet in width and a foot high. Family members may wish to quiz one another about Islamic history or salient facts about the faith and practice of Islam with Islamic game cards. Some journals contain quizzes about Islam, with the answers provided on a separate page.

Products are designed both to help Muslims affirm their identity and to make life easier and more convenient for them in a Western context. Special package tours to Saudi Arabia at the time of the *hajj* advertise "the best service and lowest prices for the pilgrimage," some geared for the traveler who would prefer economy and others combining stays in luxury hotels with the rigors of the pilgrimage. A number of travel agencies offer special service and low prices for arranging special *'umra* (the lesser pilgrimage not made

Advertisement for a watch that gives times of prayer and the direction of Mecca. COURTESY UFI, INC.

during the time of *hajj*) trips. Information on pilgrimage opportunities is available on the Internet at the Hajj & Umrah website. Muslims who want to know the exact times for prayer and breaking the daily fast during Ramadan may purchase a variety of specially designed watches and clocks. "Don't pray when you remember," advertises CASIO, "pray when it is time to pray!" What is billed as its "Amazing AL-ASR Islamic Watch" points to Mecca from any location without using a compass, gives the time of prayer for more than two hundred cities around the world, and displays a thirty-day *hijra* calendar.

The Muslim who wants to ensure that her or his diet is appropriate to the strictures of the law can send in to a number of food production companies that feature such treats as *shawarma* (a Middle Eastern mixture of

A Halal store sells Islamically acceptable food products. © THE PHOTO WORKS

rotisserie-grilled meat and spices), Vienna sausage, corned beef and pas-
trami, turkey ham, and even pizza toppings, all prepared according to strict
halal standards. The Islamic Book Center in Richmond Hill, New York,
offers *A Handbook of Halaal and Haraam Products* with more than six
thousand listings and articles on how to select one's diet wisely. Companies such as Midamar Corporation in Cedar Rapids, Iowa, assure customers that they have worked for many years with selected USDA-
approved companies to ensure product quality and integrity. Even *halal*
marshmallows are available in large and small size, prepared appropriately
from beef gelatin. Along with foods, one can order exclusive skin-care
products like eye-lift hydrating gel and mystic musk night cream, also
designed to meet Islamic requirements by avoiding the use of animal fats
or alcohol and guaranteed not to have been tested on animals. Weight-loss
programs advertise products in line with Islamic dietary requirements.
Men can even hope to have their hair restored using Islamically appropriate products for hair and scalp.

    As issues of appropriate dress, especially but not exclusively for women,
have become more prominent over the past several decades, so they are
reflected in the availability of many different kinds of Muslim clothing.
Women wishing to wear Islamic dress can find a range of products available,
from various kinds of *hijab*, or headdress (the company Small Kindnesses, for

example, advertises slip-on scarves in cotton and silk as well as more elaborate coverings), to embroidered dresses reaching the ankles and wrists. Sometimes these are for the business or daytime public sphere and are often featured in gray or tan tones. Other creations are designed for the world of full fashion. The Tekbir Company in Richardson, Texas, for instance, advertises stunning winter coats and gowns for elegant evening wear. Most Islamic clothing businesses use the terminology of *jilbab* for an overgarment, *hijab* or *khimar* for the head scarf, and *niqab* for the full face veil. Some companies feature women's clothing in a more Indian or Malaysian style, often called *shalwar khameez*, with loose trousers and tunics. Full-length robes, called *thoubs*, *jalabiyyas*, or *kurtas*, are also featured for men. Some of these are distinctively Arab or Pakistani in style, while others are modified for Western consumption, as, for example, a *thoub* advertised as having classic shirt tailoring with Mandarin collar and button cuffs. One can purchase rings, earrings, pins, pendants, and other kinds of jewelry in gold or silver featuring Islamic inscriptions such as *"Allahu akbar"* ("God is greater"). For those who would like to dress more casually but still carry the message of their identity, Islamic and Arabic T-shirts are available, custom-made for businesses, schools, and other organizations. Companies such as Rahman Imports offer full catalogs of new clothing styles for men, women, and children.

Personal Problems and Islamic Solutions

Much has been said already about the concerns Muslims raise as they try to balance the requirements of their faith with the expectations of American culture. There is no dearth of assistance in helping individuals find answers to their questions through mosques and Islamic centers, the Internet, Muslim journals and newspapers, and many other sources. *The Minaret* magazine published in Southern California assures its readers that a *fatwa* (which, technically, is a religious/legal opinion, not a ruling) is only a phone call away, urging that those with concerns call 1-800-95-FATWA for assistance in making important life decisions. "God's Will need not be searched or sought; you need not sweat or pain, you need not reflect or persevere. Instead, you make a phone call."[14] The problem for many Muslims comes in trying to determine what responses are truest to the heart of Islamic law and whether they are applicable or even possible in the American context. Following are a few of the many questions being raised in the Muslim community today, and some of the Islamic responses offered.

- Is it lawful to accept a gift from someone whose money has earned interest in a bank? The conservative response is no, although some would argue that the thought behind the gift matters more than how the money was accumulated.

- Should girls who have not yet reached puberty be allowed, or even encouraged, to wear a scarf to school? The Muslim community is deeply engaged in the issue of dress for girls, and most would argue that they should not be encouraged to wear the scarf at least until puberty. Whatever the girl's decision, it is important for the family to provide a supportive and approving context.

- Is it really un-Islamic to listen to, play, and enjoy music? All the major Islamic schools of thought prohibit the use of certain kinds of music, but clearly there are major compromises made on this issue. Yusuf Islam, the former pop singer Cat Stevens, suggests that, as in all things, moderation is the key. He believes that songs and singing are Islamically acceptable if the words are appropriate and if praise of God is always the primary intention of one's music. "[Legal prohibition] does not mean that Muslims become melodious-less monks. Muslims have to partake in every aspect of life. . . . So a lot more thought has to go into this . . . because there are songs and singing in Islam, there is melody as well as drums, but it has to be within the limits."[15] Others are less open and tend to condemn music in any Islamic setting.

- Can a Muslim attend the funeral of a non-Muslim member of his family? Should he pray for the soul of the dead? Most often the response is yes.

- If an employer does not allow time or space for a Muslim to pray during the workday, is it OK to skip the prayer? Islam recognizes that prayer can be a hardship as well as a joy, and if at all possible one should try to pray at the appropriate time. If it is absolutely impossible, then the situation falls under what are called the laws of necessity, and the prayer can be made up at another time.

- Should Muslims say prayers over meals, or is this just copying a Christian custom? Although it has not been a traditional Muslim custom, mealtime prayer is generally acceptable and is actually gaining popularity in some American Muslim families.

As one browses through question-and-answer columns in Muslim journals or joins conversations on the World Wide Web, it is evident that answers are not always clear cut. Advisers sometimes tend to lean so heavily on examples from the past that their relevance to life in contemporary America is rather obscured. Clearly, in some cases, such a focus tries to help the believer discover the answer for himself or herself. Many Muslims in American society, for example, wonder if it is acceptable or forbidden to have non-Muslims as friends. While some argue that it is most advisable for Muslims to limit their circle of friends to members of their own faith, others cite the example of the Prophet, who cared deeply even for the polytheists of Mecca and expressed his concern for them, as indicative of the importance of care for non-Muslim neighbors. Interfaith issues remain complex for many American Muslims and will be an important part of their immediate and future agenda.

Women's issues surface regularly. "I am a Muslima (female) who really enjoys exercising," writes one woman. "Although I wear loose clothing and a head covering when I exercise or jog, I have been told that any form of exercising in public by Muslim sisters is forbidden. Do I have to stay in the house to exercise?"[16] This question encompasses concerns for dress, women's public participation, and women's behavior in general, as well as the specific issue of exercise. Clearly, there is no one Muslim answer, but the fact is that girls in schools are often encouraged to participate in sports, especially if their clothing is appropriate. Female Muslim athletes sometimes compete officially in sports and games, occasionally even in the Olympics, and are generally able to modify Islamic dress to meet the requirements of modesty and of the sport itself.

Muslimas commonly raise questions about matters related to their marriages. Sometimes these are rather routine, having to do with the running of the household, such as whether a husband should help with the cleaning and child care. Interestingly, the answer in the American context almost invariably is yes, and many cite examples of the Prophet Muhammad's helping at home. Some wonder if the debts incurred by a woman before marriage should become the responsibility of her new husband, and the answer generally given is that they remain hers, although a responsible and caring husband will want to help. Muslim women whose husbands do not feel it is appropriate for them to work outside the home often seek advice about how to change their husband's mind or how to feel that they are contributing to the community while remaining at home.

Should Muslim women shake hands with men who are not members of their family? The responses vary. More urgent is the question many ask about whether birth control is Islamically acceptable. A majority of American Muslims now seem to feel that women should be able to use some form of birth control, although there is often disagreement as to which forms are approved. Even more difficult to discuss publicly, although some are courageously doing so, is the presence of HIV in the Muslim community and the importance of honest and early education about this societal menace. "When we first started hearing about the AIDS virus," says the wife of a drug user, "it was a gay thing, then it was a Haitian thing, and then they started finding out that it was affecting IV drug users. For a little while, I kept saying, 'Well I don't use drugs. I'm Muslim. I'm praying five times a day.' But that didn't sit well with me because the fact that you pray does not mean that you are exempt from adversity."[17] This courageous woman, who with her husband did in fact test positive for AIDS, is working to spread information among Muslims about the reality of this disease and urging other Muslims who might be living with the virus to undergo testing, develop support groups, and address those risks that may bring AIDS into the Muslim community.

Those in leadership positions in the American Muslim community urge members to be alert to the various ways of giving an Islamic cast to life's transitional events. They offer advice about how to conduct the ceremony for a new baby, although it is a recommended rather than a legally obligatory responsibility, including the traditional slaughtering of two sheep for a male baby and one for a female. Muslim men who wish to marry Christian women are advised on the appropriate preparations and ceremony and about the importance of meeting the conditions of an Islamic marriage, such as the offer of the bride by the bride's guardian and the acceptance by the groom in front of witnesses. Inheritance laws, carefully articulated in the Qur'an, are being interpreted for American Muslims. Muzammil Siddiqi, president of the Islamic Society of North America, urges American Muslims to prepare their wills as early as possible, providing guidance according to the stipulations of the Qur'an and Hadith. "Since one does not know when death may come, one should have a will ready at all times," he urges.[18] A "Will Kit" prepared by the ISNA is designed to help ensure the best distribution of one's estate.

The final rite of death is receiving more consistent attention, particularly in terms of an appropriate burial plot. For more than half a century, Muslims in various parts of the country have been concerned about having to adapt traditional Muslim funeral rites and customs to the requirements of American law and, increasingly, are procuring land to use as Muslim cemeteries. Traditionally, the corpse of a Muslim is wrapped in a winding cloth, then laid in the ground without a coffin, facing Mecca, according to Islamic requirements. Although American law requires that a casket be used for burial, cemeteries designated as Islamic allow for the grave to be dug so that the deceased will face Mecca. Over the last half century, many more Muslim cemeteries have been established. Among the many issues facing Muslims concerning death and dying is whether a Muslim who has never attended a local mosque or identified himself or herself as religiously practicing should be given a Muslim funeral and be buried in a Muslim cemetery.

Many of these concerns facing the Muslim community in America are being addressed in public presentations by regional and national organizations and institutions. We turn now to look at how Muslims come together for the public practice of their faith, ways in which Islam is being presented both for propagation and for better understanding by the American public, and the organizational information and support available to help Muslims live and practice their religion.

CHAPTER SEVEN

The Public Practice of Islam

Mosques (*Masjids*)

A Muslim architect who came from Pakistan to the United States as a student in 1960 describes his attempts to find a mosque in the Pittsburgh area. His host family, eager to make him feel at home, took him to the closest facsimile they could find. "As we turned onto a minor street on the University of Pittsburgh campus," Gulzar Haider writes, "[my host] pointed to a vertical neon sign that said in no uncertain terms 'Syria Mosque.' . . . Horseshoe arches, horizontal bands of different colored bricks, decorative terra-cotta—all were devices to invoke a Moorish memory. Excitedly, I took a youthful step towards the lobby, when my host turned around and said, 'This is not the kind of mosque in which you bend up and down facing Mecca. This is a meeting hall-theater built by Shriners. . . . They are the guys who dress up in satin baggies, embroidered vests, and fez caps.' "[1]

As a result of this and other fruitless attempts to find an American mosque that both looked and functioned like one, this architect has devoted his career to designing Islamic mosques for the Western context. In 1979 he was invited to draw up plans for the mosque located at the national headquarters of the Islamic Society of North America (ISNA) in Plainfield, Indiana. The movement to create an Islamic architecture for the American environment is both fascinating and challenging. It is, in effect, the latest chapter in a long struggle among American Muslims to find or create worship spaces appropriate for the particular needs of their communities and faith.

We have seen that many Muslims who came to America earlier in this century with little overt interest in participating in Islamic functions or even in identifying themselves specifically as members of the Islamic tradition soon found their attitudes changing. Their frequent frustration in not finding a social group of other Americans with whom they could feel comfortable and accepted, or the satisfaction of sharing experiences that reflected their commonality with other Muslims, encouraged them to participate more openly in religiously based activities. They gravitated toward common worship, Qur'an study groups, and other gatherings that reinforced their affiliation with the religion of Islam. As second-generation Muslims reached the age to marry and have children, they often became more aware of the importance of providing a social, cultural, and religious context for their children. Most of the new Muslim communities, however, had no easy access to trained leadership to instruct them in the elements of the faith or to lead the prayer. Those who had even a little education in the Qur'an or Islamic law were looked to for guidance. Sometimes people who had no training at all in the Islamic sciences had to gather the faithful together on Friday and perform the function of imam, or prayer leader.

Before long, a number of immigrant Muslim communities across the nation began to think about more structured ways to observe their religion and assure its continuity. They were concerned about the difficulty of finding an appropriate place in which to worship and observe the Friday prayers. Sometimes they held services in one another's homes. But as the communities began to grow, this arrangement became increasingly less feasible. Some congregations leased abandoned buildings or other spaces, while others occasionally shared space in local churches. Often these facilities were dreary and at best unsuited for sitting and praying on the floor, without pews or chairs, as is the Muslim custom. Slowly, more and more Muslims began to think and dream about establishing their own mosques. To possess such a building would, of course, make it much easier to gather together and perform the actual worship. The building would also enable the community to have pride in its identification with Islam and its ability to provide its own facility. And finally, it would serve as a means of legitimating Islam as part of the American religious scene, providing for visible structures and institutions that could "stand up and be counted," so to speak, alongside the many churches and synagogues across America.

We have already noted the pioneering efforts in New York, Massachusetts, and the Midwest in building the earliest mosques in the 1920s and 1930s. The mosque movement began to gain some real momentum by the middle of the century. The opening of the Islamic Center in Washington, D.C., completed in 1957, was an important signal to Muslims and non-Muslims alike that Islam was being recognized by Islamic countries abroad as a significant presence in the American context. The Center was built as a cooperative venture between U.S. Muslims and Islamic governments overseas. As the first building in America to have been professionally designed as a mosque, it has since attracted visitors and dignitaries from across the Muslim world. From its minaret, archways, and columns to its spacious and carpeted worship hall, the mosque of the Center was constructed according to the highest standards of Islamic architecture. Designed particularly to serve the diplomatic community of Washington, it has also been the locus of missionary and educational activities. Overseas governments have continued to support the Center, although decreases in oil revenues have caused a decline in financial aid for this mosque, as for many others in the United States.

Since the construction of the Washington, D.C. mosque, well over a hundred structures have been architecturally conceived and built for the specific purpose of serving as a mosque or Islamic center, and many hundreds of other buildings have been converted for mosque use. That there are now some thirty-three mosques in the Washington, D.C. area alone illustrates the enormous growth of the mosque movement in America over the last half century. Currently, over thirteen hundred institutions identify

The Islamic Center in Washington, D.C.　Courtesy Islamic Center, Washington, D.C.

themselves as mosques or Islamic centers in the United States. Almost 80 percent of these have been established since 1980. New York has the largest number of *masjids*, more than 130, with California next at nearly 120. Illinois, New Jersey, Texas, and Michigan all have large numbers of mosques, and only a few states cannot identify any structure functioning in this capacity. In terms of ethnic identification, African Americans and Indo-Pakistanis claim the most mosques, with Arabs next, although as racial-ethnic identities begin to give way to more integrated congregations, such distinctions become less meaningful.

While many of the structures designed as mosques follow a classical style of Islamic architecture, it appears that a new American style is gradually emerging, related to the particular locations of these edifices. The Massachusetts Institute of Technology's project to document the growth of mosques in the United States and Canada has prepared a traveling photography exhibit of this American phenomenon. Muslim architects have actually designed only a few of these buildings, and well-meaning efforts in some cases have resulted in structures actually not well conceived to meet the various needs of their congregations. Those wishing to design and build their own mosques can find assistance through such companies as KINOO, Inc. "The Principals, as Muslims, have direct concern and knowledge of contemporary and traditional norms important to the program, development, design, and construction of mosques and Islamic centers," KINOO assures potential customers.[2] Muslims themselves are increasingly "owning" the task of designing the mosque or community center in their self-conscious efforts to "create Muslim space" within the American continent.

Many different styles, then, characterize American mosques. Some are converted storefronts, offices, or houses, made to look at least somewhat Islamic by the removal of chairs and other furniture and the addition of Qur'anic verses on the wall and some kind of marker to indicate the direction of prayer. Others are well-financed, full-fledged mosques, constructed according to architecture appropriate to the Middle East or other parts of the Muslim world. Some emphasize racial or ethnic identity and serve as centers in which members work together for survival in a sometimes hostile American context. Others are more heterogeneous in character, not only serving as centers for prayer and social activities but also maintaining an active outreach to the surrounding community with various kinds of social services. Many work in the schools and other public contexts for education about Islamic beliefs and practices, as well as for better interfaith understanding. Some have even been likened to Christian "mega-churches," large racially and ethnically diverse institutions with a variety of educational and social services. These large mosques and Islamic centers often provide education at a range of levels for children and adults, with well-equipped classrooms and libraries, feature social and sporting facilities, and occasionally even have an Islamic grocery store, restaurant, funeral home, or offices to let for Islamic-oriented businesses. Muslims are encouraged by a variety of means to contribute to the construction of these large Islamic centers, assured that their contributions are tax deductible and vital to providing an Islamic environment for worship and education.

Among the several examples of this kind of mega-mosque, a few, such as the Islamic Center of Greater Cincinnati (ICGC), are particularly noticeable on the American landscape. The ICGC is a neighbor to the large Ohio Islamic center in Toledo, both eye-openers for those not expecting to see such visible evidence of the presence of Islam in the state. The ICGC is an interesting example of the way in which such centers are entering the American scene. It was born in the early 1960s when a small group of Muslims first gathered for prayer in Cincinnati. As the community grew, it began to press more steadily for a facility that could provide not only a worship context but a place for the education of the community. Constant efforts at planning and fund-raising finally paid off, with the assistance of some support from the Middle East, and the resulting center abounds with a range of facilities. At its heart is a lovely mosque with the capacity to accommodate more than one thousand worshipers. The larger facility includes a community center, gymnasium, school, recreational center, and house for the resident imam. Plans are under way for the construction of senior-citizen housing near the center to allow elderly members the chance to participate in center activities.

Despite the impressive nature of these large institutions, the vast majority of buildings currently being used as mosques were neither built for that purpose nor have facilities adequate for the various demands of their congregations. Most are converted houses, offices, former churches, or other buildings originally constructed for different purposes. In every instance, efforts are made to "Islam-ify" the structure as much as possible, including clearing space and adding carpets in the largest room to serve as the prayer hall, ensuring washing facilities are available for ablutions, marking the prayer direction in some visible way, decorating the walls with Arabic calligraphy, turning rooms into classrooms, adding a sign in the front of the building to indicate its present use, and perhaps putting a crescent in some visible place. Often most, if not all, of the labor in maintaining these facilities comes from the volunteer services of members of the congregation.

Masjid Al Faatir Islamic Center in Chicago, Illinois, can accommodate up to 3,000 worshipers. TED GRAY

Imams

Technically, nothing in Islam corresponds to the ordained clergy of Christianity and Judaism. Nonetheless, the forms of religious leadership through the history of Islam have been many and varied, with high degrees of specialization. As Islam in the United States has grown and developed, there has been increasing need of people to serve in leadership capacities. Normally, the person who assumes the function of leading the prayer in a mosque or Islamic gathering is known as the imam (to be distinguished from the technical term as applied to the hidden leader of the Shi'ites). It is not unusual to find today that those within and outside the American Muslim community see imams as functioning in ways that reflect, if not parallel, the clergy of other faiths.

Some mosque communities active since the earlier part the century, when they did not worry so much about the exact appropriateness of some of their activities, have found that with the arrival of new and more conservative co-religionists some of their mosques' activities and practices are being challenged. In some cases, imams who received their training in places like Cairo or Saudi Arabia have introduced changes. Oil-producing Muslim countries, eager to support the growth of Islam in areas in which it is a minority faith, have financed and sent these imams to America. Classically educated, and often the first trained leaders that longer established mosque communities have had, they may insist on more strict interpretations of mosque usage and practice than has been customary for some American Muslims. As one imam put it, "If you are talking about performing a wedding in the mosque, there is nothing in Islam which will say to you, 'no.' The Prophet used to do that in the mosque. But if you are talking about having the wedding in the form of music and dancing in the mosque, we will not allow it. Anyone who wants to do that, he can go and rent a hall outside, but it will not be accepted in the mosque."[3] Imams who come to the United States for the express purpose of serving and educating mosque communities here may find themselves challenged by the customs of already established communities; they are often also disadvantaged by a lack of facility in English, which can curtail their effective leadership.

If some imams assume their responsibilities with full Islamic training, others may be pressed into service when they are not well prepared because of the needs of the community for leadership. Particularly in less affluent communities, often African American, imams serve their congregations with only a partial knowledge of Arabic, the Qur'an, Islamic law, and Sunna. Sometimes they work in the capacity of imam without remuneration from their poor congregations and find themselves having to carry out those responsibilities while maintaining full-time employment elsewhere. In fact, only relatively few *masjids* in America actually have the services of a full-time trained imam. If a mosque community is located near a university, students from Muslim countries may serve as temporary imams or assist in teaching Arabic and the Qur'an. The need for better training facilities for imams in the United States is widely recognized, although at present the opportunities to receive such training, particularly when communities are under severe financial restraints, are extremely limited.

The few large Islamic centers that can afford the services of a full-time imam insist on a wide range of qualifications. An advertisement in a national Muslim journal, for example, suggests that an applicant for the position of imam/administrator be trained in the Qur'an, Hadith, and Islamic law, be fluent in English and Arabic, be a legal U.S. resident, have experience in dealing with family and community issues, possess excellent communication skills with people of all ages, and have good managerial and financial skills. Often, those who are most active in large mosques and Islamic centers, and who are their strongest financial supporters, are Muslim professionals who are trained in the sciences (especially medicine) and who have not had extensive religious instruction. Muslims in the United States, while grateful for the support that has come from the international Islamic community in sending trained religious leadership to American mosques, are deeply aware of the crucial necessity of developing an Islamically well educated but distinctively indigenous American religious leadership.

Those imams who do have classical Islamic training, however, often find that the expectations of their constituents differ from those in traditional Islamic societies. As *masjids* assume functions and activities that often make them seem more like American churches and synagogues than mosques, so imams are asked to carry out a range of responsibilities more characteristic of pastors and rabbis than has ever been the case for Muslim prayer leaders. The very word *imam* means "the one who stands in front of the congregation and leads the prayer." In traditional Muslim societies, other professionals perform weddings and funerals, give legal advice, provide education in matters of faith and practice, and the like. But in America imams are called upon to do all of these things and more. They must often raise funds for the maintenance of the mosque, provide pastoral care and counseling for congregants with particular needs, visit the sick and elderly, organize the community in cleaning up neighborhoods from drugs and other illicit activities, train members to teach in after-school and weekend mosque-school sessions, adjudicate when disputes over procedure arise among members, combat anti-Islamic prejudice and promote a better understanding of Islam, participate in interfaith community activities, and do many other things not part of the traditional role of imam. These expectations are often difficult to meet, not only because the imam may not be trained to do them but also because in so many cases he is working with the *masjid* in only a part-time capacity at best. In some cases new models are under experimentation, such as having a "team" of leaders to rotate through the responsibilities and take turns in actually leading the prayer.

Chaplains

A recent and growing phenomenon on the American scene is the presence of Muslims serving in a chaplaincy capacity in educational institutions, the military, and the prison system. Sometimes these people have imam status and sometimes not.

Slowly, a few universities are recognizing the need not only for Muslim student organizations on campus but also for chaplains to work with students and provide prayer leadership. Some smaller colleges, unable to fund a full-time Muslim chaplain, are looking for other ways to meet their Muslim students' needs. Mount Holyoke College, a women's institution, has appointed a Muslim woman to work on a part-time basis as religious adviser and counselor. The University of Alberta in Canada provides a model that some U.S. schools may wish to follow, having established an Islamic campus ministry with a retired professor serving as chaplain. Volunteering his services, this former immigrant works with international students as they face the emotional and personal, as well as spiritual, issues that confront them in the West. Many institutions enlist the services of Muslim professors or graduate students to work as advisers to Muslim students. Institutions from Harvard University in Massachusetts to Tuskegee University in Alabama are inviting Muslims in their respective Islamic communities to lead prayers in official university programs.

The 1990s have seen the first several Muslim chaplains in the U.S. armed forces. The number of Muslim men and women currently serving in all branches of the U.S. military is estimated to be some ten thousand and is probably rising, nearly a third of those said to have embraced Islam during the Gulf War. Although only a fairly small number are actually identified as Muslim in military records, the several branches of the military are beginning to recognize the importance of providing assistance for Muslim men and women. In addition to attending to their spiritual needs, chaplains help create appropriate contexts in which Muslims can observe their faith through practice, diet, and dress, and they work to ensure the granting of appropriate rights.

In 1993 Captain Abdul-Rasheed Muhammad became the first commissioned Islamic chaplain in the U.S. Army, for example, with the title of imam. Officially listed as chaplain to both Muslims and non-Muslims, he has the responsibility of creating ways in which people of all religious faiths can practice their religion, although his primary work is with Muslims. Serving both male and female Muslims, he has argued for the right of men to wear beards, for appropriate Islamic dress such as *hijab* and *kufi*, for allowing women to wear modified uniforms during physical training for purposes of modesty, for special areas in which prayers can be said, and for the right to perform Muslim wedding ceremonies and burial services. He is working on developing Muslim "ready-to-eat" meals comprised of *halal* meat and other items appropriate to an Islamic diet. "I think the Army bringing in an Islamic chaplain is a symbol of the increased sensitivity toward Islam," says Muhammad. "The armed forces have taken important steps to accommodate Muslim beliefs."[4]

The second Muslim to be commissioned as a member of the Military Chaplains Corps was Lieutenant (junior grade) Monje Malak Abd al-Muta Ali Noel, Jr., of the U.S. Navy, appointed three years after Muhammad. Chaplain Noel holds a master of divinity degree from the Lutheran School of Theology in Chicago, conferred jointly with the American Islamic College.

Thanks to the work of people like Muhammad and Noel, and aided by the continuing efforts of the Office of Armed Forces and Veteran Affairs of the American Muslim Council, Muslims in the armed services are allowed to observe the Friday prayer, to go to Mecca to perform *hajj*, and in general to practice their faith appropriately. During Ramadan 1998 the Pentagon hosted the first *iftar* meal for all Muslims on active duty in the armed services or employed by the Department of Defense. (Dress remains an issue in the military, however, and in 1996 a female Muslim soldier was discharged, albeit honorably, after she refused to stop wearing the head scarf.)

There is a great need for trained imams to work with the significant number of prison inmates who wish to learn more about and to practice Islam. In many cases, Catholic and Protestant chaplains find themselves called on to minister also to Muslims, and they are trying hard to educate themselves about Islam as well as to find ways in which to provide religious materials for Muslim inmates. A Roman Catholic priest working in a U.S. penitentiary in Colorado, for example, has written to Islamic journals, begging for assistance in procuring Qur'ans, videotapes, audio cassettes, pamphlets, and other study materials.

"The National Association of Muslim Chaplains is undergoing a nationwide recruitment effort of Muslim brothers and sisters who service Muslim inmates in county, state or federal correctional facilities; both paid and volunteer," says a national Muslim journal.[5] The Association, formed in 1979, argues that when greater numbers of people act as advocates for the rights and privileges of Muslim inmates, the organization can gain more leverage with correctional administrators. With member affiliates in many of the states, it provides an Islamic support system for Muslim prisoners, lobbies governmental agencies for prisoner rights, and offers Islamic education for the incarcerated.

Many local mosques and Islamic centers, including Sufi communities, are working actively with prisoners in their areas to provide support and instruction, members in some cases serving in the capacity of imams and chaplains. In a few cases, Muslim women are allowed to work in female correctional institutions, providing instruction and counseling to female Muslim inmates and helping them find Islamic solutions to the chronic problems of abuse, drug addiction, prostitution, and poverty that may have contributed to their incarceration.

First Muslim Navy Chaplain Monje Malak Abd al-Muta Ali Noel, Jr.
GEOFF LUMETTA/THE WASHINGTON REPORT ON MIDDLE EAST AFFAIRS

Spreading the Faith (*Da'wa*)

Muslims in America feel a particular responsibility for the exercise of *da'wa*, which as we have seen means, literally, "calling" (to God, to faith, to Islam). It has been likened to the missionary efforts of Christianity and some other religions, although it has distinctive meanings within the Islamic context. For some, *da'wa* means the active business of the propagation of Islam with the end of making conversions, and a number of immigrant groups work regularly in the United States to disseminate the faith. For others, *da'wa* involves the effort to bring those who have fallen away from Islam back to active involvement in the faith. That may involve encouraging Muslims who are not observant or who participate only in the major holidays to pray regularly, attend the mosque, and pay *zakat*. And for still others, *da'wa* means the responsibility simply to live quiet lives of Muslim piety and charity, with the hope that by example they can encourage wayward coreligionists as well as others that Islam is the right and appropriate response to God. Often they cite Qur'an 2:256, "There is no compulsion in religion," in support of their unwillingness to press for the conversion of others. Many different arenas can support any of these interpretations of *da'wa*, including mosques and Islamic centers themselves, prisons, interfaith activities, schools, and universities.

As Muslims become more self-conscious about the establishment and promotion of Islam in America, increasing numbers of books and journal articles are appearing on the subject of *da'wa*. Muslims who work actively for the propagation of Islam, and who speak openly about the possibility of the United States becoming a Muslim country in the foreseeable future, tend to be those most opposed to anything more than the most minimal assimilation of Muslims into American society. Many of the immigrants who would have been less proactive about Islam in their home country find themselves seriously involved in the identification and propagation of the faith in the West. "We have the primary task of Islamizing America. We have to carefully select our priorities, set achievable targets, and concentrate. . . . We have Allah's message, and a 250 million person-large target group."[6] Da'wa becomes part of the effort to make Islam better understood, to lobby for political and other kinds of rights for Muslims, and to offer the Islamic lifestyle as a viable alternative to the perceived perils of American secular life.

Many of those who are classified as actively pursuing da'wa are influenced by the writings of such twentieth-century Muslim leaders as Abu'l-A'la al-Mawdudi of Pakistan and Sayyid Qutb of Egypt. They argue that the more Muslims there are in America, the more opportunities they will have to express their voice in public life, and the better chance Muslims in general will have to combat American prejudice against Islam. As with the spread of Islam over much of the world, Muslims involved in active propagation in America stress its rationality, the simplicity of its beliefs and requirements, its ethical content and emphasis on responsible living in this world, and its ideals of racial harmony and human brotherhood.

The propagation of Islam in America has ranked high on the agenda of a number of other Muslim countries. The Tableeghi Jamaat (Tablighi Jama'at) regularly sends itinerant missionaries to the United States and Canada to preach and practice da'wa through meetings and lectures, using local mosques as the base for their activities. The Jamaat is a movement of spiritual renewal that began in India in the early part of the century, attempting to imitate the practice of the Prophet's community in Medina. They began their missionary work in the United States in 1952 and since then have preached spiritual revival and social isolation, directed both to wayward Muslims and to those whom they hope to convert. Urging Muslims in America to avoid any unnecessary contact with people who do not share their beliefs, they preach resistance to Western culture whenever possible and strongly oppose Muslim involvement in any kind of political activity save the propagation of the faith. A small number of mosques are directly affiliated with the Tableeghi Jamaat, although their influence extends considerably further. Tableeghi members are sophisticated in the use of new media techniques. Starting in 1980, they have held periodic annual gatherings, the one in Chicago in 1988 believed to be the largest gathering of Muslims ever held in America, with attendance near six thousand.

That some revivalist Muslim groups abroad have targeted American Muslims as the recipients of financial assistance has greatly aided the *da'wa* effort. The Salafiyya movement, supported by the Dar al-Iftar in Saudi Arabia, ideologically resembles the Tableeghi Jamaat but differs in its insistence on returning as much as possible to traditional society. Salafis are also non-political, though as conservative Sunnis they take an active stance in attempting to denounce Shi'i movements in this country and abroad. After the Iranian Revolution, tensions appeared in the Muslim Student Association over the question of Sunni vs. Shi'i identity. When an MSA Persian-Speaking Group emerged to offer support for Shi'i students, Saudi Arabia provided financing for students in an effort to "inoculate" them against the influence of Imam Khomeini. Many consider the resulting tensions to have encouraged a division between Sunnis and Shi'is in America that has not yet been fully healed. American Shi'is themselves, as has been noted, receive a great deal of attention through such institutions as the Kho'i Foundation, formerly under the leadership of Imam Kho'i from Najaf in Iraq. Such efforts, of course, illustrate not only the range of foreign-supported *da'wa* activities in America but also the tensions, being played out in the West, reflecting traditional splits and hostilities in Islam as it has developed historically and geographically.

As *da'wa* efforts continue in America, the results are noticeable. Growing numbers of African Americans, especially men, are proclaiming themselves Muslim. Other American converts are a small but growing group making a significant contribution to the Muslim community. The experience of a kind of "moment of conversion" is less evident for those becoming Muslim in America than it often is for people who find themselves "called" to Christianity. Many converts to Islam, whatever their racial-ethnic background, choose to refer to the process as "reversion" rather than "conversion." Those who choose to adopt Islam tend to view their change of religion as a gradual realization of their true faith and identity. This understanding reflects a strong movement in international Islamic apologetic that affirms the essential and basic nature of each human being as Muslim. Qur'an 7:172 says that while we were all nascent in the loins of Adam, God appeared to us and said, "Am I not your Lord?" And in that primordial time we all answered, "Yes, we do testify." That, Muslims affirm, is proof that all people are really submitters (*muslim*, at least, in their personal response to God), and if they believe otherwise it is because they have been so educated by their parents and families. The basic human submission to the oneness and lordship of God, they say, has characterized pious people since Adam. Thus, to decide to adopt Islam is not simply to change from one religion to another but to go back, to revert, to the basic. For African Americans, the term *revert* has the added meaning of going back to the faith of their ancestors, who may have been among the Muslims brought to this country in the slave trade.

Part of the *da'wa* effort in American Islam, including providing advice and counsel to those who have newly adopted the faith, is made by those who are themselves new members and understand the pressures that may come from family, the workplace, and the culture in general. That it is not easy to be Muslim in the West and sometimes less easy for the convert can temper the joy and enthusiasm of a new faith and identity. How long do you have to have given your *shahada*, some ask, before you are considered by others to be a "real" Muslim? Is it necessary to adopt a Muslim name, or can one simply choose to be called by the name on his or her birth certificate and still be considered the genuine article? (African Americans tend to be more insistent on taking a new Muslim name than Anglo converts. Some choose to combine their Muslim and Anglo names so that one could be Robert Mustafa Field, for example, or Naima Lois Marshall.) Why is it that those new to Islam often seem more concerned about understanding and following the letter of the law than those raised in Muslim countries? And why is it that African American converts sometimes find themselves treated by their immigrant brothers and sisters as somehow less "authentic" than they, even though the converts may know just as much about the Qur'an and Sunna?

The *da'wa* efforts of a number of Muslim organizations have resulted in the visibility of Islam in public places in new ways. In January 1996, Denver's new international airport became the first in America to feature a mosque. The space designated for Muslim worship is on the sixth-floor mezzanine looking out onto the main terminal, adjacent to a combined Christian and Jewish chapel. At first, discussion was held about a common worship space for all three religions, but the Muslims chose for both practical (no chairs or pews occupy a Muslim prayer hall) and religious (many Muslims would not avail themselves of a worship space that had Christian or Jewish symbols) reasons to keep the mosque separate, with its own entrance. Private donations financed half of the whole worship complex, the other half coming from the airlines servicing the airport. The international airport in Columbus, Ohio is in the process of planning an Interfaith Meditation Room that will include a separate prayer area for Muslims. John F. Kennedy International Airport in New York, along with a number of other public buildings in the city, features the Muslim crescent and star on one of its outdoor flagpoles. Such efforts intend not only to provide services for American

Muslims and those traveling from abroad but also to raise the visibility of Islam in America—one more tool in the effort to foster the faith and its better understanding.

One of the richest fields for the propagation of *da 'wa*, particularly but not exclusively among African Americans, is the prison system. In some senses, Malcolm Little's experience of finding Islam while he was incarcerated, and the way it truly changed his life, has been repeated in less dramatic ways in the lives of many hundreds of people over the last half century. Certainly, Malcolm's story is well known and influential among young blacks who hope to find in Islam a way to make serious changes in their lives. Their struggle to practice Islam while in prison has a number of interesting dimensions. On the one hand, the fight to achieve the freedom to express their faith appropriately, paralleling the struggle of members of the armed forces in terms of dress, space, diet, and opportunity, has been hard fought and is still not fully achieved. On the other, prison guards and other personnel, aware that Muslims who observe the discipline of the faith and stand by its moral code are less likely to "cause trouble" than other inmates, have often tried to support and encourage rather than obstruct their practice of Islam.

Islamic worship area of the interfaith chapel at Denver International Airport.
COURTESY DENVER INTERNATIONAL AIRPORT

While exact figures again are hard to determine, it is estimated that more than three hundred thousand prisoners are converts to Islam and that the rate of conversion may be more than thirty thousand each year. A higher proportion of ethnic minorities is represented in the American prison system than in the population as a whole, including Hispanics and Native Americans as well as blacks. Studies indicate that the rate of recidivism, the return to crime and imprisonment, is lower among Muslims than other groups, although certainly the adoption of Islam is not a firm guarantee that incarceration is a thing of the past. Muslims have also demonstrated relatively greater success in rehabilitation from drug and alcohol addiction. Given the significant numbers of Muslims converting in prison, those who do reintegrate into society form a growing segment of the population of American Muslims. While programs designed for the support of newly released Muslim converts are still not generally available, the American Muslim community shows growing awareness of the needs of these ex-convicts and is developing initiatives to continue their education in Islam and to help integrate them into the community.

When a prisoner accepts Islam, he or she recites the *shahada*, or profession of faith, before witnesses in whatever facility of the prison is set aside for Islamic practice. In some cases, the appeal of a new identity is so strong that inmates wish to "take their *shahada*" well before they have a clear idea of what they are really professing. Part of the instructional effort in the prisons is to make sure that inmates receive an adequate introduction to Islam before they decide whether they wish to convert. Once the *shahada* is made, a number of things combine to assure a new identity. Generally, one adopts an Islamic name and begins to wear whatever form of dress is allowed in a given facility. Acceptance into the community of those prisoners who are already Muslim is immediate, and the participation in communal prayers and other Islamic activities helps solidify the new convert's sense of identity and belonging. In some larger facilities, rows of Muslims can be seen praying together in exercise yards or in special rooms segregated from the rest of the prison complex. Often, the Muslim's cell reflects his or her acceptance of the faith by its neat appearance, absence of pornographic pictures, and perhaps the addition of some Islamic symbolism. Personal modesty and cleanliness become of primary importance, as does one's general appearance, with all efforts made to demonstrate that one has entered the community of Islam. Many choose to give up smoking and use particular toiletries, such as aromatic oils, to enhance the image of Muslims as different from other inmates. Rigorous programs of

study and prayer are designed to divert attention from any sexual temptations. Such disciplines are particularly important in maximum-security facilities to help maintain a sense of pride, worth, and belonging.

Both the numerous people working as chaplains, missionaries, and
teachers from the Muslim community outside the prison and those inmates
who have accepted Islam and share with fellow inmates their enthusiasm for
their new faith and discipline are carrying out the *da'wa* effort. As the influence of Imam Warith Deen grows and considerably more African American Muslims accept Sunni Islam over the teachings of the Nation of Islam,
there will inevitably be more emphasis on teaching and learning the basics
of the faith. The growing numbers of trained imams and Muslim leaders
active in the prisons, working with Christian and Jewish clergy to ensure
equal opportunities for observance, encourage such study. The Islamic Society of North America (ISNA) sponsors a national conference on the subject
of Islam in American prisons, bringing together people who have been
involved in *da'wa* and assistance to the incarcerated. Presentations at the
conference help workers introduce the message of Islam, lobby for
improved opportunities to practice the faith, and develop techniques for
rehabilitation, post-prison support, and finding jobs on release.

Still, some inmates feel that the Islamic community at large is not doing
enough to help address the plight of Muslims in prison. "I, like Malcolm X
. . . and a vast host of former political/religious prisoners, am emotionally
dismayed and disheartened by . . . the non-supportive attitudes in regards to
how Muslims think about incarcerated Muslims. . . . I hope that the Ummah
is not deaf, dumb, and blind to the fact that the catch phrases, like 'we should
be tough on crime,' and 'we need more prison and harsher sentences,' are
actually covert calls to lock-up as many non-European people as possible
and in turn limit minority people from becoming the majority power-hold-
ers in this country," writes an inmate from South Carolina.[7]

Nonetheless, significant efforts are being made, particularly among
young Muslim converts in prison. The Junior Association of Muslim Men
(JAMM), for example, was established at Sing Sing prison in 1994 under the
leadership of Imam Warith Deen Mohammed. The first program of its kind,
JAMM is designed to create a sense of responsibility in young Muslims,
training them in the elements of Islam and providing tools for their reentry
into society. Inmates under the age of thirty-five are targeted, along with
others possibly interested in adopting Islam. The message is that Islam provides the structure through which they can transform their lives, and they
can become leaders in society upon their release. JAMM, which forms a sig-

nificant bridge between prison and community life, hopes to extend its activities to other penal institutions.

These opportunities are certainly growing all the time, although the struggle for the recognition of Islam as a religion deserving constitutional protection has not been easy. For several decades, virtually the only Muslims in prison belonged to the Nation, considered by the state to be a dangerous racist cult. Since the 1960s the attempt simply to contain and manage Muslims in the prisons has gradually changed to a recognition of religious liberty and a Muslim's right as an American citizen to practice the faith. Issues have been resolved primarily as a result of Muslim prison inmates' bringing these issues to court. Slowly, the courts have come to acknowledge that Islam is a faith deserving of the same constitutional safeguards as Christianity and Judaism. Muslims have fought for, and in many cases won, the right to have *halal* food, to wear beards, to gather for Friday prayer, and to observe the fast of Ramadan with *iftar* meals at the end of the day.

Many times courts have had to try cases in which Muslim prisoners have charged authorities with First Amendment violations of discrimination and even religious persecution, and in general the decisions have supported these charges. In a few penal institutions the creation of what has been called "Islamic space" allows Muslim prisoners to feel that their religion actually allows them to exist separately defined from their fellow inmates and in some senses from the institution in which they are incarcerated. In addition to having access to facilities for performing *salat* and being allowed to observe other of the basic elements of Islam such as food and dress, some are now studying the Qur'an and Arabic as well as the elements of Islamic finance in preparation for eventual financial autonomy. Many continue to argue that Muslim converts in the prison system still do not receive religious rights equal to those accorded to Christians and Jews. That there has been great progress over the last several decades, however, is certainly acknowledged.

Islamic Organizations

Behind many of the efforts to facilitate life for Muslims living in America are the numerous organizations developed for the guidance and support of the community. The earliest movements toward such organization began in the middle of the century with the attempt to bring together for a national conference the small but growing number of mosques begun in various parts of the country. In 1952 in Cedar Rapids, Iowa, some four hundred Muslims representing the United States and Canada gathered with the intent to form a national organization. The idea for such a union came to one Abdullah Igram, a Muslim serving in the American army during the World War II. He was frustrated that the armed services did not recognize his identity as a Muslim, and no such notice could be made on his dog tag. After returning home, he began to work for the recognition of Muslims in America. After a second and third meeting, the Federation of Islamic Organizations was formed, with Igram as its president and fifty-two mosques as members, mainly Lebanese and Syrian. Later, under the expanded name Federation of Islamic Associations in the United States and Canada, and assisted by funding from Saudi Arabia, the organization moved its headquarters to Detroit, where it still continues to function. The FIA played a key role in providing an umbrella of unity for American mosques in the middle of the century and was the first attempt to provide for conversation and collaboration among Muslims in the United States. After a series of national meetings, however, it gave way as the major American Islamic organization to other groups, among which the most influential was the Muslim Student Association (MSA).

The family of Abdullah Igram, founder of The Federation of Islamic Organizations, at prayer.
COURTESY BETTY IGRAM

While the FIA had tended to emphasize ethnic identities among immi-grant Muslims, the MSA was formed to strengthen national and internation-al ties among Muslims of all national origins and ethnicities. Following the ideology of the Muslim Brotherhood of Egypt and the Jamaati Islami of the Indian subcontinent, the group was created to provide a structure through which the Muslim student associations that had begun to appear on a num-ber of American campuses could relate to one another. It soon developed into an agency with enormous influence in helping redefine Islamic identity in America as something beyond national, ethnic, and linguistic allegiances. The first national conference, held at the University of Illinois in 1963, was attended by students from countries all over the Islamic world. These stu-dents brought with them not only their hopes for an American *umma*, in which national identities would be subsumed under the banner of Islam, but also the residue of their experiences in countries that had been in political and religious turmoil for much of the twentieth century. Most of the stu-dents in America planned to return to their home countries as educated, informed, and influential participants in the process of furthering interna-tional Islam. An elaborate organizational structure was soon developed, with local chapters of the MSA established across the country, connected both nationally and regionally. Each year an annual convention was held, activities multiplied, and the influence of the association extended. Finally, in 1975 a national headquarters was set up in Plainfield, Indiana, with a gen-eral secretary and a significant support staff.

Under the general structure of the MSA, a number of subsidiary orga-nizations have been established. The North American Islamic Trust (NAIT) handles financial matters including investments, loans, mutual funds, book services, and the like. The Islamic Teaching Center (ICS) deals with mat-ters related to the education of American Muslims through the development of publications and promotional literature, materials for *da'wa*, and other means of spreading information about the faith and practice of Islam. A series of groups emerged under the aegis of the MSA, focusing on the pro-fessional expertise of those who have graduated and stay on to become employed in the United States. Among these are the Islamic Medical Asso-ciation (IMA), which holds annual conferences to discuss different aspects of medicine and health; the American Muslim Social Scientists (AMSS), dedicated to connecting social science research and Islamic tradition through its publication *The American Journal of Islamic Social Sciences;* the Associa-tion of Muslim Businessmen and Professionals (AMBP), whose purpose is to provide links for Muslims in business and commerce; and the Association of American Muslim Scientists and Engineers (AMSE). As the MSA grew and time passed, it was obviously no longer simply a vehicle for uniting student groups and working on college campuses but had become the strongest Islamic structure in North America.

By 1981, after much consultation, a plan was put forward to establish an organization that would reflect the range of activities and interests of American Muslims that the MSA, originally designed to meet the needs of students, actually carried out. That organization has been known ever since as the Islamic Society of North America (ISNA). ISNA, in effect, has become the overseeing body for a great number of emerging Islamic organizations. These include local organizations devoted to community work in specific locations, campus student groups (still referred to as MSA, one of the largest and best connected of the Islamic groupings), organizations designed to foster the activities of Muslim professionals, and those devoted to the service of the Muslim community in America and abroad (such as the Muslim Community Association) and to the youth (Muslim Youth of North America [MYNA]). The overall organization is complex and expansive, with constituent groups functioning with their own boards and committees but responsible overall to ISNA and its executive council, called the Majlis al-Shura. ISNA sponsors national weekend conferences each year, which draw large numbers of Muslims from the United States to hear speakers and to debate issues of ethical, social, and religious interest. Those who attend share common prayer and worship, meet and mix with Muslims from their home countries as well as other parts of the world, and experience a strong and reassuring sense of the strength and power of the Muslim community in America. Many youth participate in these national meetings and have an opportunity to talk with one another and with Muslim leaders about how to grow up with Islamic values intact. MSA itself also holds annual conferences for students across America.

ISNA activities range widely and attend to virtually every aspect of Islam in twentieth-century America. Instruction and sometimes financial assistance are provided to local groups wishing to organize around particular issues of Islamic interest, and its national services include a great repertoire of instructional materials, workshops, library facilities, housing assistance, a marriage bureau operating a computerized database for matching partners, certificates for marriage and for taking the *shahada*, a *zakat* fund, *da'wa* literature, an Islamic book service and audiovisual center, the AMANA Mutual Trust Fund, and the ISNA women's committee. Among the journals ISNA publishes are *Islamic Horizons*, *American Journal of Islamic Studies*, and *Al-Ittihad*.

While ISNA is designed as an organization of all American Muslims, and while it is clearly more universal in scope than the FIA, some African Americans still perceive it as devoted primarily to the needs of members of the immigrant community. Although Imam Warith Deen Mohammad serves on the ISNA Shura Council, his followers in the Muslim American Society tend not to go to annual ISNA conferences but to hold their own national meetings to address topics of particular interest to African American Muslims. In some cases, blacks even feel that they are unwelcome and unappreciated by those involved in ISNA, although the clear movement of most African Americans to identify with Sunni Islam will, many believe, serve to ameliorate that problem.

Another national organization of Muslims, which has been present on the American scene for more than two decades but claims considerably fewer affiliates than ISNA, is the Islamic Circle of North America. ICNA is known for its strict adherence to the spirit and the law of Islam, exemplified in its national meetings at which separate sessions are arranged for women. Most of ICNA's members are from the East Coast and Canada. While there are occasional tensions between ICNA and ISNA, increased efforts are being made to build bridges between the organizations. Representatives of each group generally attend the meetings and conferences of the other, and efforts are made to see that their respective conventions, workshops, and seminars are not scheduled in conflict. ICNA focuses less on pressing social and political concerns than ISNA and more on the spiritual regeneration of American Muslims and the direction of youth to righteous living. Its primary publication is the monthly journal *The Message*.

An organization formed in 1993 specifically for the pursuit of *da'wa* in the United States is the Islamic Assembly of North America (IANA). Its stated goal is to gather all energies and potential resources, human and financial, to revive Islam and meet the needs of Muslims.

National Muslim women's organizations are growing up rapidly in America. KARAMA, the Muslim Women Lawyer's Committee for Human Rights, devotes itself to helping Muslim women understand and work for their legal rights. The North American Council for Muslim Women, headquartered in northern Virginia, and the Toronto-based Canadian Council of Muslim Women work to promote the welfare of American Muslim women. They host annual conferences on issues such as violence against women, law and policies applicable to women, youth concerns, and the like. Various other associations bring Islamic education to the women of the community.

In addition, women are becoming connected on an international scale through such groups as IMAN, the International Muslimah Artists Network, created by and for Muslim women artists, and the World Council of Muslim Women Foundation, a nonprofit organization whose goals are the teaching of women's rights, global peace, and interfaith education from a worldwide perspective. American Muslim women are also active in women's groups not specifically geared toward Islam, such as the Sisterhood Is Global Institute in Bethesda, Maryland.

A great many organizations function at the national level to bring together special groups and to promote particular causes related to Muslim life in America. The recently formed North American Association of Muslim Professionals and Scholars (NAAMPS) is designed to attract Muslim intellectuals and scholars from different ethnic and cultural groups interested in discussing the challenge of Muslim community life in America. Some organizations are geared to particular ethnic and professional identities, such as the Association of Pakistani Physicians in North America (APPNA), offering its members opportunities to develop their organizational skills within an Islamic ethos. APPNA works to sponsor grassroots activities, such as free clinics for local communities, to emphasize that Islam teaches love and care for neighbors.

Sometimes aided by and sometimes independent of these national organizations, Muslims are forming groups at all local and regional levels. Islamic councils in many areas of the United States serve as organizing units for centers and mosques. In many cases, a membership fee for local congregations provides a budget for annual meetings and services such as financial assistance, family counseling, and support of international Muslim causes. Also developing at the local and regional levels are numbers of shura councils (consultative bodies). The Islamic Shura Council of New York, for example, evolved from a small study group of Muslim city leaders. Members of the Council now meet monthly to work for the promotion of Islam, better prison conditions for Muslim inmates, drug control, and other forms of community service. Warith Deen Mohammed has recently reactivated the Illinois Shuraa of Imams into a newly formed Illinois Shuraa to support the imams' ministry in the state. It supervises the work of a number of subcommittees headed by male and female Muslim leaders and works for the establishment of schools and mosques throughout the state.

Increasing numbers of organizations at both the national and local levels concentrate specifically on the political arena. The American Muslim Council (AMC) in Washington, D.C. is a nonprofit, sociopolitical organization established in 1990 that works to promote ethical values among Muslims and to educate voters about the electoral process. Interested in developing increased political power for Muslims, it holds national conventions on such topics as "Muslim America: Becoming a Political Reality." The AMC regularly puts on registration drives in coordination with local Muslim groups. First Lady Hillary Rodham Clinton now regularly invites the AMC to host an *'eid al-fitr* celebration at the White House. The AMC is campaigning for official recognition of the two Islamic *'eids* as national holidays and hopes that the U.S. Postal Service will issue *'eid* stamps by the year 2000. The Muslim Public Affairs Council (MPAC) is a bipartisan organization that also concentrates on voter education, helping Muslims understand the issues and how to make political decisions within the context of Islam. The MPAC is present at both political party conventions.

Combating Anti-Muslim Prejudice

One of the primary tasks of many of the Muslim organizations mentioned above is to identify ways in which prejudice against Islam and Muslims continues to be present on the American scene. As we have noted, consistent efforts attempt to ensure that information about Islam in textbooks and other curricular materials in the public schools is accurate and unbiased. Some organizations work to identify ways in which the public media regularly distort and misrepresent information about Islam in America as well as on the international scene and to call to public attention instances in which U.S. and Canadian Muslims experience prejudicial or unfair treatment in the workplace or other public arenas. The American Muslim community is deeply concerned that anti-Islamic feelings on the part of the general public are growing rather than abating, exacerbated by international incidents of violence carried out in the name of Islam and abetted by the unfortunate portrayal of Muslims and Islam in the media. The most uninformed readers have no difficulty identifying the Muslim portrayed in cartoon form. He is the one with squinty eyes, huge nose, and *kafiyya* (Arab headdress) rubbing his hands and asking where he can get a pickup truck and some TNT. Or standing with a sign saying, "Death to all Infidels" next to a pastor whose sign reads "Pray for Peace." Or pointing to a chart that targets nursery schools, nursing homes, and maternity wards and asking whether there are other nominations before the vote on which to bomb first.[8] Some Muslim and non-Muslim observers now label the systematic distortion of Islam as

"Islamophobia," a fear of everything Islamic. This is encouraged, many feel, when certain elements of the American government identify Islam as the "new enemy," replacing the old demon of Communism on the world scene, a kind of sinister threat to representative democracy.

Muslims are particularly concerned about the potential for even greater misinformation and propagation of prejudice with the rapid development of Internet use. Increasingly, school children and teenagers can access the "net" for school reports and other projects, and much of what they find is propaganda fostering a negative image of Islam. The threat of Islam is real, warns a book available on the Internet, more than Communism was, because Muslims are willing to die for the cause of Islam, spreading their faith through "jihad," or holy war. We must work to stop the spread of Islam before it is too late, warns the author. Those concerned with the easy dissemination of such materials note that Islam is the only monotheistic religion that has become the object of such insults and false accusations. Other anti-Muslim prejudice can be found expressed more informally, but not less effectively, if one accesses Internet chat rooms.

One of the organizations specifically dedicated to identifying and combating anti-Muslim prejudice in the United States and Canada is the Council on American-Islamic Relations (CAIR) in Washington, D.C. Its American-

A 1998 newspaper cartoon associating Islam with violence. Bruce Beattie/Copley News Service

Muslim Research Center (ARC) documents incidents and events that affect Muslim civil rights in America, such as the harassment and violence following the 1995 Oklahoma City bombing, for which Muslims were immediately (and incorrectly) targeted as responsible. ARC, recognizing that most Americans are woefully ignorant and misinformed about Islam, encourages local Muslim communities to reach out and educate other segments of American society through the dissemination of accurate information. CAIR regularly publicizes, on the Internet, incidents in which Muslims in the United States have received unfair or prejudicial treatment. (Anyone may request to join CAIR-NET, its read-only mailing list.) Descriptions of these incidents are often followed by specific information as to where readers may write or be in contact with an appropriate party to influence positive resolution of an issue. Here are some of the kinds of concerns that CAIR shares with its readers:

A cartoon in a Canadian newspaper featured a snarling dog wearing an Arab headdress, clearly identified as emblematic of Islamic extremism and linked specifically to the killing of tourists in Egypt. The cartoon's subheading read, "with our apologies to dogs everywhere." CAIR contacted the newspaper, expressing its deep concern and a request for some kind of retraction, after which an apology was proffered.

A worker was fired from her job at a national doughnut chain store for refusing to remove her head-scarf on the grounds that it was a religious requirement. After CAIR's intervention, she was reinstated and allowed to wear a head covering consistent with health and safety requirements.

After another incident in which a Muslim employee allegedly was kicked while he was at prayer in the workplace, at CAIR's urging the company initiated a thorough investigation that resulted in a formal apology and the institution of sensitivity training for supervisors.

A teacher in a high school in the South, having made bigoted remarks to a fourteen-year-old female student about her Islamic dress, after CAIR's intervention made a formal apology to the student. The school, as a result, agreed to facilitate a discussion about Islam and the need to respect others' beliefs, to provide sensitivity training about Islam, and to assign a room to be used by Muslim students during Ramadan.

CAIR deeply appreciated the response of President Clinton to the vandalism committed on the Muslim symbol, which was displayed for the first time in 1997, along with the national Christmas tree and the Jewish menorah, on the White House ellipse. The star had been removed and replaced with a swastika.

In 1995, inspired by the response to the Oklahoma City bombing, CAIR issued a special report on anti-Muslim stereotyping, harassment, and hate crimes titled "A Rush to Judgment." This has been followed by other reports on the status of Muslim civil rights in the United States, including "The Price of Ignorance" (1996) and "Unveiling Prejudice" (1997). These lengthy reports both chronicle the sad progression of incidents revealing Muslims' constant difficulties in America and provide hope for Muslims, who see the increasingly organized and effective efforts of such groups as CAIR in working to address their concerns. A number of non-Muslim scholars and advocates for Islam work with CAIR, whose activities are closely coordinated with the work of other organizations such as ISNA and ICNA.

Not all Muslims living in the United States, of course, are concerned with efforts such as those outlined here to protect and foster Islam, nor do all participate in the various forms of Muslim religious life increasingly evident in communities across America. Yet for a growing number of those who consciously identify with Islam and want to live in ways that support their understanding of the faith and its requirements, structures are increasingly being put in place. Prejudice against their religion is a reality with which all American Muslims must deal in one way or another, but both Muslim and non-Muslim individuals and organizations are stepping up efforts to identify and address incidents of misrepresentation and unfair treatment. Local and national groups provide instruction and support, and information is available in a variety of forms to help Muslims address virtually any concerns. In the meantime, Muslims are finding increasing support in many segments of American society for their efforts to present Islam fairly and reasonably. With the help of colleagues in education, other religious organizations, and even some quarters of the political establishment, they may come to find that combating anti-Muslim prejudice and offering a picture of a reasonable religious community working for the betterment of American society will become easier to accomplish.

CHAPTER EIGHT

Looking to the Future

"The impact of Islam on the future of the American society will depend, to a great extent, on how relevant Islamic principles are to this society. Islamic ideas and ideals need to be articulated in a language that is understood by the masses, and carried out by institutions that can effectively deal with issues that are relevant to the people. Our goal is to reach the minds and hearts of those who aspire for a better future."[1]

So says Dr. Maher Hathout of the Islamic Center of Southern California, one of the prominent spokespersons for contemporary American Islam, in an article identifying areas that he feels must be on the agenda for discussion in the coming years. Key here is the term "relevant." As we have seen, a great range of interpretations of Islam characterizes its faith and practice in the United States. It is clear that there is no overriding understanding to which all those who call themselves Muslim will be able to subscribe. But each group must continue to ask itself if its own interpretation of Islam, and the corresponding implications for how its members choose to live and comport themselves, is indeed relevant in contemporary American society. Will the youth of their community continue to find it relevant? Those who up to now have tried to lead lives of relative isolation, fearful that too much contact with America will compromise their own faith and culture, may have to question whether generations to come will find it necessary to be more open, more receptive to the culture of which they find themselves a part. Those who have opted for complete identification with America, abandoning many of the elements of Muslim observance, may find that they have lost some of the clarity and distinctiveness of what it means to be Muslim.

While the discussion sometimes seems to polarize participants into "iso-lationists" on the one hand and "accommodationists" on the other, Muslims try to resist this kind of terminology. Neither isolation nor absorption is generally seen as a goal in the conversations among Muslims who are search-ing for guidelines and principles that can speak to the majority of the mem-bers of the complex body that is American Islam. While agreement on all matters is naturally not to be expected, there are growing efforts to identify matters on which there can be consensus. A major task for Muslims, many believe, is to clarify what matters are flexible and may be reinterpreted in the Western context and what issues are so clearly part of God's design for human life and response that they cannot be negotiated. "A difference must be made between the permanent (divine) and the changeable," says Fathi Osman, noted Muslim spokesperson and author of a large compendium on the Qur'an. "The two are not interchangeable."[2]

Few would disagree. The problem comes in discerning what falls into each category. When is it advisable, for example, to follow classical interpre-tations of Sunna and *shari'a* while living in the United States, and when must adjustments and accommodations be made? Which elements of law and cus-tom are mandatory for all faithful Muslims, no matter where they live, and which allow for more flexible interpretation? Muslims in all American com-munities are asking these questions with interest and concern, and advisers representing a range of perspectives, cultures, and interpretations are attempting to provide answers. Traditionally, Muslims have seen the world as divided into two realms. One is the *dar al-harb*, literally, the "abode of war," which is applied to territories in which Islam is not dominant. The other is the *dar al-Islam*, the realm in which Muslims as the majority are free to follow Islamic law. Sometimes the terminology *dar al-kufr*, or "abode of apostasy," is substituted for the former. For some Muslims, these categories are still applicable, and as members of a religious minority they feel conflict and tension with American culture. If one sees America as basically an alien context in which participation in society is to be avoided whenever possible, more "conservative" responses to basic questions will prevail. "Some indi-viduals affirm that were it not for the 'decadent' and generally *kuffar* [unbe-lieving, even apostate] culture of the 'West,' Muslim communities would not suffer from the problems of homelessness, allegations of child abuse, domes-tic violence, substance abuse, and foster care."[3] Those who choose to believe that America can be a land of Islam, even if Muslims do not constitute a majority, tend to be more flexible in their interpretation of the solutions to various problems faced by Muslims in America. Some writers compare the emigration of Muslims to the United States, for example, with the *hijra*, or migration, of Prophet Muhammad from Mecca to Medina. As he was able to establish the community of Islam in that initially alien environment, they say, so Muslims must work toward such a goal in America.

Many Muslims living in the United States, both the more recently arrived and members of second- and third-generation Muslim families, do want to assimilate as much as possible into American culture and try not to emphasize elements of their identity that would differentiate them from others. This disinclination to over-identify with Islam has characterized a significant number of American Muslims since the early days of immigrant arrival, fostered, as we have seen, by such factors as the search for employment, intermarriage, dissatisfaction with mosque leadership, and various forms of engagement with American culture. For some, the increase in anti-Muslim prejudice in light of terrorist activities, pro-Israeli sentiment, anti-American rhetoric from many Arab Muslim leaders, and a number of other highly publicized international realities in the last several decades has encouraged this assimilation.

For other members of America's Muslim community, however, these very factors, including the rise in revivalist Islam in many parts of the world, have reinvigorated their religious awareness and responsibility. Encouraged by the challenge that Islam poses internationally to Western secularism and worried about the influences of that very secularism on their own children in America, they have increasingly looked to and advocated Islam as both a faith and way of life. Certainly, many first-, second-, and third-generation Muslims do not want to identify themselves too openly in American society for fear of becoming, or having their children become, targets of prejudice and discrimination. Many others, however, are tired of what they see as the biased and unfair representations of Islam and Muslims in the American media and take the opportunity to correct those images by providing in their own lives public examples of what "real Islam" looks like when practiced by conscientious and faithful adherents. For these Muslims—including immigrants, African Americans, and others who have converted to Islam—it is crucial to find ways in which to live and express their faith and their Islamic identity at the same time that they acknowledge the necessity of adapting to and participating in American life. They are working out many different modes of participation, and American Islam is now at what many would consider a crucial stage as Muslims attempt to move toward a viable future in the American context.

What, then, are some of the most crucial issues on the public agenda for

Muslims in America? A survey of the current literature, review of the agendas of current national and regional meetings and conferences, and conversations with those who are assuming leadership positions in various quarters of the Muslim community suggest that a number of concerns are being identified as areas to which attention must be given. Among them we note the following, recognizing that they are neither exhaustive nor mutually exclusive, and that to some extent all reflect a common body of concerns.

Authority

In a community in diaspora—which American Islam most certainly is—who has the right to be the authoritative interpreter of the "good" or the "true" Islamic way of life? For African Americans the issue has a number of dimensions. Those who were once members of the Nation of Islam and lived through the death of their beloved Messenger, the Honorable Elijah Muhammad, have had to decide whether to follow the leadership of Louis Farrakhan and the reconstituted Nation of Islam or trust the bold initiatives of Warith Deen Mohammed and his new understanding of what it means to be black and Muslim. Many other African American leaders have emerged over the last several decades, Sunni and sectarian, claiming authority over their followers and seeking to enhance the membership of their groups. The other side of the authority issue for many African Americans is the extent to which they, most as relative newcomers to the religion of Islam, need to heed the claimed authority of immigrants coming from countries with many centuries of Islamic tradition. "What right does a Pakistani or a Saudi have to tell me how to practice my Islam?" says an African American who has been Muslim for many years. "I don't see how being a Muslim *longer* necessarily means he knows how to be a Muslim *better*!"[4] As Warith Deen and others move to assume leadership positions in the American Muslim community as a whole, such issues may recede, but they still serve as tension spots for some blacks.

Authority is also a highly significant issue for those who are members of America's immigrant Muslim communities, particularly the more recently arrived. America has been cited as a place where new understandings of Islam can be developed precisely because it is free of the watchful eyes of the religious authorities present in predominantly Muslim countries. "America . . . offers immense opportunities for Muslims to really develop and strengthen their faith," says Dr. Waheed Akbar, president of the Association of Pakistani Physicians in North America (APPNA). "In this country Muslims have the opportunity to practice Islam as it should be practiced because there is no government edict to restrict religion, nor is there sectarian control over belief."[5] This very freedom, however, while liberating for some, makes others very nervous. Having been reared with the strong understanding that certain religious figures are very (even absolutely) authoritative, many in both the Sunni and Shi'i communities who have come from conservative Muslim countries may continue to look to those figures and interpretations of Islam as authoritative for their lives in America.

Finances can be significant in the matter of authority and influence. Determining when certain interpretations of Islam are or are not appropriate to the practice of the faith in the West can become particularly complex when foreign financial support of American Muslim religious and educational institutions is tied to the ideological interpretations and political interests of the donors.

Unity

The search for what, if anything, unifies all Muslims in America is an ongoing concern with a great many dimensions. Is there, the question is asked in a great variety of ways, anything that distinguishes American Islam such that there can be an identifiable American *umma*? We have seen in the foregoing chapters many of the ways in which the quest for such unity is elusive. Immigrants have squabbled over differences in culture and custom. Some newly arrived Pakistanis, for example, may think second- and third-generation Arab Muslims are too liberal in their practice of Islam, and the Arabs in response may resent the "bossy" way in which the Pakistanis tell them how to be Muslim. Many Sunnis vigorously affirm that relations between Sunnis and Shi'ites are wonderful in America, while voices within the Shi'i community protest that all indeed is not harmonious.

Blacks, Hispanics, Native Americans, and others struggle to find their identity both under the greater umbrella of American Islam and also specifically as members of their respective racial-ethnic groupings. African Americans who are followers of Warith Deen are unhappy that Louis Farrakhan's Nation of Islam, which they consider to be dangerously heterodox, continue to get so much publicity in the American press. They also resent the fact that when they dress conservatively, or sometimes even identify themselves as Muslim, others often think them members of the Nation. Just as problematic for black Sunni Muslims are sectarian movements like the Ansar Allah or the Five Percenters, whose beliefs and practices are generally seen to be well off the mark of true Islam.

Then there are the concerns about what binds together African American and immigrant Muslims, alluded to above. "There has emerged a distinct division between the Pakistani, the Indian, Arabian, and African American communities which can be seen clearly in publications, organizational structures, and at social gatherings," argues Aminah Beverly McCloud of DePaul University. "It has been postulated that, for immigrants, there is a monolithic Islam in the Muslim world which is normative and the real experiences of African American Muslims should be rejected; instead they should aspire to effect something called 'orthodox' Islam. This assertion continues in some quarters of the Muslim community as a stimulus to divisiveness."[6] Other Muslims deeply regret not only that African American Muslims feel subject to such pressures but that attention is drawn to them rather than to the significant efforts being made to subsume immigrants, African American converts, and others under the arch of American Islam.

While most national Muslim organizations are predominantly either immigrant or African American, and while there is still lingering resentment among some blacks that they are not directly included in the work of an organization like the ISNA, it is also true that a number of coordinating councils now include both immigrant and African American leaders in positions of leadership. There is no question that continuing the efforts already under way to foster better appreciation, understanding, and cooperation among the different groups that comprise American Islam is an issue extremely high on the agenda for Muslims in the United States.

Leadership

For all Muslim Americans, the issue of attracting and appropriately training an indigenous leadership for mosques and Islamic centers is of utmost importance. Almost all of those people serving in immigrant communities as imams who are considered to be well qualified have received their training abroad, often in Egypt, Saudi Arabia, or Iran. Unfortunately, it has often been the case in the United States that men with little or no training have been called on to lead the prayers and fulfill other responsibilities now put on American imams simply because no trained leadership has been available. Clearly, one of the ways in which American Muslims can begin to extricate themselves from the influences of overseas Islam, to the extent to which this is considered desirable or necessary, is by developing their own education and training for imams. When asked what is the single most important concern facing American Muslims today, a leader of the American Muslim Council immediately answered, "Providing for the preparation of men to serve in leadership positions, especially as Imams."[7]

A few Muslim institutions, as we have seen, are in the fledgling stages of offering such programs. Most notable is the School of Islam and Social Sciences in Virginia. In a few cases, cooperative programs are being developed with Protestant Christian schools, such as Hartford Seminary in Connecticut and the Lutheran School of Theology in Chicago, to pool resources for training Muslim leadership. As the expectations for imams have mushroomed, so have the areas in which imams need adequate training. In addition to knowledge of Arabic, the Qur'an, and the fundamentals of Islamic law, theology, and history, imams should know how to preach and conduct the ceremonies essential to the Islamic life cycle. They should be familiar with pastoral care and counseling, understand finances related to the running of the mosque, and know how to set up appropriate educational programs for children, youth, and adults. In addition, imams are often called on to participate in community and interfaith activities and need to know how to operate in these broader contexts. American Muslims have yet to fully address most of these challenges.

Women

Across the Islamic world women are emerging—sometimes quietly, sometimes rather dramatically—as major players in their respective Islamic communities. While many women remain uneducated, unemployed (although working long hours in unpaid occupations), and uninformed about their Islamic rights, others are speaking and writing articulately about their roles as participants in emerging Islamic societies and are giving new and exciting interpretations to material from the Qur'an and the traditions classically understood to isolate women from the public realm. Many movements of Islamic revival abroad are encouraging women to claim their rightful roles in the public functioning of the community and are supporting their participation in politics and government as well as in the more traditional realms of education and home care.

Muslim women in America are subject to influences from a great many directions. Some are persuaded that the conservative traditions in which they may have been raised still offer the most appropriate understanding of how they should behave and what roles they should play. Others hear and are deeply influenced by the exciting new interpretations coming from various areas of the Muslim world or have themselves made those contributions in different contexts before coming to America. They are increasingly raising their voices in conversations about what is most appropriate and effective for American Muslim women. The conversations among American women who identify themselves as feminist or womanist influence men and women in a variety of ways. While initially many Muslim women found feminist discourse elitist, racist, and irrelevant to their concerns, many more attempts are now being made by Muslim and non-Muslim women to engage in conversations that are mutually enriching and beneficial. The extent to which any or all of these different voices will affect the role of women in the Western *umma* is just beginning to be seen.

Meanwhile, the leadership of national organizations is encouraging Muslim women who are professionally trained and who have opted to stay home until their children are sufficiently grown to find ways to make their opinions known and their contributions to the community visible. Many are participating in mosque activities, not only in the educational programs but often on mosque councils and other supervising structures. Some women are volunteering to assist in public school education, finding opportunities to teach their own children, as well as those who know little about Islam, what Muslim beliefs and practices are all about and how holidays are celebrated. Others, as we have seen, are active in after-school programs at the mosque or are developing forms of home education for their children. Some of the different roles played by American Muslim women are illustrated in "Profiles." To the extent to which Muslims do succeed in defining a peculiarly American Islam, women will provide much of that definition.

Politics

Until fairly recently, most American Muslims stayed clear of political involvement for a number of reasons. Immigrants from countries in which little or no effective political participation is possible sometimes find it hard to understand that the situation is different in America. Some Muslims have been persuaded that their vote or involvement cannot make any difference, and they believe that American national and international policies are never going to benefit Muslims. Others have felt that involvement in politics is actually *haram*.

This situation, however, is changing rather dramatically. Muslims are realizing that if they become organized, they can, indeed, wield significant influence in American politics. The Qur'anic verse 13:11, "God does not change the condition of a people until they [first] change what is in their hearts," is cited as evidence that Muslims must take the initiative in bringing about beneficial changes. Some are beginning to cite Muslim passivity as responsible for many of the problems the community currently faces. In an article titled "Muslim Self-Determination—It's Time!" for example, a Pakistani physician challenges Muslims to wake up to their responsibilities:

> Considering that Muslims worldwide are one billion (a fair number sitting on heaps of oil and other natural resources), our voice is akin to dead silence. . . . We have lost the forest for the trees, and energetically differ, harangue and hinder one another—at an individual level, community level and national level. . . . More news guys! God guarantees the livelihood of every soul—so whether you get out there and write letters to the newspapers, participate in a protest, write to your political representatives, stand for office or just sit in mental sloth in your mansions and your Mercs—your due shall come from God. What would it take to awaken America's slumbering Muslims? How can one correct our collective myopia? What should we imagine our children suffering in order for us to metamorphose from spectators into participants?[8]

A recent national gathering of the American Muslim Alliance, a young organization dedicated to organizing Muslims into a major voting bloc at the national level, featured the theme "How to Get 2000 Muslim Americans Elected to Public Offices in 2000." Its focus, echoed in current literature and discussion, was on providing Muslim candidates for school boards and municipal posts, working for the election of Muslim mayors and state legislators, and planning for an eventual Muslim presence on the American Supreme Court. "I believe we can be a major force first in getting Muslims to register to vote, then to participate in the American political system, and finally to become effective political activists," says Dr. Agha Saeed, founder and general secretary of the American Muslim Alliance.[9] For that to happen, he insists, Muslims must look beyond their cultural identities and focus on their commonality as Muslims. Some groups expend considerable effort to encourage Muslim women to run for public office. Since the middle 1980s a number of Political Action Committees (PACs) have emerged, such as the ISNA-PAC, and much attention is being given to the importance of having more Muslim lobbyists. Some people are even asking whether it would be important to have a separate League of Muslim Voters.

Many local groups work to encourage political participation by helping register voters and encouraging Muslim candidates to run for public office. Savvy advisers even counsel voters about when too enthusiastic public support from members of the Muslim community may actually embarrass a candidate and hinder his or her election. Current estimates are that Muslims in America divide fairly evenly among Democrats, Republicans, and independents. At the national level, concentrated efforts have been made recently to coordinate the advice given to Muslim voters about the issues and positions of candidates. A national Coordination Committee consisting of six member organizations, including the AMC, MPAC, and CAIR (see below), is working for the exchange and dissemination of information. Similarly, Warith Deen Mohammed and his associates have founded the Coalition for Good Government to provide political vision for Muslim Americans. The changes that Warith Deen has effected in the process of bringing Muslims into Sunni Islam and denouncing NOI's policy of urging its members not to participate in American society have led directly to a greater engagement of Muslims in local and national political life. Some project that in the coming years both immigrants and African Americans will be playing prominent roles on the American political scene.

Key in the thinking of those who advocate greater political involvement is influencing the ways foreign policy will deal with Muslim countries and the impact these policies will have on how the American populace views Islam. The goal toward which many are thus working is greater cooperation between American Muslims and the American political establishment. "The possibility of mutually beneficial outcomes, both at home and abroad, of a Muslim-U.S. partnership, are enormous," says one commentator. "One can have a lot of respect for the American system's potential to respond to its national interests. But the onus of repositioning Islam as an element of American national interest and not as a threat to it lies with the American Muslims."[10]

Many questions face the community as it looks to the immediate future. How will Muslims and thus American Islam itself change as second, third, and fourth generations of immigrants become more distant from their places of origin? Non-Muslim Americans can no longer talk about Islam as "foreign" or even as an "Eastern" religion. Islam has become part of America, and Muslims a growing and vital segment of its population. How will this affect both external and internal perceptions of Islam and Muslims? Will the majority of Muslims identify themselves as Americans who happen to be Muslim or as Muslims who happen to live in America, and what differences will such identification make in their public and private lives? Will Islam in America achieve its currently stated goal of becoming a significant political force? Is it likely that American resentment and prejudice against Islam will subside as the result of greater contact with Muslims and better understanding of their faith and practices? Who will provide the authoritative voices for American Muslims as they are increasingly able to choose where to go for direction?

The search for an American *umma* distinct from the racial-ethnic identities that have often served to divide and separate rather than unify is high on the agenda of many Muslims today and is particularly important to the youth who will be the new leaders of the community. The coming decades will be crucial as Muslims in the United States and Canada get clearer about who they are, what they need, and how they must organize to make their voices heard amid the competing claims of a diverse American society. Whatever patterns of religious, social, and personal life develop, clearly they will have to represent both a continuity with the life and faith of the Prophet and his community and the emergence of a new entity with its own qualities and characteristics—a truly American Islam.

American Muslims of Note

The preceding chapters have presented information about the history of Islam and its various manifestations in America in as narrative a style as possible, attempting to allow the lives of individual Muslims to illustrate the range of backgrounds, interests, and interpretations that have contributed to and continue to make up the picture of Islam in the West. Following are brief biographical sketches of twelve men and women not detailed earlier, whose lives exemplify some of the contributions Muslims have made to life in America. They are immigrants, African Americans, and Anglo converts, men and women, scholars and athletes and religious leaders, living and deceased. In different ways all are or have been public figures, and all have contributed to the efforts made over the course of this century to formulate and participate in American Islam.

Alexander Russell Webb

A white journalist named Alexander Russell Webb established the first documented Islamic institution in New York, the American Moslem Brotherhood, in 1893. A native New Yorker, Webb was named U.S. consul to Manila in the Philippines in 1887. Long an avid student of religious literature, he became fascinated with the religion of Islam as practiced by believers in the East. Ahmadis claim that his correspondence with Ghulam Ahmad in the 1880s was key to his conversion to Islam. He decided to declare the *shahada*, by which he converted from Presbyterian Christianity to Islam, and his wife and children soon followed suit. Webb sought financial support for the spread of

Islam in North America from Muslims overseas, especially in India and Saudi Arabia. In addition to establishing the first Muslim house of worship in America, among his many activities were publishing for several years a journal called *Moslem World*, authoring a number of books intended to introduce Americans to Islam, founding the first Islamic press in America, and representing Islam at the 1893 World's Parliament of Religions in Chicago.

Webb's Manhattan mosque was short-lived, however, and disagreements among its members undermined his organization. Internal dissensions were leaked to the press, publicizing allegations of Webb's financial mismanagement. Webb admitted to having secured little in the way of international funding and concluded finally that his efforts had not resulted in any lasting effect on the religious culture of America. *The New York Times* even published an article titled "Fall of Islam in America," signaling the virtual end of his attempts to introduce his faith to the American public. Nonetheless, Webb was extremely serious about his dedication to Islam and his desire to bring its message to his native city and country. Muslims acknowledge him as the pioneer of *da'wa*, or missionary activity, to white America. Webb died in 1916.

Betty Shabazz

The wife, and then widow, of the popular and controversial Malcolm X never had an easy life. While she often professed her conviction that Malcolm truly loved her and their five children, she also admitted that his long absences (despite letters and phone calls) and his treatment of her according to traditional patterns of male dominance were difficult to deal with. When Malcolm was shot, it was Betty Shabazz who shielded her daughters with her own body. Describing her sitting in widow's black in the second row at Malcolm's funeral, with police escort, one writer thought he was paying her a compliment by referring to her as a "black Jacqueline Kennedy." Betty's own life ended in 1997, again in tragic circumstances, when she suffered third-degree burns over most of her body after her own grandson set fire to the residence in which they were living.

As is recorded in FBI records, in 1956 then Betty Saunders joined New York's Temple Number 7 of the Nation of Islam and was renamed Sister Betty X. Malcolm writes in his biography that he merely noticed her for a while, not with any real interest, and that she probably would not even have known he knew who she was. Describing Betty as tall and with darker skin than his own, Malcolm identified her as a native of Detroit who was currently working at a school of nursing in a New York hospital, lecturing on hygiene to classes of Muslim girls and women. When Betty's family discovered that she had become a Muslim, they threatened to cut off financial support for her schooling. Malcolm reports having discussed the possibility of marriage with Elijah Muhammad and obtained his approval. Six years after he was released from prison, in January of 1958, Malcolm took Betty as his wife.

Betty herself reports that Malcolm was cool, even brusque, as a suitor but could be tender and solicitous as a husband. According to her, he became a supportive instructor in how to love as a woman and be true to her responsibilities as a mother. Nonetheless, his claim to authority in the marriage, and his tendency to show her off as the model of a good Muslim woman, were sufficiently irritating that Betty actually left him after the births of each of their first three children. She admitted that while she had to share him with the rest of the community, he was highly possessive of her. Still, her memories of Malcolm were generally ones of love and even gratitude, and it is from Betty, after Malcolm's death, that we have learned much about the private character of her husband and his relationship and responses to Elijah Muhammad.

Soon after Malcolm's death, Betty Shabazz went on her own pilgrimage to Mecca, tracing her husband's journey and writing back to her friends in Harlem about the beauty and serenity of the holy city of Islam. Over the years she became a popular lecturer and developed a close circle of friends, including Coretta Scott King and poet Maya Angelou. Politicians, activists, educators, and others sought her counsel. Professing herself then a Sunni Muslim, she educated her six daughters by Malcolm Islamically and worked behind the scenes with government officials and representatives of different Muslim communities for the advancement of Islam.

Much of her time in the hospital where she died was spent listening to recordings of Qur'an recitation. An obituary for Betty Shabazz in *The Message* concludes: "Her case, as will eventually be all of ours, is with Allah. The responsibility to give Dawah to the Shabazz family members is a religious duty to those who have access to them. May Allah strengthen the family and help the Ummah to meet the challenges of the day."[1]

Isma'il and Lois Lamya al Faruqi

Both the Muslim and academic communities in America were deeply shocked, grieved, and angered when on May 24, 1986, Isma'il al Faruqi and his wife, Lois Lamya, were assassinated in their Pennsylvania home while they were preparing for the celebration of 'Id al-Fitr. Known by their Muslim students as "Momma and Papa," both played roles of unusual significance in mentoring young Muslims and assisting in their intellectual and moral development. The funeral was attended by national and international leaders as well as by many of their American scholarly colleagues.

A native Palestinian born in Jaffa in 1921, Isma'il al Faruqi came from a religiously educated family. After receiving his higher education in the United States, he studied traditional Islamic sciences in al-Azhar in Cairo, combining Western and Eastern scholarship. Time spent at McGill's Institute of Islamic Studies, along with influences from the political climate in which was

Ismail al Faruqi, late Palestinian professor of religion at Temple University.
AP/WIDE WORLD PHOTOS

raised, fostered his interest in Arabism. For al Faruqi, Arabism was not a narrow nationalism, however, but a focus on Arab consciousness as part of Islamic universalism. Especially after coming into contact with the Muslim Student Association after 1965, he dedicated his work to what he called "the Islamization of knowledge." One of the founders of the Association of Muslim Social Scientists (AMSS), he was committed to recapturing the excellence of the Islamic past in the effort to highlight the intellectual content of its future. From 1968 until his death, Isma'il al Faruqi taught at Temple University, where he established a major graduate program in Islam and social sciences.

Al Faruqi was one the relatively few Muslim scholars who have taken serious academic interest in Christianity, having done a major study of Christian ethics, and for years was a participant in Christian-Muslim intellectual engagement. He worked diligently for Islamic *da'wa*, sometimes claiming that American academia was his realm for outreach activities. Involved in the creation of the American Islamic College in Chicago, he was also instrumental in founding the International Institute of Islamic Thought (IIIT) in Herndon, Virginia, dedicated to the Islamization of social and natural sciences. Just before his death he had been planning to open branches of the IIIT in other Muslim and non-Muslim countries.

Lois Lamya al Faruqi was also a scholar of Islam, particularly in the areas of religion, art, and music. An American convert, she was knowledgeable in Arabic and traveled over the Islamic world, lecturing and teaching. She also wrote basic text materials on women in Islam, condemning the excesses of Western feminism and fostering the distinction of clearly defined roles and responsibilities for men and women. Lois Lamya dedicated her life to helping Muslims reclaim their artistic and cultural heritage, particularly those living in a Western context or subject to the pressures of Westernization. Both Isma'il and Lamya al Faruqi worked with enormous strength, energy, and dedication in preparing young Muslims for the task of formulating an Islam that would be vibrant and viable in the contemporary world. Their loss was acute for American Islam.

Muhammad Ali

One of the first public figures in America to be identified with Islam was boxer Muhammad Ali, to whom more media attention has been given than to any other athlete. He has appeared on the cover of *Sports Illustrated* more than thirty times, and his name and face are known to people all over the world.

Ali was born Cassius Marcellus Clay in 1942 in Louisville, Kentucky, of a Baptist mother and Methodist father. He started boxing at a young age so as to be able to buy his parents a car; by the time he was in his twenties, many considered him the greatest fighter of all time. After winning the Rome Olympics in 1960, he became the darling of the American public—handsome, charming, and greatly successful. In 1963 he recorded an album in which he extolled his own merits ("I am the greatest") in a stunt that brought him even greater publicity but also earned him some ridicule.

Eighteen days before he defeated Sonny Liston to become heavyweight champion of the world, Clay joined the "Black Muslims," influenced by Malcolm X. After his conversion he seems visibly to have changed, bragging less about his own accomplishments and stressing the importance of Islam as a spiritual force in his life. Adopting the Muslim name Muhammad Ali, he has always insisted, was one of the most important occurrences of his life. He did it, however, at a time when the Nation of Islam was unpopular in the United States. The boxing commission was furious, and from a hero Ali quickly became the object of suspicion. Meanwhile, when the rift in the Nation occurred between Elijah Muhammad and Malcolm, Ali, to the deep disappointment and hurt of his friend Malcolm, sided with Elijah, whom he believed to be God's messenger. In 1967, in opposition to the Vietnam War, Ali refused to be inducted into the armed forces on the grounds that he was a minister in the religion of Islam. The New York State Athletic Commission suspended his boxing license and withdrew his recognition as champion.

Muhammad Ali's later career has been extremely checkered, and it is generally recognized that he fought well beyond the time that his physical condition allowed. He was finally diagnosed with Parkinson's Disease. Meanwhile, he also did a great deal of public speaking about his life and about Islam, while the government continued

Muhammad Ali, one of the first well-known American athletes to become a Muslim.
© TED GRAY

surveillance on him as a member of the NOI. Never a strong advocate of the Nation's racist doctrines, he did preach racial pride and became a hero of black Americans.

Today, Ali continues to practice Islam, lending his name to the distribution of Islamic educational materials. He has been a significant contributor to the financing of Islamic institutions such as the Masjid Al-Faatir, the first mosque built from the ground up in the city of Chicago. He prays five times a day, believing that it cleans the mind, as taking a shower cleans the body. The truly great men of history, he has said, want not to be great themselves but to help others and be close to God.

Mahmoud Mustafa Ayoub al-Faqih

Participants in sessions on Islam at the American Academy of Religion and other academic and professional gatherings have long been accustomed to the contributions of one of the academy's most articulate spokespeople, Mahmoud Ayoub. A highly gifted intellectual and a man of deep personal piety, Ayoub has served as the voice of scholarly integrity and sympathetic appreciation throughout his career. Born into a poor farming family in 'Ayn

Qana, South Lebanon, he has pursued an academic career that has included education at the American University of Beirut, the University of Pennsylvania, and Harvard University. His doctoral dissertation, published under the title *Redemptive Suffering in Islam*, deals with the meaning of the martyrdom of Imam Husayn, Shi'i life and piety, and his own battles with family poverty and the loss of his sight to congenital glaucoma as an infant. His vast scholarly work includes extensive commentary on the Qur'an and numerous essays on Christian-Muslim relations.

Interfaith concern is a direct outgrowth of Ayoub's background and training. Coming from a Shi'i family, he was sent to a Presbyterian British missionary school, where he learned the fundamentals of Christian devotional life. He thus had both a Muslim and Christian upbringing and from early on displayed a deep appreciation of religious diversity. "I grew up in Lebanon," says Ayoub, "where the voice of the *mu'adhdhin* and the church-bell can be heard together calling the faithful to God. Moreover, perhaps due to the Shi'i ethos of suffering and martyrdom, expressed in moving religious rites and rituals to which I was exposed at a very early age, I have always been religious."[2] Time spent with the Society of Friends at a Quaker college in England, he attests, helped him to rediscover his Islamic roots. Through his studies and reflections on what he sees as the rich spiritual heritage of Islam and Christianity, Mahmoud Ayoub has developed a special affinity to Sufism and the mystical life.

Professor of Islamic studies at Temple University since 1988, Mahmoud Ayoub has persevered in the task of presenting Islam to students and other audiences in its clearest and most comprehensible form. He participates regularly in interfaith dialogue and activities, describing himself not as a member of a particular legal or theological school of thought but as one who tries to interiorize the Islamic tradition as both a scholar and spiritual seeker. Ayoub cites the Qur'anic encouragement for people of piety to vie with one another in the performance of righteous works and the New Testament affirmation that though we see through a glass darkly we shall someday know the truth as models for faithful and righteous living.

Imam Siraj Wahaj

A highly visible Muslim personality in the public arena today is Imam Siraj Wahaj, congregational leader of Masjid al-Tawqa in Brooklyn, New York. He is vice president of ISNA and vice president of the Majlis al-Shura (consultative council) of New York. Imam Siraj travels around the world, speaking to Muslim and other groups about a wide range of issues from an Islamic perspective. Originally a Baptist, the Imam has been a Muslim since the late 1960s. He is an extremely enthusiastic speaker who knows how to ignite a crowd, never hesitating to identify what he sees to be the current ills of American society and the solutions provided by Islam as both a social system and a set of religious beliefs. He is regularly invited to address national meetings of Muslim organizations and is especially popular with young people. At a recent summer conference of the MYNA, Muslim Youth of North America, he addressed more than eight hundred young men and women. Encouraging them to remember that time is "tic, tocking" away, he asked, "Are you prepared to die?" assuring them that they should hold each moment dear because it is a gift from God. We must live our lives aware of the passing of time, since we never know when we will die and be accountable to God.[3]

Among the imam's many local activities is an active program spearheading an antidrug campaign in New York City, which has resulted in the closure of some fifteen drug houses. In 1991 Siraj Wahaj was the first Muslim invited to give the invocation prayer at the opening session of Congress in Washington, D.C. Prior to that only Christian and Jewish prayers had been offered. This occasion paved the way for invitations to other Muslims, although thus far the numbers have been limited, to participate more actively in public affairs.

Seyyed Hossein Nasr

Perhaps no Muslim living in America is called on more often to represent and interpret Islam to the general public than Seyyed Hossein Nasr, University Professor of Islamic Studies at George Washington University in Washington, D.C. Born in Teheran, Iran, Nasr is a Shi'ite who speaks on behalf of the unity of Islam and the complementarity of its traditional doctrines and traditions. He is a model of the well-rounded intellectual, his broad classical education beginning with the study of geology and physics and moving to Eastern and Western philosophy, the history of science, social science, Muslim and Christian historical and contemporary theology, and the development of Islamic mysticism, spirituality, art, and culture. After completing his education in the West, Nasr returned to Iran to teach at Teheran University. He was director of the Imperial Iranian Academy of Philosophy when the revolution occurred in 1979 and he was forced to flee the country.

Underlying Hossein Nasr's teaching and writing is the central theme that the modern world, especially the West, no longer understands and appreciates what he calls "the sacred." "While even in this world," he writes, "man is able to move to the other shore of existence, to take his stance in the world of the sacred and to see nature herself as impregnated with grace."[4] He is an articulate opponent of such contemporary ideologies as modernism, rationalism, secularism, and materialism, seeing the immutable principles of traditional Islam to be their most effective antidote. His attempt to encourage the integration of science, philosophy, and art, which he believes was most effectively achieved in classical Islam, is a reflection of his conviction that the central unity of all things reflects the unity of God. Contemporary problems such as ecological disasters he attributes to the loss of the sacred sciences, in which there is a relationship between the earthly and the celestial and in which human and divine history coalesce.

Nasr is deeply opposed to the rise of what in the West is called Islamic fundamentalism, seeing it as a dangerous duplication of some of the mistakes made by the modern West. He engages with serious intent in conversation with persons of various religious traditions, calling on all people to return to what is most deeply spiritual in their own faiths. Being Muslim in America today is a particularly challenging matter, he acknowledges, because Muslims are cut off from their Islamic history, tradition, and culture. Nasr is devoted to working for the spiritual enrichment of all Muslims in the West by helping connect them with their heritage and the spiritual sources of unity found in the arts, sciences, and philosophical traditions of classical Islam.

Kareem Abdul-Jabbar

Acknowledged by many sports fans as the greatest basketball player of all time, voted six times the National Basketball Association's most valuable player, Kareem Abdul-Jabbar is also one of the most visible Muslims in the American public arena. The 7' 2" native of upper Harlem, born Ferdinand Lewis Alcindor, starred for UCLA before entering the National Basketball Association with the Milwaukee Bucks in 1969. Alcindor later went to the Los Angeles Lakers. He was so dominant in college basketball that "dunking," at which he excelled, was formally banned from the intercollegiate sport. As a result, Lew Alcindor developed the shot for which he is personally the most famous—the "skyhook"—which has been called the shot that changed basketball, and with the help of which he was to score more than thirty-eight thousand points in regular-season NBA play. When Milwaukee won the NBA title in 1970–71, Alcindor, who was by then Kareem Abdul-Jabbar, was the acclaimed king of basketball.

Lew Alcindor first learned his Islam from Hammas Abdul Khaalis, a former jazz drummer and founder of the Hanafi Madhhab in Washington, D.C. According to his own testimony, he had been raised to take authority seriously, whether that of nuns, teachers, or coaches, and in that spirit he followed the teachings of Abdul Khaalis closely. It was by him that Alcindor was given the name Abdul Kareem, then changed to Kareem Abdul-Jabbar, literally "the noble one, servant of the Almighty." Soon, however, he determined to augment Abdul Khaalis's teachings with his own study of the Qur'an, for which he undertook to learn basic Arabic. In 1973 he traveled to Libya and Saudi Arabia to get a better grasp of the language and to learn about Islam in some of its "home" contexts. Abdul-Jabbar was not interested in making the kind of public statement about his Islam that he felt Muhammad Ali had in his opposition to the Vietnam War, wishing simply to identify himself quietly as an African American who was also a Muslim. He stated clearly that his name Alcindor was a slave name, literally that of the slave-dealer who had taken his family from West Africa to Dominica to Trinidad, from where they were brought to America.

As a member of the Hanafi Madhhab, Kareem Abdul-Jabbar affirms his identity as a Sunni Muslim, although he has never been overly observant. Because he was on the road so much, and because games and practices often occurred during scheduled prayer times, he never disciplined himself to the five-times-a-day routine of *salat*. He professes a strong belief in what he calls the Supreme Being and is clear in his understanding that Muhammad is his prophet and the Qur'an his revelation. Objecting to having been pushed into the Catholic faith by his father, he insists that his children (who, incidentally, are from a Buddhist mother) will be free to make their own choices.

In 1998 Kareem was again in the spotlight, this time not for his basketball skills but for appearing in a beer commercial. "I didn't see a problem with it," Kareem said. "We made sure they understood that I don't drink, Coors knew that I have taken a public posture of not drinking. I think it was tastefully done."[5] After talking with members of the Muslim Public Affairs Council, however, he apologized for any embarrassment he may have caused to the Muslim community. For his part, Kareem accepts his responsibility to live as good an Islamic life as possible, but it must be one in which religion is sometimes adapted to the requirements of being a professional athlete in America.

Laleh Bakhtiar

Angels in the Making is a book about seven American women who have joined the growing Sufi movement, in this case members of the popular Naqshbandi Sufi Order. Its author is Laleh Bakhtiar, associate of Islamic KAZI Publications on Belmont Avenue in Chicago. In it Bakhtiar describes the experiences of these women who have chosen the path of mysticism, attempting to show that the psychology available through traditional Islamic modes of response is a viable alternative to modern methods of psychological treatment. This volume, and many others written by Laleh Bakhtiar, illustrates her conviction that the traditional Muslim emphasis on ethics and morality is basic to sound mental health.

Trained both in philosophy, with a specialty in religious studies, and psychology, Bakhtiar describes her work as being like that of an archaeologist searching through the classics of the Middle Ages. Her discovery has been a wonderful system of psychology with roots in Judeo-Christian-Islamic, as well as Greek, thought. She urges that here in the realm of psychology, rather than in what she believes to be the rather fruitless efforts of theology, is where commonalities of insight and understanding are to be found. A three-volume work she has recently completed explains traditional psychology and the Islamic/Sufi origins of the Anagram. On the basis of this research she is working on a self-questionnaire to be administered to a range of groups in the attempt to find commonalities based on people's knowledge of self. Currently, Laleh Bakhtiar is counseling Muslim teenagers, using traditional psychology as the basis for psychotherapy. She finds that while girls and young women are usually open to this method, they often encounter resistance from parents who have been nurtured in a system that she sees simply does not work in America. Bakhtiar describes one of her primary goals, for which she teaches, lectures, and writes, to be training and educating Muslim counselors in traditional psychology. In her monthly advice column in *The Muslim Magazine*, Laleh helps women and girls deal with some of life's problems. In response to a wife whose husband is so miserly she and her children find it hard to live with him, she replies, "You should try to help him see what this vice of his is doing to you and his children. Help him learn to give and praise him when he does. If he comes to understand the greater struggle (*jihad al-akbar*) then he will learn that he has to overcome his miserliness because it comes from his ego and not his nature originated by God."[6]

An American Muslim who grew up in the West, Laleh Bakhtiar identifies two basic issues facing Muslims living in America: learning how to successfully parent their children in this culture and staying in touch with their

Islamic heritage while also assuming an American identity. She sees great hope in the young adult generation, especially those who have been able to survive a parenting system often inappropriate to current American culture. The trick, she says, is to figure out how they can become effective members of this society without completely losing identification with their Islamic roots. Such a loss, she fears, would only serve to haunt American Muslims in succeeding generations.

Muzammil H. Siddiqi

A prominent figure on the American Muslim scene today is Muzammil Siddiqi, director of the Islamic Society of Orange County in Garden Grove, California. A member of the Fiqh (Islamic law) Council of North America and a founding member of the Council of Mosques in the United States and Canada, Siddiqi is a Muslim intellectual who is also deeply concerned with helping Muslims live authentically in America. His weekly religious radio program has been broadcast from Pasadena since 1982. Siddiqi is a visible presence on the international Muslim scene, serving as a member of the Supreme Islamic Council of Egypt and the Supreme Council of Mosques in Mecca, Saudi Arabia.

Born in India in 1943, Muzammil Siddiqi was educated at Aligarh Muslim University and Darul Uloom Nawatul Ulama in Luckow, India. He has also received degrees from the Islamic University of Medina in Saudi Arabia and Birmingham University in England and holds a doctorate in comparative religion from Harvard University. During his career, Siddiqi has exemplified the life of an activist Muslim, working with national and international Islamic organizations. He has chaired the Religious Affairs Committee of the MSA, served as head of the Department of Religious Affairs at the Muslim World League Office, and been director of the Islamic Center of Washington,

Muzammil Siddiqi, President of the Islamic Society of North America (ISNA).
Courtesy Dr. Muzammil H. Siddiqi

D.C. In 1997 he was elected president of the Islamic Society of North America (ISNA). This professional involvement is balanced with significant academic activity, including lectures at universities and institutions in many parts of the world, teaching assignments in numerous universities, and currently an adjunct professorship at California State University.

Muzammil Siddiqi also models a deep concern for interreligious dialogue and exchange, having participated in meetings and seminars of both the National and World Council of Churches and the National Council of Christians and Jews in the U.S.A. (now called simply the National Council, indicative of its move to include Muslims in many of its activities). He serves as vice president of the Academy of Judaic-Christian and Islamic Studies in California and has participated in more than two hundred dialogue presentations with Christian and Jewish colleagues.

Amina Wadud

Viewers of a documentary film on Islam titled *Paradise Lies at the Feet of the Mother* may be struck by the eloquent explanation of the role of women in Islam offered by Amina Wadud, professor at Virginia Commonwealth University in Richmond. For a number of years Professor Wadud has taken upon herself the responsibility to share with other Americans her understanding of Islam and the special opportunities it offers to women to be creative participants in religious and social life. On the board of advisers of KARAMA, Muslim Women Lawyers Committee for Human Rights, she also dedicates considerable time to working for social justice in Western as well as other societies and particularly for the rights of women. She has lectured in various parts of the world on women in Islam in general and African American Muslim women in particular, as well as on spirituality and feminism from an Islamic perspective.

For three years Amina Wadud taught at the International Islamic University in Kuala Lumpur, Malaysia, where she became part of "Sisters in Islam," a small NGO women's study and activity group composed of professional women representing many different occupations. That experience, she says, has helped her think concretely about what concepts like "justice" and "social change" really mean. Of the various NGO experiences that Amina has had, she stresses this as the most important ("the litmus test for all other networks") because she and the other women not only discussed strategies for change but saw in concrete ways how those strategies could really make a difference in women's lives. Noting the great rise in the number of

Islamic organizations in the United States, she worries that they tend to be both provincial, with little sense of a broad U.S. agenda, and somewhat hierarchical in structure—even women's groups. She continues to ponder how to make her Malaysian experience applicable in the American context, always stressing the importance of thinking globally and acting locally.

And so she continues her research and writing, especially on women and new concepts of the family, and speaks in a wide range of contexts. Her best contribution to American Islam, perhaps, is in her living example of what it means to hold a Muslim identity. "I think 'islam' exists in every kind of activity," says Wadud. "What is important to my identity as a Muslim applies to whatever Allah places before me: from laundry, to travel, to sleep, to writing."[7] One of the most important concerns facing American Muslims today, she believes, is the achievement of unity as a body with minority status. This means internal cohesion and institutional development that would facilitate growth and development as a community, including schools, mosques, associations, and social services on both the local and the national levels. The important thing is to focus on the development of a strong ethical base predicated on the Qur'an, with careful consideration given to the application of the Sunna in the contemporary world. Wadud applauds the progress made in Muslim education and scholarship, at the same time that she regrets the overemphasis on geopolitics, as a result of the still perceived "threat" of Islam, rather than on the spiritual-moral principles of Islam as a sacred system.

Talal Y. Eid

"Imam Talal Eid To Deliver First Muslim Commencement Prayer," read the headline of the Harvard University *Gazette*.[8] For the first time in its long history, Harvard University in 1997 invited a Muslim to offer the opening prayer at its commencement. Imam Talal Eid, Religious Director of the Islamic Center of New England since 1982, is at home at Harvard, holding a degree from the Divinity School and completing his doctor of divinity degree there. For his community of thirty to forty thousand Muslims in the greater Boston area it was a time of honor and recognition and an opportunity to illustrate that Muslims, along with Christians, Jews, and others, are an active part of the university community as well as of the neighborhoods and communities in whose midst Harvard is situated.

Imam Eid is a native of Lebanon, where in the city of Tripoli he founded a mosque and served as religious leader until the Lebanese civil war. He recalls with great sadness his efforts to remain neutral between the two war-ring militia groups who controlled his neighborhood. "I was speaking the language of peace," he says, "while all they understood was the language of war."[9] The imam is firmly convinced that the struggles in the Middle East are essentially conflicts among ethnic groups rather than among Muslims, Christians, and Jews as such. A call from the Muslim World League to serve in the United States as imam to Muslims of Boston came as a welcome opportunity, although he never intended to make America his permanent home. A graduate of al-Azhar University in Cairo, Eid tries to combine his Islamic and Western training to help the people of his congregation address the problems of city life from an Islamic perspective. In addition to his stud-ies and service to the mosque, the imam works with youth and ministers to the Children's Hospital of Boston.

Imam Eid identifies two goals for himself and the members of his Islam-ic Center. The first is to work for unity among Muslims who come from many different countries and cultural backgrounds. This is not always easy, he confesses. The second is to open channels of communication with persons who are not Muslim to help change misperceptions and break down stereo-types. Drawing from his experiences in Lebanon, he is persuaded that living in isolation leads to fear of the other. The pluralist society of America, he believes, presents a unique opportunity for people of different faiths to live together, to better understand one another, and to work together for peace.

CHRONOLOGY

1950	Ahmadiyya headquarters moved to American Fazl Mosque in Washington, D.C.
1952	Malcolm (now X) released from prison and begins preaching NOI doctrines
1952	Federation of Islamic Organizations formed
1957	Islamic Center in Washington, D.C. completed
late 1950s	Hanafi Madhdhab Center established in Washington, D.C.
early 1960s	Darul Islam Movement grows up in Brooklyn
1960s	Pir Vilayat Khan emerges as leader of the Sufi Order in the West
1961	Malcolm X founds *Muhammad Speaks* newspaper
1963	Muslim Student Association (MSA) formed at the University of Illinois
1964	Boxer Cassius Clay becomes Muhammad Ali
1964	Malcolm X removed as Minister of Temple Number 7 in New York
1964	Allah's Nation of the Five Percenters founded in Harlem
1964	Malcolm X makes the pilgrimage to Mecca, breaks with the NOI
1965	Malcolm (now El Hajj Malik el-Shabazz) assassinated
1965	Repeal of immigration quotas leads to great increase in Muslim immigration
1968	Islamic Circle of North America (ICNA) founded
1970s	Nimatullahi Order of Sufis in America (Shi'ite) founded in San Francisco
1971	Bawa Muhaiyaddeen Fellowship founded in Philadelphia
1975	Elijah Muhammad dies; Wallace Muhammad becomes leader of NOI
1975	Muslim Student Association headquarters set up in Plainfield, Indiana
1975	Isa Muhammad changes Nubian Islamic Hebrews to Ansaru Allah movement
1977–85	Wallace Muhammad brings his followers to orthodox Islam
1978	Louis Farrakhan breaks with Wallace and begins to rebuild the NOI
1980s–90s	Worldwide Muslim immigration for political, social, and economic reasons
1980s–90s	Emergence of a number of Muslim political action committees
1980	Wallace Muhammad becomes Warith Deen Mohammed
1981	Islamic Society of North America (ISNA) formed

1983   American Islamic College established in Chicago

1985   Warith Deen declares his followers members of Sunni Islam

mid-1980s   PIEDAD Latino Community and Alianza Islámica founded in New York City

1990   Warith Deen the first Muslim to open the U.S. Senate with prayer

1990   American Muslim Council (AMC) organized in Washington, D.C.

1993   First commissioned Islamic chaplain in the U.S. Army

1993   Islamic Assembly of North America (IANA) founded

1994   Junior Association of Muslim Men established at Sing Sing prison

1994   Council on American Islamic Relations (CAIR) established in Washington, D.C.

1996   First commissioned Islamic chaplain in the U.S. Navy

1996   Denver International Airport first to feature a mosque

1996   School of Islamic and Social Sciences (SISS) begun in Virginia

1997   Muslim symbol displayed on White House ellipse

1998   Pentagon hosts Muslims for Ramadan meal

NOTES

Introduction

1. Michael Wolfe, *The Hadj: An American's Pilgrimage to Mecca* (New York: Grove-Atlantic Press, 1998), 6–9.

2. Diana L. Eck and the Pluralism Project, Harvard University, *On Common Ground: World Religions in America* (New York: Columbia University Press, 1997). A Multimedia CD-ROM for Windows and Macintosh (Order Dept., 136 South Broadway, Irvington, NY 10533).

3. Azam Nizamuddin, "What Muslims Can Offer America," *Islamic Horizons* (March/April 1998):35.

4. John E. Woods, "Imagining and Stereotyping Islam," in *Muslims in America: Opportunities & Challenges* 66 (Chicago: International Strategy and Policy Institute, 1996).

5. Muzammil H. Siddiqi, "Striving for Moral Excellence," *Islamic Horizons* (September/October 1997):28.

6. Ismail Al Faruqi, "Islamic Ideals in North America," cited by Larry Poston, "The Future of *Da'wah* in North America," *The American Journal of Islamic Social Sciences* 8/3 (December 1991): 511.

7. Syed Rifat Mahmood, "For Your Kind Attention," *United Muslims of America Update* 1/1 (November 1996): 1.

1. Muslim Faith and Practice

1. Gai Eaton, *Islam and the Destiny of Man* (Albany: State University of New York Press, 1985), 123.

2. Released on the Internet 6/4/98 by the Council on American-Islamic Relations.

3. Wormser, *American Islam*, 21.

4. Ibid.

5. "Ramadan: The Month of Fasting as Observed by Young Muslims," *The Minaret* (January 1997):25–27.

6. Ibid.

7. Related to the author in a private conversation in 1992.

8. Suad Lawrence Islam, "Nectar of My Life," *Al Jumuah* (issue 12 1418 H): 30.

9. Spoken to a women's interfaith group at which the author was present in the spring of 1995.

10. Michael Wolfe, *The Hadj: An American's Pilgrimage to Mecca* (New York: Grove-Atlantic Press, 1998).

11. Athar, *Reflections of an American Muslim*, 208.

2. Contributors to the Development of Islam

1. Salman Rushdie, *The Satanic Verses* (London: Viking, 1988), 394.

2. Cited by W. Montgomery Watt, *The Faith and Practice of al-Ghazali* (London: George Allen and Unwin, 1953), 56–57.

3. Cited by Seyyed Vali Reza Nasr, *Mawdudi and Making of Islamic Revivalism* (New York: Oxford University Press, 1996), 83.

3. Islam Comes to America

1. See Allan D. Austin, *African Muslims in Antebellum America: A Sourcebook* (New York: Garland Publishing, 1984).

2. Marc Ferris, "To 'Achieve the Pleasure of Allah': Immigrant Muslims in New York City," in Haddad and Smith, *Muslim Communities in North America*, 226–27.

3. Asad Husain and Harold Vogelaar, "Activities of the Immigrant Muslim Communities in Chicago," in Haddad and Smith, *Muslim Communities in North America*, 254.

4. M. K. Hermansen, "The Muslims of San Diego," in Haddad and Smith, *Muslim Communities in North America*, 171.

5. Mary Lahaj, "Building an Islamic Community in America." M.A. thesis for Hartford Seminary, Hartford, Conn., May 1992.

6. Allen E. Richardson, *Islamic Cultures in North America: Patterns of Belief and Devotion of Muslims from Asian Countries in the United States and Canada* (New York: The Pilgrim Press, 1981).

7. Abdulaziz Sachedina, "A Minority Within a Minority: The Case of the Shi'a in North America," in Haddad and Smith, *Muslim Communities in North America*, 3–14.

8. Linda Walbridge, "The Shi'a Mosques and their Congregations in Dearborn," in Haddad and Smith, *Muslim Communities in North America*, 354.

9. Haddad and Smith, *Mission to America*, 48.

10. *The Message* (February 1997):29.

II. *The Message* (August 1997), cover page.

12. Hazrat Inayat Khan, *The Sufi Message of Hazrat Inayat Khan*, volumes 1–13 (Geneva: International Headquarters Sufi Movement, 1966–82).

13. Gisela Webb, "Tradition and Innovation in Contemporary American Islamic Spirituality: The Bawa Muhaiyaddeen Fellowship," in Haddad and Smith, *Muslim Communities in North America*, 75–108.

14. Javad Nurbakhsh, *In the Paradise of the Sufis* (New York: Khaniqahi-Nimatullahi Publications, 1979).

4. Islam in the African American Community

1. Alex Haley, *Roots* (Garden City, N.Y.: Doubleday & Company, 1976).

2. Quoted from Albert J. Raboteau, *Slave Religion* (New York: Oxford University Press, 1978), 44–47 in Adib Rashad, *Islam, Black Nationalism and Slavery* (Beltsville, Md. Writers Inc., 1995), 45.

3. Quoted by Bakthiar, *Sufi Women of America*, 32.

4. "Noble Drew Ali—A Centennial Remembrance (1886–1986)," n.p.

5. Author's observation. See Lincoln, *Black Muslims in America*.

6. Barboza, *American Jihad*, 141.

7. Said during a meeting with Hartford Seminary faculty and mosque members, June 1997.

8. Malcolm X, in Haley, *The Autobiography of Malcolm X*, throughout.

9. Malcolm X, "The Truth about the Black Muslims," address at the Boston University School of Theology, May 24, 1960, cited by Lincoln, *Black Muslims in America*, 19.

10. Gardell, *In the Name of Elijah Muhammad*, 97.

II. Haley, *The Autobiography of Malcolm X*, 210.

12. Barboza, *American Jihad*, 104.

13. Ibid., 143.

14. R. Mukhtar Curtis, "Urban Muslims: The Formation of the Dar ul-Islam Movement," in Haddad and Smith, *Muslim Communities in North America*, 51–74.

15. Yusuf Nuruddin, "The Five Percenters: A Teenage Nation of Gods and Earths," in Haddad and Smith, *Muslim Communities in North America*, 109–32.

5. Women and the Muslim American Family

1. Comment made to the author in a private conversation in 1997.

2. Said by a participant in a 1997 regional conference on women.

3. Comment made to the author in a private conversation in 1998.

4. This remark, made privately to the author, refers particularly to the courageous efforts of pioneers such as Huda Sha'rawi and her colleagues in the early part of the twentieth century, who upon returning to Egypt from a women's conference in Rome, defied tradition and threw their veils into the harbor.

5. Anway, *Daughters of Another Path*, 20–21.

6. From a conversation among Christian and Muslim women at Harvard Divinity School in the late 1980s.

7. M. Riaz Khan, "Domestic Violence: American Muslim Families Not Immune," *Islamic Horizons* (July/August 1995):29.

8. Advice column by Dr. Nashiha al-Sakina in *The Minaret* (August 1996): 43.

9. Shahed Amanullah, "Cyber Muslims and Internet," *The Minaret* (February 1996):36.

10. Ummil-Khary Tawwab, "Selecting a Mate: First Step to a Sound Marriage," *The Message* (March 1996):34.

11. See, e.g., Sultana Rosa Ocasio, " 'Yo Sam' Growing Up Muslim in North America," *The Message* (June 1996):35.

12. Farhad Ara Bhuiyan, "Raising Muslim Children in North America," *The Message* (March 1997):25.

13. Related to the author by the daughter of Muslim friends in 1998.

14. Letter to the editor, *Islamic Horizons* (November/December 1996):5.

15. Ama F. Shabazz, "Finding Halaal Options to Maintain Our Deen," *The Message* (July 1997):26.

16. Haddad and Lummis, *Islamic Values in the United States*, 87.

17. Dr. Shahid Athar, "Taking Care of the Elderly and Infants," *The Minaret* (December 1997):8.

6. Living a Muslim Life in American Society

1. Jameila Al-Hashimi, "The Public School System Versus Islamic School," *Islamic Horizons* (June/July 1997):55.

2. Cynthia R. Sulaiman, "The 'S' Word, Academics and College: Questions Muslim Home Schooling Families Are Asked," *Islamic Horizons* (June/July 1997):47.

3. Sabah E. Karam, "Muslim Parents' Recipe for Children's Success in School," *Islamic Horizons* (June/July 1997):46.

4. Mahdi Bray, "School Prayer: The Need for Muslim Proactive Involvement," *Islamic Horizons* (January/February 1995):18.

5. Alia Amer and Abul Hadi Harman Shah, "Guiding Principles for Islamic Social Behavior," *Al Jumuah* (4&5 1418 H):23.

6. Jahan-zaib Hassan Gilani, "Muslim Youth in College," *The Message* (November 1997):34.

7. Abdul-Aziz Al-Fawzan, "Fatawa," *Al Jumuah* (7 1418 H):16.

8. "Multiply Assets Through Investment Clubs," *Islamic Horizons* (March/April 1997):54.

9. A. Rushdi Siddiqui, "Finances Take a Chair," *The Message* (November 1997):42.

10. Judi Muhammad, "Islamic Hospital Care Comes to Detroit," *Islamic Horizons* (September/October 1996):36.

11. Haddad and Lummis, *Islamic Values in the United States*, 106–7.

12. "Islam Day to Day," *The Message* (July 1996):24.

13. Vernon Schubel, "The Muharram Majlis: The Role of a Ritual in the Preservation of Shi'a Identity," in Waugh, Abu-Laban, and Qureshi, eds., *Muslim Families in North America*, 118.

14. *The Minaret* (October 1997):43.

15. Yusuf Islam, "Music: The Good and the Bad," *Islamic Horizons* (September/October 1997):56.

16. "Islam Day to Day," *The Message* (March 1996):41.

17. Tarajee Abdur Rahim, "Living with HIV in the Muslim Community," *The Message* (May 1996):27.

18. Muzammil H. Siddiqi, "Where There's a Will There's a Way," *Islamic Horizons* (July/August 1996):38.

7. The Public Practice of Islam

1. Gulzar Haider, "Muslim Space and the Practice of Architecture," in Metcalf, ed., *Making Muslim Space in North America and Europe*, 31.

2. From an advertisement in *The Muslim Magazine* (April 1998):42.

3. Haddad and Lummis, *Islamic Values in the United States*, 53.

4. Bonne Lovelace, "U.S. Military Designates First Muslim Chaplain," *Islamic Horizons* (May/June 1995):46.

5. "Muslim Prison Workers Sought," *The Message* (August 1997):14.

6. Omar Afzal, "Beyond Brown, Black and White: Muslims in North America," *The Message* (July 1997):21.

7. Tahrim S. C. Jihad in "Letters," *The Message* (February/March 1998):8.

8. John Woods, "Imagining and Stereotyping Islam," in *Muslims in America: Opportunities & Challenges* (Chicago: International Strategy and Policy Institute, 1996), 45–75.

8. Looking to the Future

1. Maher Hatout, "The Nature of Islamic Discourse in America," *The Minaret* (January 1998):21.

2. "Muslim Professionals Meet to Discuss Issues of Common Concern," *The Minaret* (May 1996):41.

3. "Muslim Social Services Take a Step Forward," *Islamic Horizons* (July/August 1996):24.

4. Said in a private conversation with the author in 1998.

5. Omer Bin Abdullah, "Eyes on the Muslim Future in America," *Islamic Horizons* (May/June 1995):37.

6. McCloud, *African American Islam*, 169–70.

7. Said to the author in June 1998.

8. Mahjabeen Islam-Husain, "Muslim Self-Determination—It's Time!" *The Washington Report on Middle East Affairs* (May/June 1998):116.

9. Richard H. Curtiss, "Dr. Agha Saeed: Dynamic Leader of Expanding American Muslim Alliance," *The Washington Report on Middle East Affairs* (December 1997): 25.

10. "American Muslims/US Policy Shaping: A Crucial Partnership, Now," *The Message* (December 1995):33–34.

Profiles: American Muslims of Note

1. "Betty Shabazz Succumbs," *The Message* (July 1997):8.

2. A private communication to the author, January 1998.

3. "MYNA Summer Conference," *Islamic Horizons* (November/December 1996):45.

4. Seyyed Hossein Nasr, *Knowledge and the Sacred* (New York: Crossroad Publishing, 1981), 168.

5. "Kareem in the Midst of Beer Ad Controversy," *The Minaret* (February 1997):19.

6. "Dr. Laleh," *The Muslim Magazine* (April 1998):75.

7. A private communication to the author, March 1998.

8. *Gazette* XCII (June 5, 1997):1.

9. Mary DeRosia, "An Imam's Great Hope," *Living City* (March 1996):11.

GLOSSARY

Following are terms that have been used throughout this volume, reflecting the concepts and vocabulary relevant to understanding the experience of American Islam. They are given in transliteration from the Arabic with a brief definition.

'Abd servant, the believer in relation to God

Adhan call to prayer given five times daily; *Mu'adhdhin*—the one to give the call

Ahl al-Bayt "People of the House," referring to the members of the Prophet's family; descendants of the Prophet's son-in-law 'Ali

Ahl al-Kitab "People of the Book," the Qur'anic reference to Christians, Jews, and others who possess Scripture

Arkan "pillar," referring to the five basic responsibilities incumbent on all Muslims

Ashura the "tenth" of the month of Muharram, the time when Shi'is remember the martyrdom of Imam Husayn

Dar al-harb "abode of war," referring to lands outside of Islam (sometimes called *dar al-kufr*, "abode of apostasy")

Dar al-Islam "abode of peace," referring to lands where Islamic law is enforced

Da'wa "call or invitation" summoning others to heed the call of God to Islam; propagation of the faith

Dhikr "remembrance," the congregational Sufi ritual of remembering God

'Eid holiday or festival; *'Eid al-Fitr*—observance of the end of Ramadan; *'Eid al-Adha*—observance on the last day of the *hajj* or pilgrimage to Mecca

Fiqh Islamic jurisprudence; codification of the sacred law, or *shari'a*

Hadith traditions that report the words and deeds of Prophet Muhammad

Hajj pilgrimage to Mecca prescribed for every Muslim, if possible, once in a lifetime

Halal legally permissible

Hanif one of the pious believers before Muhammad, not Christians or Jews, who submitted to God's oneness

Haram unlawful, prohibited

Hijab head covering worn by women as a sign of piety and Muslim identity

Hijra emigration of Prophet Muhammad and his followers from Mecca to Medina in 622 C.E.

Iftar breaking of the daily fast during the month of Ramadan

Ijma' consensus of the community; one of the four accepted sources of Islamic law

Ijtihad individual reasoning or interpretation

Imam for Sunnis a religious leader, or one who leads the prayer; for Shi'ites a direct descendant of the Prophet who is the divinely mandated leader of the community

Iman faith, submission to God through the heart

Islam personal submission to the will of God through which one enters Islam, the community of the faithful

Jahiliyya the time of ignorance, said to apply to the Arabian society before the revelation of the Qur'an

Jihad struggle against the lower forces of one's nature or against the enemies of God

Ka'ba the Holy House, or shrine of Islam, in the Grand Mosque at Mecca

Kalam word (of God); the speculative theology of Islam

Khalifa caliph, the one who comes after the Prophet, the titular leader of Muslims until the caliphate was abolished in 1924

Khatm seal or stamp, referring to the fact that Muhammad is the last of the prophets

Kufr rejection of the reality and being of God; unbelief

Mahdi the divinely guided leader who will return to establish justice on earth before the resurrection

Masjid mosque; place where one prostrates before God

Mi'raj the journey taken by Muhammad with the angel Gabriel through the heavens into the presence of God

Mufti jurisconsult; one who gives a legal opinion (*fatwa*) based on his knowledge of the law

Mujaddid renewer of the faith, said to come once in each century

Nabi prophet; a recipient of a communication from God intended for a specific community

Niyya declaration of intention to carry out a religious responsibility, as in *salat*, or prayer, in the right spirit of mind and heart

Qadi judge, one who decides civil and criminal cases according to the *shari'a*

Qibla the direction of prayer facing the Ka'ba in Mecca

Qiyas reasoning by analogy; one of the four accepted sources of Islamic law

Raka' bending at the waist in the ritual prayer, followed by prostrations

Rasul messenger, the recipient of a universal message from God

Riba usury, or interest in excess of the legal rate

Salat the formal or ritual prayer to be performed five times a day

Saum fasting during the daylight hours of the month of Ramadan

Shahada bearing witness that there is no God but God and that Muhammad is his Prophet

Shari'a Islamic sacred law; prescribed conduct for the believer

Shaykh a Sufi master; one who initiates followers into the spiritual and esoteric disciplines (also called *pir* or *murshid*)

Shi'a, Shi'ite the identifying name for those who are of the party of 'Ali, as distinguished from the majority Sunnis or Sunnites

Shirk the sin of associating anything or anyone with God

Shura the principle of consultation by which decisions in the Islamic community are made

Sufi one who follows one of the schools of mystical thought in Islam

Sunna the life example or way of the Prophet Muhammad

Sunni the identifying name for the great majority of Muslims (generally as distinguished from the Shi'a or Shi'ites)

Takbir saying *"Allahu akbar,"* literally "God is greater," often used as a signal of commendation

Tariqa way or path under the leadership of a *shaykh* or *pir;* a Sufi order or brotherhood

Tawhid the essential unity of God; affirmation of God's oneness and consequent human responsibility to live ethically

'Ulama' the learned religious and legal scholars of Islam

Umma the community of all of those who affirm Islam

'Umra the lesser *hajj*, or pilgrimage to Mecca performed at any time of the year

Wahy revelation, specifically used for the sending down of the message of the Qur'an by God to Prophet Muhammad

Wali a "friend of God," a holy person or saint

Wudu' ritual washing before performance of the *salat*, or prayer

Zakat the alms payment or welfare tax

RESOURCES FOR THE
STUDY OF AMERICAN ISLAM

Bibliography

Anway, Carol L. *Daughters of Another Path: Experiences of American Women Choosing Islam.* Lee's Summit, Mo.: Yawna Publications, 1996. Interviews of women whose daughters have married Muslims and converted to Islam, sharing both concerns and pleasures.

Athar, Shahid. *Reflections of an American Muslim.* Chicago: KAZI Publications, 1994. A practicing Muslim physician communicates his understanding of Islam to North America, attempting to remove misconceptions as well as express what he sees as problems in Muslim communities.

Bakhtiar, Laleh. *Sufi Women of America: Angels in the Making.* Chicago: KAZI Publications, 1996. Interviews with women who have joined Islam through the Naqshbandiyya Sufi movement.

Barazangi, Nimat Hafez, guest editor. *Religion & Education* 25/1&2 (Winter 1998). A special edition devoted to articles about Islamic education in North America.

Barboza, Steven. *American Jihad: Islam After Malcolm X.* New York: Doubleday, 1994. Brief biographical sketches of American Muslims, some well known and others not, who have converted to Islam.

Gardell, Mattias. *In the Name of Elijah Muhammad: Louis Farrakhan and the Nation of Islam.* Durham, N.C.: Duke University Press, 1996. A scholarly and intensive study by a Swedish observer of Nation of Islam ideology and development from the early twentieth century to the present.

Haddad, Yvonne Yazbeck, ed. *The Muslims of America.* New York: Oxford University Press, 1991. Essays on the history, organization, challenges, responses, outstanding leaders, and future prospects of the Muslim community in the United States and Canada, including immigrants and African Americans.

Haddad, Yvonne Yazbeck, and Adair T. Lummis. *Islamic Values in the United States: A Comparative Study.* New York: Oxford University Press, 1987. Interviews with Muslims in five communities about life in America, Islamic institutions, American culture, and roles of women and men.

Haddad, Yvonne Yazbeck, and Jane Idleman Smith. *Mission to America: Five Islamic Sectarian Communities in North America.* Gainesville, Fla.: University Press of Florida, 1993. A study of five sects that label themselves Muslim but whose identity is challenged by other Muslims.

————, eds. *Muslim Communities in North America.* Albany: State University of New York Press, 1994. Descriptions and analyses of twenty-two communities representing different racial-ethnic and national groupings.

Haddad, Yvonne Yazbeck, and John L. Esposito, eds. *Muslims on the Americanization Path?* Atlanta: Scholars Press, 1998.

Haley, Alex. *The Autobiography of Malcolm X.* New York: Ballantine Books, 1964 (1992). The life of Malcolm told in his own words, from his early days as an East Coast drug dealer to his prison conversion to his movement out of the Nation of Islam and his murder.

Kepel, Giles. *Allah in the West: Islamic Movements in America and Europe.* Stanford, Calif.: Stanford University Press, 1997. Along with Islam in Britain and France, the volume looks at the birth of black Islam in America, the life of Malcolm X, and Louis Farrakhan's Nation of Islam.

Koszegi, Michael A., and J. Gordon Melton, eds. *Islam in North America: A Sourcebook.* New York: Garland Publishers, 1992. Articles cover waves of Islam in North America, sectarian movements, Islamic mysticism, and Islamic-Christian relations in the West; useful directory of North American Islamic organizations and centers.

Lee, Martha F. *The Nation of Islam: An American Millenarian Movement.* Syracuse: Syracuse University Press, 1996. Looks at the Nation of Islam as a failed millenarian movement that branched into the different movement of the American Muslim Mission and the reconstituted Nation.

Lincoln, C. Eric. *Black Muslims in America,* rev. ed. Boston: Beacon Press, 1973. The first significant sociological study of the Nation of Islam before the death of Elijah Muhammad.

Mallon, Elias. *Neighbors: Muslims in North America.* New York: Friendship Press, 1989. Brief stories told in interview format of American Muslims from a variety of ethnic, cultural, and geographical backgrounds.

Marsh, Clifton E. *From Black Muslims to Muslims: The Transition from Separatism to Islam, 1930–1980.* Metuchen, N.J.: The Scarecrow Press, Inc., 1984. A treatment of the transition of African American Islam from its earlier separatist ideology to Sunni Islam.

McCloud, Aminah Beverly. *African American Islam.* New York: Routledge, 1995. An introduction to the different expressions of African American Islam, focusing on five early and thirteen contemporary communities.

Metcalf, Barbara Daly, ed. *Making Muslim Space in North America and Europe*. Berkeley: University of California Press, 1996. A collection of essays on the different ways Muslims in America and Europe have translated physical and psychological space to fit their needs as Muslims.

Poston, Larry. *Islamic Da'wah in the West: Muslim Missionary Activity and the Dynamics of Conversion to Islam*. New York: Oxford University Press, 1992. A brief history of *da'wa* in the East and West, noting influences on American Islam, treatment of "paramosque" structures and strategies, and the literature of Muslim apologetic.

Shaheen, Jack G. *Arab and Muslim Stereotyping in American Popular Culture*. Washington, D.C.: Center for Muslim Christian Understanding, History and International Affairs, 1997. Muslims as portrayed on television, in the movies, and in print and broadcast news, contesting the stereotypes.

Turner, Richard Brent. *Islam in the African-American Experience*. Bloomington, Ind.: Indiana University Press, 1997. An exploration of the roots of American Islam overseas and in antebellum America, and the stories of leaders of urban-based twentieth-century African American Muslim movements.

Waugh, Earle H., Sharon M. Abu-Laban, and Regula B. Qureshi, eds. *Muslim Families in North America*. Edmonton, Alberta: The University of Alberta Press, 1991. Looks at critical issues facing Muslims in the United States and Canada, especially the situation of women, adjustment of families, and strategies for coping in an alien environment.

Waugh, Earle H., Baba Abu-Laban, and Regula B. Qureshi, eds. *The Muslim Community in North America*. Edmonton, Alberta: The University of Alberta Press, 1983. Leading scholars from America and overseas discuss a range of issues relevant to the lives of Muslims in the United States and Canada.

Wolfe, Michael. *One Thousand Roads to Mecca: Two Centuries of Travelers Writing about the Muslim Pilgrimage*. New York: Grove-Atlantic Press, 1998.

Wormser, Richard. *American Islam: Growing Up Muslim in America*. New York: Walker and Company, 1994. Interviews with Muslim teenagers about everyday concerns such as family, school, relationships, to see how they maintain and adapt their Muslim identity in America.

Muslim Journals and Periodicals

The American Journal of Islamic Social Sciences: The Association of Muslim Social Scientists, The International Institute of Islamic Thought, published simultaneously in Washington, D.C., and Kuala Lumpur, Malaysia.

The American Muslim: Quarterly publication of The American Muslim Support Group, P.O. Box 5670, Bel Ridge, MO 63121 with the cooperation of Al-Ribat al-Islami, P.O. Box 601, La Jolla, CA 92038-0601.

The Final Call: Weekly newspaper of Minister Louis Farrakhan, FCN Publishing, 734 W. 79th Street, Chicago, IL 60620. Tel: (773) 602-1230. Fax: (773) 602-1013. Website: http://www.finalcall.com

Iqra: Monthly magazine of the South Bay Islamic Association of San Jose, 3325
    North Third Street, San Jose, CA 95112.

Islam in America: Quarterly survey of books, periodicals, and newspapers pub-
    lished by the Alduvai Humanities Library, P.O. Box 2411, Olympia, WA
    98507-2411.

Islamic Horizons: Bimonthly publication of the Islamic Society of North America
    (ISNA), P.O. Box 38, Plainfield, IN 46168-0038.

Journal of Muslim Minority Affairs: Published twice a year as a forum for discus-
    sion of issues relating to the life of Muslims in non-Muslim societies. Car-
    fax Publishing Ltd., P.O. Box 25, Abingdon, Oxfordshire OX14 3UE,
    United Kingdom.

Al Jumuah Magazine: Published monthly by the Islamic Revival Association
    U.S.A., P.O. Box 5387, Madison, WI 53705-5387.

The Light and Islamic Review: The Lahore Ahmadiyya Movement, 1315 Kingsgate
    Road, Columbus, OH 43221-1504.

The Message: Monthly journal published by the Islamic Circle of North America
    (ICNA), 166-26 89th Avenue, Jamaica, NY 11432-4254.

The Minaret: Published monthly by The Islamic Center of Southern California,
    434 South Vermont, Los Angeles, CA 90020.

Muslim Journal: Weekly newspaper of the ministry of W. D. Muhammad, pub-
    lished by Muslim Journal Enterprises, Inc., 910 W. Van Buren, Suite 100,
    Chicago IL 60607. Tel: (312) 243-7600. Fax: (312) 243-9778. E-mail: mus-
    limjrnl@aol.com. Website: http://www.worldforum.com/muslimj

The Muslim Magazine: Monthly journal started in 1998, designed for both Muslim
    and non-Muslim readership, with issues focusing on special topics. Editor,
    607A W. Dana Street, Mountain View, CA 94041.

Washington Report on Middle East Affairs: Published eight times a year at 1902
    18th Street, NW, Washington, D.C. 20009-1707. Regular sections on Islam
    in the United States and Canada. Tel: (202) 939-6050.

Islamic Educational Organizations

Council of Islamic Schools in North America (CISNA), American Muslim
    Council, 1212 New York Avenue, NW, Suite 400, Washington, D.C.
    20005. Tel: (202) 789-2262. Fax: (202) 789-2550. Director: Sabah E.
    Karam.

Council on Islamic Education, 9300 Gardenia Street, Suite 3-B, Fountain Valley,
    CA 92708. Tel: (714) 839-2929. Fax (714) 839-2714. Director: Shabbir
    Mansouri.

The Institute of Islamic Information and Education, P.O. Box 41129, Chicago, IL
    60641-0129. Tel: (773) 777-7443. Fax: (773) 777-7199.

Islamic Schools Department, ISNA, P.O. Box 38, Plainfield, IN 46168. Tel: (317)
    839-8157. Fax: (317) 839-1840. Director: Dr. Shaban Ismail.

Muslim Education Council, 902 McMillan Court, Great Falls, VA 22066. Tel: (703) 759-7698. Fax: (703) 759-9461. Director: Sharifa Alkhateeb.

National Education Board, Clara Muhammad Schools, 560 Fayetteville, SE, Atlanta, GA 30316. Tel: (404) 378-1600. Fax: (404) 377-0043. Director of Education: Imam Plemon El-Amin, Convener of National Shura.

Videotapes About American Islam

Note: This is only a representative sample of the many videotapes available. A few are designed for the presentation of Islam to non-Muslims; most are prepared for use by Muslims living in America.

EcuFilm, 810 12th Avenue, South, Nashville, TN 37203. Tel: (800) 251-4091.
- *A Tale of Two Mosques*. Life and evolution of the Muslim community of Edmonton and its search for a refined sense of Islamic identity in Canada. 30 minutes.
- *Islam, America*. Speakers at a University of Massachusetts conference on understanding Islamic Americans addresses the history of Islam in the United States, stereotypes and prejudices, and the relationship of Islam to Christianity. 30 minutes.

Astrolabe Pictures, Inc., 585 Grove Street, #300, Herndon, VA 20170. Tel: (800) 392-7876.
- *Islam—A Closer Look*. Documentary that informs non-Muslims about Islam, particularly focusing on North America. 30 minutes, ages 12 to adult.
- *Malcolm X*. Film starring Denzel Washington, telling the story of Malcolm's life and conversion to Islam. 3 hours, 21 minutes, ages 14 to adult.
- *Pathways to Islam*. Account of three young American students discovering Islam, told through interviews. 25 minutes, ages 12 to adult.

International Books & Tapes Supply (IBTS). Tel: information (800) 337-4287. Tel: order (718) 721-2425. Fax (718) 728-6108.
- *Americans Becoming Muslim*. Story of the conversion of Prof. Jeffery Lang of the University of Kansas.
- *Documentary: Malcolm X*. Traces Malcolm's journey from Harlem through prison to civil rights leadership.
- *Interview: Minister Louis Farrakhan*. Farrakhan's discussion of his interpretation of the Shahada, the Nation of Islam, and *da'wa* efforts in the United States.
- *Islam in the Lives of American Muslims*. Sr. Aminah Assilmy & Sr. Cathy Bullock.
- *Living in America—Ethical and Moral Behavior*. Lecture by Dr. Jamal Badawi.

- *Looking Ahead: A Vision for a Better America*. Imam W. Deen Mohammed, Imam Jamil Al Amin, Dr. Muhamma Yunis, and A. Idris Ali.
- *Muslim Women in Mosques and Islamic Centers*. Lecture by Dr. Jamal Badawi.
- *My Journey from Christianity to Islam*. Story of Sr. Nancy Ali, a former nun converted to Islam.
- *Riba—Can We Avoid It? Or Is It a Must in America?* Lecture by Dr. Jamal Badawi.

IQRA' International Educational Foundation, IQRA' Book Center, 6410 North Campbell Avenue, Chicago, IL 50545. Tel: (312) 274-8733, (800) 521-2472. Fax: (312) 274-8733.
- *From Darkness to Light*. Yusuf Islam on his journey to Islam.
- Jamal Badawi Audio Series. 11 volumes looking at various tenets of Islam by Dr. Jamal Badawi.
- *Living Islam*. 6-volume series on what it means to be Muslim in today's world. 50-minute presentations.
- *Women's Rights & Roles*. Debate between a Muslima and a Western journalist writing against Islam's treatment of women.

Sound Vision, 843 W. Van Buren, Suite 411, Chicago IL 60607. Tel: (312) 226-0205. Fax (312) 226-7537; E-mail GetInfo@SoundVision.Com.
- *Choosing Islam*. Presents Islam to non-Muslims through the personal experiences of Americans who have accepted it.
- *Hakeem Olajuwon*. Interview with Hakeem about winning the World Championship of basketball and the role Islam has played in his life.
- *Islam in North America*. Lectures on Spanish-speaking Muslims in America, Islam and its roots in America, challenges for Muslims.
- *Muslim Leadership in America*. Leaders of the Islamic Shura Council of North America share their thoughts on unity among Muslims in North America.
- *Muslims in America Yesterday & Today*. History of Muslims in America and the challenges they face today.
- *Muslims in the Americas Before Columbus*. Roots of Muslims in the Americas from Arabic sources and findings of Western scholars.

Radio and Television Broadcasts
- *Imam W. Deen Mohammed Speaks*. Information, products, and support services; economic growth through the promotion of improved health. Radio broadcast listings in local areas in twenty-eight states.
- *Islam*. The only national weekly TV broadcast on Islam and Muslims, a program that explains Islam to Muslims and non-Muslims. Started as a local program of the Islamic Center of Southern California, it has

grown into a major national source of Islamic information. Saturday at 10:30 A.M. (EST). Islamic Information Service, P.O. Box 6220, Altadena, CA 92003. Tel: (800) 531-4447 or (818) 791-9818.

Internet Resources

A great range of resources on the Internet are being made available on a regular basis. Muslims or others can key into discussions or information on almost any subject. Following are a few of the materials that can currently be accessed. The enterprising browser will easily be able to discover more.

Islamic Web sites: http://www.mpac.org/network.html

American Muslim Alliance (AMA): http://mercury.hypersurf.com/ama/

American Muslim Council (AMC): http://www.amermuslim.org/

Council on American-Islamic Relations (CAIR): http://www.mpac.org/cair.html

Islamic Intellectual Forum: http://www.islamforum.org/

Muslim Student Network: http://www.mpac.org/msn.html

Muslim Women's League: http://www.win.net/mwl/

Mosques and Muslim Institutions: http://www.mpac.org/network/mosques.html

Muslim Student Associations in the U.S.: http://www.mpac.org/network/msa.html

Links to Muslim Countries: http://www.mpac.org/network/country.html

Working with Peace Organizations: http://www.mpac.org/network/other.html

Interfaith Gateway: http://www.mpac.org/network/interfaith.html

The Shi'a Home Page: http://shia.org/

All about Ashura: http://www.ashsura.com/

Islamic Human Rights Commission: http://members.tripod.com/

IslamiCity News Search Service: http://www.islamicity.org/

CyberBookstore: http://www.islamicity.org/bookstore/default.htm

Announcements and News:
        http://www.islamicity.org/media/ANCMTS/default.htm

Cyber Yellow Pages: http://islam.org:81/cyberpages/FMPro?-db=yellow pages

IslamiCity Chat and Conference Center: http://islam.org/Chat/default.htm

Islamic Circle of North America: http://www.icna.com/main/shtml

Voice of Islam lectures, sermons, and news in Real Audio format:
        http://www.islamicity.org/voi/ [you need a sound card and Real Audio Player software]

Cyber TV Network: http://www.islamicity.org/cyberTV/default.htm [you need a sound card and Real Audio Player software]

Muslim World Journey (information on Muslim countries):
  http://www.islamicity.org/world/default.htm

Holy Quran: http://www.islamicity.org/Mosque/Quran.htm

Virtual Mosque: http://www.islamicity.org/mosque/default.asp

Ask the Imam: http://www.islamicity.org:81/imam/default.htm

*Culture: http://*www.islamicity.org/culture/default.htm

News: http://www.islamicity.org/media/default.htm

Economic and Business Plaza: http://www.islamicity.org/economic/default.htm

Education Parkway: http://www.islamicity.org/education/default.htm

Science and Technology Square: http://www.islamicity.org/science/default.htm

Public Affairs and Political Center: http://www.islamicity.org/politics/default.htm

CyberPort: http://www.islamicity.org/port/default/htm

Muslim Matrimonial Link.
      http://www.matrimonials.com/MML/? —or—
      http://www.ummah.net/comfort/

INDEX